英语专业系列教材

A COURSEBOOK IN APPRECIATING CLASSIC ENGLISH ESSAYS

英语散文名家名篇赏析教程

吕晓志　编著

清华大学出版社
北京

内容简介

本教材以英语散文发展的历史为经,以文学史上的名家名篇为纬,既注重不同历史时期散文作家不同的写作风格以及他们对散文发展的推动作用,又注重微观分析每一篇经典散文的遣词造句、文体风格与思想内容。本教材分为英国和美国两个部分,包括12个单元的英国散文作家及其作品,6个单元的美国散文作家及其作品。

版权所有,侵权必究。举报:010-62782989,beiqinquan@tup.tsinghua.edu.cn。

图书在版编目(CIP)数据

英语散文名家名篇赏析教程 / 吕晓志编著. —北京:清华大学出版社,2017(2024.9重印)
(英语专业系列教材)
ISBN 978-7-302-46031-2

Ⅰ.①英… Ⅱ.①吕… Ⅲ.①英语-阅读教学-高等学校-教材②散文-文学欣赏-世界 Ⅳ.①H319.4:1

中国版本图书馆CIP数据核字(2017)第002608号

责任编辑:蔡心奕
封面设计:平　原
责任校对:王凤芝
责任印制:刘海龙

出版发行:清华大学出版社
网　　址:https://www.tup.com.cn,https://www.wqxuetang.com
地　　址:北京清华大学学研大厦A座　邮　编:100084
社 总 机:010-83470000　邮　购:010-62786544
投稿与读者服务:010-62776969,c-service@tup.tsinghua.edu.cn
质量反馈:010-62772015,zhiliang@tup.tsinghua.edu.cn
印 装 者:天津鑫丰华印务有限公司
经　　销:全国新华书店
开　　本:170mm×230mm　印　张:22　字　数:399千字
版　　次:2017年12月第1版　印　次:2024年9月第3次印刷
定　　价:69.00元

产品编号:068255-01

Preface

在异彩纷呈的英美文学的大花园里，小说、诗歌、戏剧向来占据了最重要的位置，有着最夺目的光辉。而散文，常常是其中最默默无闻、最不引人注目的一个分支。然而在这个略显清淡的园地，如若细细品味，其中也有着沁人心脾的美好和芳香。笔者在中国传媒大学讲授英美散文名篇课程的这几年，与同学们徜徉在散文花园的课堂时光是永远难忘的宝贵记忆。同学们被散文迷住的样子深深感动了我，他们时而激烈讨论、时而高声朗读、时而会心浅笑、时而凝神沉思的神态令我从心底感受到做老师的快乐，也促使我有勇气将这几年的讲义编纂出版。

笼统地给散文下定义是很困难的。散文在英语中可以用两个词来表达，一是 prose，另一个是 essay。散文（prose）就其广义而言，泛指不属于韵文的任何书面或口头作品，包括除诗歌之外的一切体裁，比如小说、戏剧、传记、文学评论、随笔、演说、日记、书信等；狭义的散文（essay），很难把它翻译成恰当的中文。"随笔"或"小品文"似乎也不能概括英文"essay"的全部含义。大致说来，essay 指的是一种篇幅不长、不以叙事为目的、有一定风格的非韵文写作。除了活泼短小、含义隽永的小品文外，有着严肃论、犀利笔触的正式论文（formal essay）也是散文大家庭中的重要成员。可以说，这些独具风格的散文凭借其独特的思想内涵和文字魅力征服了一代又一代的读者。对于想学好英文的学生来说，浸润在风格各异的散文王国里，细读经典文本，是培养学生自身文学审美能力、思辨能力、语言敏感度和语言运用能力的一个有效途径。

《英美散文名家名篇赏析教程》共分 18 个单元，分为英国和美国两个部分。考虑到英国散文的博大精深和源远流长，笔者精选了12 个单元的英国散文作家的作品；其余 6 个单元为美国散文作家的作品。所选散文家包括英国的 Francis Bacon（培根）、Jonathan Swift（乔纳森·斯威夫特）、Joseph Addison（约瑟夫·艾迪生）、Samuel Johnson（塞缪尔·约翰逊博士）、Charles Lamb（兰姆）、Thomas De Quincey（德·昆西）、Virginia Woolf（伍尔芙）、Betrand Russell（罗素），美国的 R. W. Emerson（爱默生）、E. B. White（E. B. 怀特）等。这些作家的作品可以帮助读者浸润在优美的英语散文中，在潜移默化中提高英语语言能力。

本教材的编写与同类教材相比有以下特点：

一、系统化。散文名篇赏析课程虽然是对经典散文名篇的学习，但又不应止于此，文学史的学习也同样重要。本教材在编写过程中对教材内容进行了系统化设计。本教材以英语散文发展的历史为经，以文学史上的名家名篇为纬，力图编织出一幅美丽又有序的英语散文的灿烂织锦。选文分为英国与美国两大部分，每部分按时代顺序排列。在内容编排上既注重不同历史时期不同散文家的写作风格及其对散文发展的推动作用，又注重微观分析每一篇经典散文的遣词造句、文体风格与思想内容。系统化的编排方式可以帮助读者清晰地勾勒出英语散文发展的历史以及不同时期散文的特色。

二、专业化。本书的编排完全突破"散文集子"的做法，将更多的专业内容融于一体。每一单元都包括了导读、作者简介、精选散文、妙语警句四部分。第一部分的"本章导读"起导航的作用，该部分用中文提纲挈领地介绍和剖析了作者的写作风格和文学地位以及将要学习的散文，让同学们有一个初步的了解和印象。第二部分的"About the Author"是对作者生平、在散文领域的成就及写作特色的英文介绍，旨在让读者调整语言模式，为进入英文的学习做好准备。第三部分包括 A 和 B 两篇精读散文。每篇文章后附有详细的词汇注释和阅读理解练习。A 篇散文之后还设有语言和写作风格讨论题，以培养学生对每位作家遣词造句、谋篇布局的个人风格的敏感性。此外，每一单元结尾增加了相应作家最脍炙人口的警句和妙语，以利于读者更深入地了解其思想和语言风味。除"本章导读"部分为中文外，其他内容都为英文。这样的编排方式更加专业化、学术化，也更利于教师在课上对教学内容的讨论和引领。

三、深入化。本教材所选的文章不是一般的英语泛读读物，而是著名散文家的精品之作。在英美两国诸多经典散文作品中，本书试图选录不同题材、不同风格的精品代表作。在题材方面，有社会风情、人物写生、哲理辩论、灵性追求等内容；在风格上，有字字珠玑的议论直陈、浓墨重彩的抒情写意、雷霆万钧的辛辣讽刺，也有深刻细腻的娓娓道来。编者的用意是希望同学们都能有机会采撷和品尝一下散文百花园中丰富多彩的果实。此外，为了让同学们静心细读文本，本书所选的散文除了如培根的《论治学》和约翰逊博士的《致切尔斯菲尔德伯爵书》等个别比较短小的篇章外，大部分散文的篇幅都达到了2500—3500字。这是对同学们耐心与意志的考验和磨炼，也是在润物无声中提高语言能力的不二法门。同时，为了让读者对各位散文家的思想、风格及作品有更深刻地体察，本教材将每位散文家及其作品列为一单元，每单元精选此作家的两篇散文，由短到长，由易到难。这样的编排方式既丰富了学习内容，让学生对作家作品有更深入地了解，又便于教师根据学生的不同水平来安排教学内容。

本书可供英语专业本科生高年级或研究生一年级教学使用。教学内容可根据课程性质（选修还是必修）、学生程度、课时、教学目的等进行调整和取舍。本书也可以作为具有一定文学功底的英语爱好者自学之用。

由于编者水平有限，所选作品难以概其全貌，而且导读分析中也一定会有很多不足之处，敬请读者批评指正。

编者
2017 年 6 月

Contents

PART I
English Essays and Essayists

Chapter 1   Francis Bacon 弗朗西斯·培根 (1561–1626) 2
- Text A   Of Studies 4
- Text B   Of Marriage and Single Life 9

Chapter 2   Jonathan Swift 乔纳森·斯威夫特 (1667–1745) 13
- Text A   A Modest Proposal 15
- Text B   The Spider and the Bee 27

Chapter 3   Joseph Addison 约瑟夫·艾迪生 (1672–1719) & Richard Steele 理查德·斯梯尔 (1672–1729) 34
- Text A   The Spectator's Account of Himself 37
- Text B   The Spectator Club 44

Chapter 4   Samuel Johnson 萨缪尔·约翰逊 (1709–1784) 53
- Text A   A Letter to Lord Chesterfield 56
- Text B   On Idleness 60

Chapter 5   Charles Lamb 查尔斯·兰姆 (1775–1834) 65
- Text A   Dream-Children 68
- Text B   New Year's Eve 75

Chapter 6   William Hazlitt 威廉·哈兹里特 (1778–1830) 85
- Text A   On Familiar Style (Excerpt) 87
- Text B   On Going A Journey (Excerpt) 91

Chapter 7   Thomas De Quincey 托马斯·德·昆西 (1785–1859) 101
- Text A   On the Knocking at the Gate in Macbeth 104
- Text B   A Happy Home 111

Chapter 8   Bertrand Russell 伯特兰·罗素 (1872–1970) 118
- Text A   What I Have Lived For 120
- Text B   On Human Nature and Politics 123

Chapter 9   Edward Morgan Forster 爱德华·摩根·福斯特 (1879–1970) 132
- Text A   My Wood 135
- Text B   People 142

Chapter 10   Virginia Woolf 弗吉尼亚·伍尔芙 (1882–1941) 153
- Text A   Street Haunting: A London Adventure (Excerpt) 156
- Text B   A Room of One's Own (Excerpt) 163

Chapter 11   D. H. Lawrence D. H. 劳伦斯 (1885–1930) 179
- Text A   Whistling of Birds 182
- Text B   Give Her a Pattern 189

Chapter 12   George Orwell 乔治·奥威尔 (1903–1950) 196
- Text A   Some Thoughts on the Common Toad 199
- Text B   Reflections on Gandhi 206

PART II
American Essays and Essayists

Chapter 13 **Benjamin Franklin 本杰明·富兰克林 (1706–1790)** .. 220
    Text A   The Way to Wealth 222
    Text B   The Art of Procuring Pleasant Dreams 233

Chapter 14 **Washington Irving 华盛顿·欧文 (1783–1859)** 240
    Text A   Old Christmas 242
    Text B   Westminster Abbey 250

Chapter 15 **Ralph Waldo Emerson 拉尔夫·瓦尔多·爱默生 (1803–1882)** 263
    Text A   Nature 266
    Text B   Beauty 271

Chapter 16 **Henry David Thoreau 亨利·大卫·梭罗 (1817–1862)** 280
    Text A   Economy (Excerpt) 283
    Text B   Solitude 290

Chapter 17 **Henry Louis Menken 亨利·路易斯·门肯 (1880–1956)** 302
    Text A   The Penalty of Death 304
    Text B   The Libido for the Ugly 310

Chapter 18 **Elwyn Brooks White 埃尔文·布鲁克斯·怀特 (1899–1985)** 318
    Text A   Once More to the Lake 321
    Text B   Farewell, My Lovely! 331

PART I
English Essays and Essayists

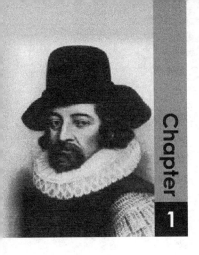

Francis Bacon
弗朗西斯·培根
(1561—1626)

Chapter 1

本章导读

弗朗西斯·培根（Francis Bacon，1561—1626），英国著名的哲学家、思想家、作家和科学家，文艺复兴时期哲学史和科学史划时代的人物，被马克思称为"英国唯物主义和整个现代实验科学的真正始祖"。同时他也是英国文艺复兴时期最重要的散文作家，被誉为"英国散文之父"。

弗兰西斯·培根出生于伦敦的一个高级官员家庭，拥有特殊的家庭背景和社会关系，再加上才华出众，培根很早就有了出入宫廷的机会，早在孩提时代，他就被伊丽莎白女王称为"我的小掌玺大臣"。雄心勃勃的培根很希望找到一条谋取功名利禄的捷径，并立志为官。他曾就读于剑桥大学三一学院，此后仕途一帆风顺，曾任副检察长、检察长、掌玺大臣、大法官等，被授予"维鲁拉姆男爵"的称号，后晋爵为圣阿尔本子爵。晚年因贪污受贿而被终身逐出宫廷，不得担任任何政府官。遭遇官场的失败后，培根闭门著书，虽生活颇为凄凉，却在学术上卓有成就。

他的著作中最负盛名的就是散文集《随笔集》（*Essays*），其中收录散文共58篇。这些文章以贵族和资产阶级上层人士为目标读者，谈论哲学、宗教、政治制度和国家以及处世、修身、养性等问题。培根以睿智的眼光洞察社会，解析生活。他撰写的散文透彻精辟、幽默隽永、意趣盎然、风格独具，享有世界性的声誉。培根的《随笔集》被誉为"英国散文发展史上的重要里程碑"，开创了英国文学的随笔体裁，从此英国散文文学进入了繁荣且具有自身特点的发展之路。培根的散文无论在思想内容和语言风格上都给后世的英国散文文学带来了巨大的影响。《随笔集》中的很多句子被作为警世格言而广为流传。

Chapter 1
Francis Bacon
弗朗西斯·培根

About the Author

Sir Francis Bacon was an English reformer, philosopher, champion of modern science, lawyer, statesman, essayist and historian. Early in his career, he claimed "all knowledge as his province" and afterwards he dedicated himself to a wholesale revaluation and re-structuring of traditional learning. While he was founding and promoting this new project for the advancement of learning, Bacon was also moving up the ladder of state service. His career aspirations had been largely disappointed under Elizabeth I, but, with the ascension of James, his political fortunes rose. Knighted in 1603, he was then steadily promoted to a series of offices, including Solicitor General (1607), Attorney General (1613) and eventually Lord Chancellor (1618). While serving as Chancellor, he was indicted(指控) on charges of bribery and forced to leave public office. He then retired to his estate where he devoted himself full time to his continuing literary, scientific and philosophic work. He died in 1626, leaving behind a cultural legacy that, better or worse, includes most of the foundation for the triumph of technology and for the modern world as we currently know it.

In Bacon's day, it was the common opinion of educated men that anything worth careful consideration ought to be published in Latin. In 1597, however, 10 little essays of Bacon appeared in vernacular (白话文) and met with instantaneous success. They were merely observations from notebooks put together in essay form and not considered by the author important enough to demand expression in Latin. Fifteen years later, 38 essays were published, and in 1625, the complete number—58 came out. These were the first example of the genre in English literature, which has been recognized as the important landmark in the development of English prose. Bacon is therefore generally regarded as the "Father of English essays".

Unlike Montaigne, the French originator of the genre essay, who wrote pieces more on personal rumination and humanity, Francis Bacon wrote to inform and educate, generally, the young people of his class. His compact essays on various subjects were pithy, packed with wisdom, brilliantly concise and epigrammatical. The explicit, direct and terse prose style exerts great influence on subsequent English writing.

Text A

Of Studies

Francis Bacon

Studies serve for delight, for ornament, and for ability. Their chief use for delight is in privateness and retiring; for ornament, is in discourse; and for ability, is in the judgment and disposition of business. For expert men[1] can execute, and perhaps judge of particulars, one by one; but the general counsels, and the plots and **marshalling** of affairs, come best from those that are learned. To spend too much time in studies is **sloth**; to use them too much for ornament, is affectation; to make judgment wholly by their rules, is the humour[2] of a scholar. They perfect nature, and are perfected by experience: for natural abilities are like natural plants, that need pruning, by study; and studies themselves do give forth directions too much at large, except they be bounded in by experience. Crafty men **contemn** studies, simple men[3] admire them, and wise men use them; for they teach not their own use; but that is wisdom without them, and above them, won by observation. Read not to contradict and confute; nor to believe and take for granted; nor to find talk and discourse; but to weigh and consider. Some books are to be tasted, others to be swallowed, and some few to be chewed and digested; that is, some books are to be read only in parts; others to be read, but not curiously[4]; and some few to be read wholly, and with diligence and attention. Some books also may be read by **deputy**, and **extracts** made of them by others; but that would be only in the less important argument and the meaner sort of books, else distilled

---

1 expert men: experienced men 有经验之人
2 humour: (old English) a person's mental qualities; temperament. Here it means the queer temperament. 怪癖
3 simple men: simple minded and easily cheated men 头脑简单之人
4 curiously: (old English) with care 谨慎地

Chapter 1

Francis Bacon
弗朗西斯·培根

books are like common distilled waters, flashy things.

Reading maketh a full man; conference a ready man; and writing an exact man. And therefore, if a man write little, he had need have a great memory; if he **confer** little, he had need have a present wit: and if he read little, he had need have much cunning, to seem to know that he doth not. Histories make men wise; poets witty; the mathematics **subtle**; natural philosophy deep; moral grave; logic and rhetoric able to contend. Abeunt studia in mores[1]. Nay, there is no stond or **impediment** in the wit but may be **wrought** out by fit studies; like as diseases of the body may have appropriate exercises. Bowling is good for the stone and **reins**; shooting for the lungs and breast; gentle walking for the stomach; riding for the head; and the like. So if a man's wit be wandering, let him study the mathematics; for in demonstrations, if his wit be called away never so little, he must begin again. If his wit be not apt to distinguish or find differences, let him study the Schoolmen; for they are cymini sectores[2]. If he be not apt to beat over matters, and to call up one thing to prove and illustrate another, let him study the lawyers' cases. So every defect of the mind may have a special receipt.

I Words and Phrases

marshal ['mɑːʃl]	v.	to arrange in logical order 整理
sloth [sləʊθ]	n.	laziness, especially with regard to work 懒惰
contemn [kən'tem]	v.	to treat or regard with contempt; scorn 蔑视，轻视；侮辱
deputy ['depjʊtɪ]	n.	a person appointed to represent or act on behalf of others 副手；代表
extract ['ekstrækt]	n.	an extract from a book or a piece of writing

---

1 Abeunt studia in mores: (Latin) Studies pass into the character; what one has studied will eventually become part of his character. 凡有所学，皆有所成。
2 cymini sectores: (Latin) dividers of cumin seeds; hair-splitters; people who care too much of the details 吹毛求疵之人

		that is printed or published separately 摘录，选段
confer [kən'fɜː]	v.	have a conference in order to talk something over 协商
subtle ['sʌtl]	adj.	able to make fine distinctions 敏锐的
impediment [ɪm'pedɪmənt]	n.	any structure that makes progress difficult 妨碍，阻止
wrought [rɔːt]	adj.	shaped to fit by or as if by altering the contours of a pliable mass (as by work or effort) 锻造的，加工的
reins [reɪnz]	n.	the kidneys or loins 肾，腰

II Reading Comprehension Questions

1. The first sentence summarizes the functions of studies. Can you think of any other functions of studies?
2. How do you understand the sentence "To spend too much time in studies is sloth"?
3. What is the relation between "studies" and "experience"?
4. The author introduces his method of reading books to us. Do you agree with him?
5. Do you believe every defect of the mind may have a special receipt? How does the author make his point convincing?

III Questions on Writing Style and Language

1. Have you noticed any stylistic feature of Francis Bacon's writing? Are his sentences long or short? What particular effect is produced by these sentences?
2. Parallelism means giving two or more parts of the sentences a similar form so as to give the passage a definite pattern. Can you identify parallel sentences in the essay? What is the effect?

Chapter 1

Francis Bacon
弗朗西斯·培根

3. Epigram states a simple truth pithily and pungently. It is usually terse and arouses interest and surprise by its deep insight into certain aspects of human behavior or feeling. Can you find some examples of epigram in this essay?
4. The author enumerates different aspects of studies. How does the author arrange his points? Do you see the logic between the sentences?
5. The following is a translation of "OF Studies" by Professor Wang Zuoliang. Do you think it is a good translation? Why or why not?

论学习

王佐良　译

　　读书足以怡情，足以傅彩，足以长才。其怡情也，最见于独处幽居之时；其傅彩也，最见于高谈阔论之中；其长才也，最见于处世判事之际。练达之士虽能分别处理细事或一一判别枝节，然纵观统筹，全局策划，则舍好学深思者莫属。读书费时过多易惰，文采藻饰太盛则矫，全凭条文断事乃学究故态。读书补天然之不足，经验又补读书之不足，盖天生才干犹如自然花草，读书然后知如何修剪移接，而书中所示，如不以经验范之，则又大而无当。有一技之长者鄙读书，无知者羡读书，唯明智之士用读书，然书并不以用处告人，用书之智不在书中，而在书外，全凭观察得之。读书时不可存心诘难读者，不可尽信书上所言，亦不可只为寻章摘句，而应推敲细思。书有可浅尝者，有可吞食者，少数则须咀嚼消化。换言之，有只需读其部分者，有只须大体涉猎者，少数则须全读，读时须全神贯注，孜孜不倦。书亦可请人代读，取其所作摘要，但只限题材较次或价值不高者，否则书经提炼犹如水经蒸馏，淡而无味。

　　读书使人充实，讨论使人机智，笔记使人准确。因此不常做笔记者须记忆力特强，不常讨论者须天生聪颖，不常读书者须欺世有术，始能无知而显有知。读史使人明智，读诗使人灵秀，数学使人周密，科学使人深刻，伦理学使人庄重，逻辑修辞之学使人善辩；凡有所学，皆成性格。人之才智但有滞碍，无不可读适当之书使之顺畅，一如身体百病，皆可借相宜之运动除之。滚球利睾肾，射箭利胸肺，慢步利肠胃，骑术利头脑，诸如此类。如智力不集中，可令读数学，盖演题需全神贯注，稍有分散即须重演；如不能辩异，可令读经院哲学，盖是辈皆吹毛求疵之人；如不善求同，不善以一物阐证另一物，可令读律师之案卷。如此头脑中凡有缺陷，皆有特效可医。

Chapter 1

Francis Bacon
弗朗西斯·培根

Of Marriage and Single Life

Francis Bacon

He that hath wife and children hath given hostages to fortune; for they are impediments to great enterprises, either of virtue or **mischief**. Certainly the best works, and of greatest merit for the public, have proceeded from the unmarried or childless men; which both in affection and means, have married and endowed the public. Yet it were great reason that those that have children, should have greatest care of future times; unto which they know they must transmit their dearest **pledges**. Some there are, who though they lead a single life, yet their thoughts do end with themselves, and account future times **impertinences**. Nay, there are some other, that account wife and children, but as bills of charges. Nay more, there are some foolish rich **covetous** men that take a pride, in having no children, because they may be thought so much the richer. For perhaps they have heard some talk, "Such an one is a great rich man", and another except to it, "Yea, but he hath a great charge of children", as if it were an **abatement** to his riches. But the most ordinary cause of a single life, is liberty, especially in certain self-pleasing and humorous minds, which are so sensible of every restraint, as they will go near to think their **girdles** and **garters**, to be bonds and shackles. Unmarried men are best friends, best masters, best servants; but not always best subjects; for they are light to run away; and almost all fugitives, are of that condition. A single life doth well with churchmen; for charity will hardly water the ground, where it must first fill a pool. It is indifferent for judges and magistrates; for if they be facile and corrupt, you shall have a servant, five times worse than a wife. For soldiers, I find the generals commonly in their hortatives, put men in mind of their wives and children; and I think the despising of marriage amongst the Turks, maketh the vulgar soldier more **base**. Certainly wife and children are a kind of discipline of humanity; and single men, though they may be many times more charitable, because their means are less exhaust, yet, on the other side, they are more cruel and hardhearted (good to make severe inquisitors), because their tenderness is not so oft called upon. Grave natures, led by custom, and therefore constant, are commonly loving husbands, as was said of Ulysses, vetulam suam praetulit immortalitati[1]. **Chaste** women are often proud and **froward**, as presuming upon the merit of their chastity. It is one of the best bonds, both of chastity and obedience, in the wife, if she think her husband wise; which she will never do, if she find him jealous. Wives are young men's mistresses; companions for middle age; and old men's nurses. So as a man may have a quarrel to marry, when he will. But yet he was reputed one of the wise men[2], that made answer to the question, when a man should marry: "A young man not yet, an elder man not at all." It is often seen that bad husbands, have very good wives; whether it be, that it raiseth the price of their husband's kindness, when it comes; or that the wives take a pride in their patience. But this never fails, if the bad husbands were of their own choosing, against their friends' consent; for then they will be sure to make good their own folly.

Words and Phrases

mischief ['mɪstʃɪf]	n.	the quality or nature of being harmful or evil 伤害，祸害
pledge [pledʒ]	n.	a deposit of personal property as security for a debt 抵押（品）
impertinence [ɪmˈpɜːtɪnəns]	n.	the trait of being rude and impertinent 鲁莽，无礼
covetous [ˈkʌvətəs]	adj.	a covetous person has a strong desire to

---

1 vetulam suam praetulit immortalitati: He preferred his old wife to immortality. This is what Cicero said of Ulysses. 此句引自古罗马著名演说家、政治家西塞罗的《论演说家》第一章，意思是"他对老妻的爱情胜过他对不朽的追求"。

2 one of the wise men: refers to Thakes of Miletus (640–550BC), who was one of the Seven Sages of Greece. 指米利都的泰勒斯，古希腊所谓"希腊七贤"之一。

Chapter 1

Francis Bacon
弗朗西斯·培根

		possess something, especially something that belongs to another person 贪婪的，垂涎的
abatement [ə'beɪtmənt]	n.	an interruption in the intensity or amount of something 减少，消除
girdle ['gɜːdəl]	n.	a band of material around the waist that strengthens a skirt or trousers 束腰带
garter ['gɑːtə]	n.	a band (usually elastic) worn around the leg to hold up a stocking (or around the arm to hold up a sleeve) 吊袜带
base [beɪs]	adj.	having or showing an ignoble lack of honor or morality 卑鄙的，低劣的
chaste [tʃeɪst]	adj.	abstaining from unlawful sexual intercourse 纯洁的，贞洁的
froward ['frəʊəd]	adj.	habitually disposed to disobedience and opposition 刚愎的；难驾驭的

II Reading Comprehension Questions

1. According to the author, what is "the most ordinary cause of a single life"?
2. According to the author, what kind of vocations suit unmarried men better than married ones? What are his reasons?
3. How do you understand the sentence "A single life doth well with churchmen; for charity will hardly water the ground, where it must first fill a pool"?
4. Which one do you prefer, an old company or immortality? Why?
5. Do you agree with the author's opinion on marriage and single life?

Quotes of the Author

A wise man will make more opportunities than he finds.

By far the best proof is experience.

Certainly virtue is like precious odours, most fragrant when they are incensed, or crushed: for prosperity doth best discover vice, but adversity doth best discover virtue.

Choose the life that is most useful, and habit will make it the most agreeable.

Death is a friend of ours; and he that is not ready to entertain him is not at home.

Chapter 2

Jonathan Swift
乔纳森·斯威夫特
(1667—1745)

本章导读

乔纳森·斯威夫特是英国 18 世纪杰出的政论家和讽刺小说家。他出生于爱尔兰都柏林的一个贫苦家庭。15 岁时就读于都柏林三一学院，获学士学位；1692 年获牛津大学硕士学位；1701 年获三一学院神学博士学位。1688 年，斯威夫特前往英国，做了穆尔庄园主人威廉·邓波尔爵士的私人秘书，直到 1699 年邓波尔去世。在担任秘书期间，他阅读了大量古典文学名著。1699 年，斯威夫特回到爱尔兰，在都柏林附近的一个教区担任牧师，但因为教会中的事务常去伦敦，后来卷入了伦敦的辉格党与托利党之争，受到托利党首领的器重，担任过该党《考察报》的主编。1714 年托利党失势，他回到爱尔兰，任都柏林圣帕特里克教堂主持牧师，同时着手研究爱尔兰现状，积极支持并投入争取爱尔兰独立自由的斗争。1745 年 10 月 19 日，斯威夫特辞世，终年 78 岁，葬于圣帕特里克大教堂。

斯威夫特的文学才能很早就显露出来，分别创作于 1696 年与 1697 年的《桶的故事》和《书的战争》就是其讽刺才华的最初展现。《桶的故事》表面上是三兄弟背弃了亡父遗嘱的故事，实质上则是对宗教论争的尖刻模仿，讽刺了那些自诩为基督教正宗教徒的道貌岸然，揭露了他们对教义阳奉阴违的事实。该书被英国启蒙主义者们用作攻击教会的重要武器。《书的战争》则将矛头直指当时贫乏的学术、浅薄的文学批评和各种社会恶习，对当时学究式的烦琐考证和脱离实际的学术研究提出批评，还提出了"文艺与科学应当为人民服务"的观点。斯威夫特最著名的文学作品是寓言小说《格列佛游记》(1726)。作者借船长格列佛之口逼真地描述了其四次航海的奇异经历，通过这种幻想旅行的方式来影射现实，极尽讽刺之能事，对英国的君主政体、司法制度、殖民政策和社会风气进行了批判。

《一个小小的建议》是斯威夫特最负盛名的讽刺政论文，写于1729年，至1732年共重印了七次，可见当年读者之众，流传之广。爱尔兰在16世纪后沦为英国的属国，至18世纪虽设有单独的国会，但事实上已完全成为英国政府的傀儡。爱尔兰人民在英国政府专制统治和爱尔兰地主的双重剥削下处于水深火热之中。在这篇文章中，斯威夫特借献策者之口，行讽刺抨击统治、剥削者之实。文章构想巧妙，文笔犀利，讽刺辛辣，为世界文坛所罕见，堪称一篇奇文。

About the Author

Jonathan Swift, the greatest English satirist, is best remembered as the author of *Gulliver's Travels*, a wonderful satirical novel which has been translated into many languages and is still read throughout the world.

Swift was born in Dublin, Ireland. At school, Swift was not a very good student and his teachers noted his headstrong behavior. He made several trips to London and gained fame with his essays. Throughout the reign of Queen Anne (1702–1714), Swift was one of the central characters in the literary and political life of London. In 1710, Swift tried to open his political career among Whigs, but changed his party and took over the Tory journal, *The Examiner*. With the accession of George I, the Tories lost political power. Swift withdrew to Ireland. In the years followed, he made frequent visits to England, getting deeply involved in politics and literature.

Swift is one of the greatest masters of English prose. Simple, clear, vigorous, he seems to have no difficulty in finding the exact word for his purpose. He once said "proper words in proper places make the true definition of a style." His satire is usually masked by an outward gravity and an apparent seriousness which renders his satire all the more powerful, as can be seen from his most renowned political satirical essay "A Modest Proposal".

Chapter 2

Jonathan Swift
乔纳森·斯威夫特

A Modest Proposal

For Preventing the Children of Poor People in Ireland
From Being a Burden to Their Parents or Country
and For Making Them Beneficial to the Public

Jonathan Swift

It is a melancholy object to those who walk through this great town or travel in the country, when they see the streets, the roads, and cabin doors, crowded with beggars of the female sex, followed by three, four, or six children, all in rags and **importuning** every passenger for an **alms**. These mothers, instead of being able to work for their honest livelihood, are forced to employ all their time in strolling to beg sustenance for their helpless infants: who as they grow up either turn thieves for want of work, or leave their dear native country to fight for the Pretender[1] in Spain, or sell themselves to the Barbadoes[2].

I think it is agreed by all parties that this **prodigious** number of children in the arms, or on the backs, or at the heels of their mothers, and frequently of their fathers, is in the present **deplorable** state of the kingdom a very great additional **grievance**; and, therefore, whoever could find out a fair, cheap, and easy method of making these children sound, useful members of the commonwealth, would deserve so well of the public as to have his statue set

---

1 the Pretender: The Pretender refers to James Francis Edward Stuart (1688–1766), the son of James II, who was claimant ("pretender") to the throne from which the Glorious Revolution had barred his succession. Catholic Ireland was loyal to him, and Irishmen joined him in his exile on the Continent. 觊觎王位者（伪装者）：詹姆斯·弗兰西斯·爱德华·斯图尔特，詹姆斯二世之子。在光荣革命中詹姆斯二世被剥夺王位，王位落到了他信奉新教的女儿玛丽二世和女婿威廉三世手中。詹姆斯·弗朗西斯·爱德华一直策划恢复詹姆斯派的王位，但没有成功。

2 the Barbadoes: an island in the west Indies, a British colony at the time 巴巴多斯，西印度的一座岛屿，当时为英国殖民地

up for a preserver of the nation.

But my intention is very far from being confined to provide only for the children of professed beggars; it is of a much greater extent, and shall take in the whole number of infants at a certain age who are born of parents in effect as little able to support them as those who demand our charity in the streets.

As to my own part, having turned my thoughts for many years upon this important subject, and maturely weighed the several schemes of other projectors, I have always found them **grossly** mistaken in the computation. It is true, a child just dropped from its dam may be supported by her milk for a solar year, with little other **nourishment**; at most not above the value of 2 shillings, which the mother may certainly get, or the value in **scraps**, by her lawful occupation of begging; and it is exactly at one year old that I propose to provide for them in such a manner as instead of being a charge upon their parents or the parish, or wanting food and **raiment** for the rest of their lives, they shall on the contrary contribute to the feeding, and partly to the clothing, of many thousands.

There is likewise another great advantage in my scheme, that it will prevent those voluntary abortions, and that **horrid** practice of women murdering their bastard children, alas! too frequent among us! sacrificing the poor innocent babes I doubt more to avoid the expense than the shame, which would move tears and pity in the most savage and inhuman breast.

The number of souls in this kingdom being usually reckoned one million and a half, of these I calculate there may be about two hundred thousand couple whose wives are breeders; from which number I subtract thirty thousand couples who are able to maintain their own children, although I apprehend there cannot be so many, under the present distresses of the kingdom; but this being granted, there will remain an hundred and seventy thousand breeders. I again subtract fifty thousand for those women who miscarry, or whose children die by accident or disease within the year. There only remains one hundred and twenty thousand children of poor parents annually born. The question therefore is, how this number shall be reared and provided for, which, as I have already said, under the present situation of affairs, is utterly impossible

Chapter 2
Jonathan Swift
乔纳森·斯威夫特

by all the methods hitherto proposed. For we can neither employ them in handicraft or agriculture; we neither build houses (I mean in the country) nor cultivate land: they can very seldom pick up a livelihood by stealing, till they arrive at six years old, except where they are of towardly parts, although I confess they learn the **rudiments** much earlier, during which time, they can however be properly looked upon only as **probationers**, as I have been informed by a principal gentleman in the county of Cavan, who protested to me that he never knew above one or two instances under the age of six, even in a part of the kingdom so renowned for the quickest proficiency in that art.

I am assured by our merchants, that a boy or a girl before twelve years old is no **salable** commodity; and even when they come to this age they will not yield above three pounds, or three pounds and half-a-crown[1] at most on the exchange[2]; which cannot turn to account either to the parents or kingdom, the charge of nutriment and rags having been at least four times that value.

I shall now therefore humbly propose my own thoughts, which I hope will not be **liable** to the least objection.

I have been assured by a very knowing American of my acquaintance in London, that a young healthy child well-nursed is at a year old a most delicious, nourishing, and wholesome food, whether stewed, roasted, baked, or boiled; and I make no doubt that it will equally serve in a fricassee or a ragout.

I do therefore humbly offer it to public consideration that of the hundred and twenty thousand children already computed, twenty thousand may be reserved for breed, whereof only one-fourth part to be males; which is more than we allow to sheep, black cattle or swine; and my reason is, that these children are seldom the fruits of marriage, a circumstance not much regarded by our savages, therefore one male will be sufficient to serve four females. That the remaining hundred thousand may, at a year old, be offered in the sale to the persons of quality and fortune through the kingdom; always advising the mother to let them suck plentifully in the last month, so as to render

---

1 crown: British coins at the time. A crown was worth 5 shillings. 克朗，当时的英国钱币，1 克朗大概等于 5 个先令。
2 exchange: the market 市场

them plump and fat for a good table. A child will make two dishes at an entertainment for friends; and when the family dines alone, the fore or hind quarter will make a reasonable dish, and seasoned with a little pepper or salt will be very good boiled on the fourth day, especially in winter.

I have reckoned upon a medium that a child just born will weigh 12 pounds, and in a solar year, if tolerably nursed, increaseth to 28 pounds.

I grant this food will be somewhat dear, and therefore very proper for landlords, who, as they have already devoured most of the parents, seem to have the best title to the children.

Infant's flesh will be in season throughout the year, but more plentiful in March, and a little before and after; for we are told by a grave author[1], an **eminent** French physician, that fish being a prolific diet, there are more children born in Roman Catholic countries about nine months after Lent[2] than at any other season; therefore, reckoning a year after Lent, the markets will be more glutted than usual, because the number of popish infants is at least three to one in this kingdom: and therefore it will have one other collateral advantage, by lessening the number of papists[3] among us.

I have already computed the charge of nursing a beggar's child (in which list I reckon all cottagers, labourers, and four-fifths of the farmers) to be about two shillings per **annum**, rags included; and I believe no gentleman would **repine** to give ten shillings for the **carcass** of a good fat child, which, as I have said, will make four dishes of excellent nutritive meat, when he hath only some particular friend or his own family to dine with him. Thus the squire will learn to be a good landlord, and grow popular among his tenants; the mother will have eight shillings net profit, and be fit for work till she produces another child.

Those who are more thrifty (as I must confess the times require) may flay

---

1. a grave author: an ironical reference to the French satirist and humorist Francois Rabelais（1494?-1553）指法国人文主义讽刺作家拉伯雷，著有政治讽刺小说《巨人传》，他的作品充满谐趣，人物间插科打诨很多，此处作者故意把他说成是一位严肃作家，是为了把下面那句玩笑话（fish being a prolific diet）当真理来引用。
2. Lent: an annual season of fasting and penitence beginning on Ash Wednesday and lasting 40 days to Easter 大斋节（亦称"封斋节"）。基督教的斋戒节期。教会通常在圣灰礼拜三也就是大斋节的首日开始，斋戒时长40天。
3. papists: a disparaging term for Roman Catholics 对天主教徒的污蔑称呼

Chapter 2
Jonathan Swift
乔纳森·斯威夫特

the carcass; the skin of which artificially dressed will make admirable gloves for ladies, and summer boots for fine gentlemen.

As to our city of Dublin, shambles may be appointed for this purpose in the most convenient parts of it, and butchers we may be assured will not be wanting; although I rather recommend buying the children alive, and dressing them hot from the knife, as we do roasting pigs.

A very worthy person, a true lover of his country, and whose virtues I highly esteem, was lately pleased in discoursing on this matter to offer a refinement upon my scheme. He said that many gentlemen of this kingdom, having of late destroyed their deer, he conceived that the want of venison might be well supplied by the bodies of young lads and maidens, not exceeding fourteen years of age nor under twelve; so great a number of both sexes in every country being now ready to starve for want of work and service; and these to be disposed of by their parents, if alive, or otherwise by their nearest relations. But with due **deference** to so excellent a friend and so deserving a patriot, I cannot be altogether in his sentiments; for as to the males, my American acquaintance assured me, from frequent experience, that their flesh was generally tough and lean, like that of our schoolboys by continual exercise, and their taste disagreeable; and to fatten them would not answer the charge. Then as to the females, it would, I think, with humble submission be a loss to the public, because they soon would become breeders themselves; and besides, it is not improbable that some scrupulous people might be apt to censure such a practice (although indeed very unjustly), as a little bordering upon cruelty; which, I confess, hath always been with me the strongest objection against any project, however so well intended.

But in order to justify my friend, he confessed that this expedient was put into his head by the famous Psalmanazar[1], a native of the island Formosa[2],

---

1 Psalmanazar: George Psalmanazar, a most notorious impostor in the 18th century. Born in France, he successfully posed as a native of the island of Formosa (present-day Taiwan) and published a book about Formosan life, language and religious practices. George Psalmanazar（1679-1763），一个臭名昭著的法国大骗子。他自称是台湾岛岛民，胡编乱造了一部有关台湾岛的书，其中描写人祭以及吃人习俗。

2 island Formosa: 16世纪葡萄牙殖民者对我国台湾的称呼

who came from thence to London above twenty years ago, and in conversation told my friend, that in his country when any young person happened to be put to death, the executioner sold the carcass to persons of quality as a prime dainty; and that in his time the body of a plump girl of fifteen, who was crucified for an attempt to poison the emperor, was sold to his imperial majesty's prime minister of state, and other great mandarins of the court, in joints from the gibbet, at four hundred crowns. Neither indeed can I deny, that if the same use were made of several plump young girls in this town, who without one single groat to their fortunes cannot stir abroad without a chair, and appear at playhouse and assemblies in foreign fineries which they never will pay for, the kingdom would not be the worse.

Some persons of a desponding spirit are in great concern about that vast number of poor people, who are aged, diseased, or maimed, and I have been desired to employ my thoughts what course may be taken to ease the nation of so grievous an encumbrance. But I am not in the least pain upon that matter, because it is very well known that they are every day dying and rotting by cold and famine, and filth and vermin, as fast as can be reasonably expected. And as to the young labourers, they are now in as hopeful a condition; they cannot get work, and consequently pine away for want of nourishment, to a degree that if at any time they are accidentally hired to common labour, they have not strength to perform it; and thus the country and themselves are happily delivered from the evils to come.

I have too long digressed, and therefore shall return to my subject. I think the advantages by the proposal which I have made are obvious and many, as well as of the highest importance.

For first, as I have already observed, it would greatly lessen the number of papists, with whom we are yearly overrun, being the principal breeders of the nation as well as our most dangerous enemies; and who stay at home on purpose with a design to deliver the kingdom to the Pretender, hoping to take their advantage by the absence of so many good protestants, who have chosen rather to leave their country than stay at home and pay tithes against their conscience to an episcopal curate.

Chapter 2

Jonathan Swift
乔纳森·斯威夫特

Secondly, the poorer tenants will have something valuable of their own, which by law may be made liable to distress and help to pay their landlord's rent, their corn and cattle being already seized, and money a thing unknown.

Thirdly, whereas the maintenance of a hundred thousand children, from two years old and upward, cannot be computed at less than ten shillings a-piece per annum, the nation's stock will be thereby increased fifty thousand pounds per annum, beside the profit of a new dish introduced to the tables of all gentlemen of fortune in the kingdom who have any refinement in taste. And the money will circulate among ourselves, the goods being entirely of our own growth and manufacture.

Fourthly, the constant breeders, beside the gain of eight shillings sterling per annum by the sale of their children, will be rid of the charge of maintaining them after the first year.

Fifthly, this food would likewise bring great custom to taverns; where the vintners will certainly be so prudent as to procure the best receipts for dressing it to perfection, and consequently have their houses frequented by all the fine gentlemen, who justly value themselves upon their knowledge in good eating: and a skilful cook, who understands how to oblige his guests, will contrive to make it as expensive as they please.

Sixthly, this would be a great inducement to marriage, which all wise nations have either encouraged by rewards or enforced by laws and penalties. It would increase the care and tenderness of mothers toward their children, when they were sure of a settlement for life to the poor babes, provided in some sort by the public, to their annual profit instead of expense. We should see an honest emulation among the married women, which of them could bring the fattest child to the market. Men would become as fond of their wives during the time of their pregnancy as they are now of their mares in foal, their cows in calf, their sows when they are ready to farrow; nor offer to beat or kick them (as is too frequent a practice) for fear of a miscarriage.

Many other advantages might be enumerated. For instance, the addition of some thousand carcasses in our exportation of barrelled beef, the propagation of swine's flesh, and improvement in the art of making good bacon, so much wanted among us by the great destruction of pigs, too frequent at our tables; which are no way comparable in taste or magnificence to a well-grown, fat, yearling child, which roasted whole will make a considerable figure at a lord mayor's feast or any other public entertainment. But this and many others I omit, being studious of brevity.

Supposing that one thousand families in this city, would be constant customers for Infant's Flesh, besides others who might have it at merry meetings, particularly at weddings and christenings, I compute that Dublin would take off annually about twenty thousand carcasses, and the rest of the Kingdom (where probably they will be sold somewhat cheaper) the remaining eighty thousand.

I can think of no one objection, that will possibly be raised against this proposal, unless it should be urged, that the number of people will be thereby much lessened in the Kingdom. This I freely own, and 'twas indeed one principal design in offering it to the world. I desire the reader will observe, that I calculate my remedy for this one individual kingdom of Ireland, and for no other that ever was, is, or I think, ever can be upon Earth. Therefore let no man talk to me of other expedients: of taxing our absentees at five shillings a pound: of using neither clothes, nor household furniture, except what is of our own growth and manufacture: of utterly rejecting the materials and instruments that promote foreign luxury: of curing the expensiveness of pride, vanity, idleness, and gaming in our women: of introducing a vein of **parsimony**, prudence and temperance: of learning to love our country, wherein we differ even from Laplanders, and the inhabitants of Topinamboo: of quitting our animosities, and factions, nor act any longer like the Jews, who were murdering one another at the very moment their city was taken: of being a little cautious not to sell our country and consciences for nothing: of teaching our landlords to have at least one degree of mercy towards their tenants. Lastly, of putting a spirit of honesty, industry, and skill into our shop-keepers, who, if a resolution could now be taken to buy only our native goods, would immediately unite to cheat and exact upon us in the price, the measure and the goodness, nor could ever yet be brought to make one fair proposal of

Chapter 2
Jonathan Swift
乔纳森·斯威夫特

just dealing, though often and earnestly invited to it.

Therefore I repeat, let no man talk to me of these and the like expedients, till he hath at least some glimpse of hope, that there will ever be some hearty and sincere attempt to put them into practice.

But as to my self, having been wearied out for many years with offering vain, idle, visionary thoughts, and at length despairing of success, I fortunately fell upon this proposal, which as it is wholly new, so it hath something solid and real, of no expense and little trouble, full in our own power, and whereby we can incur no danger in disobliging England. For this kind of commodity will not bear exportation, the flesh being of too tender a consistence, to admit a long continuance in salt, although perhaps I could name a country, which would be glad to eat up our whole nation without it.

After all, I am not so violently bent upon my own opinion as to reject any offer proposed by wise men, which shall be found equally innocent, cheap, easy, and effectual. But before something of that kind shall be advanced in contradiction to my scheme, and offering a better, I desire the author or authors will be pleased maturely to consider two points. First, as things now stand, how they will be able to find food and raiment for an hundred thousand useless mouths and backs. And secondly, there being a round million of creatures in human figure throughout this kingdom, whose whole subsistence put into a common stock would leave them in debt two millions of pounds sterling, adding those who are beggars by profession to the bulk of farmers, cottagers, and labourers, with their wives and children who are beggars in effect: I desire those politicians who dislike my overture, and may perhaps be so bold as to attempt an answer, that they will first ask the parents of these mortals, whether they would not at this day think it a great happiness to have been sold for food, at a year old in the manner I prescribe, and thereby have avoided such a perpetual scene of misfortunes as they have since gone through by the oppression of landlords, the impossibility of paying rent without money or trade, the want of common sustenance, with neither house nor clothes to cover them from the inclemencies of the weather, and the most inevitable prospect of entailing the like or greater miseries upon their breed forever.

I profess, in the sincerity of my heart, that I have not the least personal interest in endeavouring to promote this necessary work, having no other motive than the public good of my country, by advancing our trade, providing for infants, relieving the poor, and giving some pleasure to the rich. I have no children by which I can propose to get a single penny; the youngest being nine years old, and my wife past child-bearing.

I Words and Phrases

importune [ˌɪmpɔːˈtjuːn]	v.	to beg persistently and urgently 强求；向某人要求
alms [ɑːmz]	n.	money or goods contributed to the poor 捐献，救济物
prodigious [prəˈdɪdʒəs]	adj.	very large or impressive 巨大的；给人印象深刻的
deplorable [dɪˈplɔːrəbəl]	adj.	bad; unfortunate; of very poor quality or condition 可叹的，凄惨的
grievance [ˈɡriːvəns]	n.	a feeling of having been treated unfairly 委屈，不满
grossly [ˈɡrəʊslɪ]	adv.	greatly 很，非常
nourishment [ˈnʌrɪʃmənt]	n.	a source of materials to nourish the body 食物，营养品，滋养品
scraps [skræps]	n.	food that is discarded (as from a kitchen) 残羹剩饭
raiment [ˈreɪmənt]	n.	clothing 衣服
horrid [ˈhɒrɪd]	adj.	exceedingly bad; causing horror 可怕的，恐怖的；极讨厌的
rudiment [ˈruːdɪmənt]	n.	a statement of fundamental facts or principle 入门，初步，基础知识
probationer [prəˈbeɪʃnə]	n.	someone who is still being trained to do a job and is on trial 见习生，试用人员

Jonathan Swift
乔纳森·斯威夫特

salable ['seɪləbəl]	*adj.*	capable of being sold; fit for sale 畅销的，适于销售的
liable ['laɪəbəl]	*adj.*	at risk of or subject to experiencing something usually unpleasant 有……倾向的，易于……的
eminent ['emɪnənt]	*adj.*	well-known and respected 卓越的，有名望的
annum ['ænəm]	*n.*	(Latin) year <拉>年，岁
repine [rɪ'paɪn]	*v.*	to express discontent 抱怨，不满
carcass ['kɑːkəs]	*n.*	the dead body of an animal especially one slaughtered and dressed for food（人或动物的）尸体或残骸
deference ['defərəns]	*n.*	courteous regard for people's feelings 顺从，尊重
parsimony ['pɑːsɪmənɪ]	*n.*	extreme care in spending money; reluctance to spend money unnecessarily 吝啬，过度节俭

II Reading Comprehension Questions

1. What kind of social problems does Swift's proposal address?
2. Who, according to Swift, are the "principle Breeders of the Nations"?
3. What will be the average price of a child, according to Swift's calculations?
4. What are the alternative "expedients" the author rejects? Why?
5. What evidence does the author offer to support his pure motive in making the proposal?

III Questions on Writing Style and Language

1. Swift's opening paragraph offers a starkly realistic, although compassionate, portrait of families of beggars in Ireland. Please analyze it sentence by sentence.
2. In whose tone does the author make the proposal? When did it first become apparent to you that Swift's proposal was not serious? How did you respond?

3. Verbal irony is a figure of speech in which the actual intent is expressed in words which carry the opposite meaning. Can you find some examples of irony in this essay?
4. How do you evaluate the author's closing statement?
5. Swift is regarded as a master of satire. What techniques does the author use to achieve the most astounding satirical effect?

Chapter 2

Jonathan Swift
乔纳森·斯威夫特

Text B

The Spider and the Bee[1]

Jonathan Swift

Things were at this crisis when a material accident fell out. For upon the highest corner of a large window, there dwelt a certain spider, swollen up to the first magnitude by the destruction of infinite numbers of flies, whose spoils lay scattered before the gates of his palace, like human bones before the cave of some giant. The avenues to his castle were guarded with **turnpikes** and **palisades**, all after the modern way of fortification. After you had passed several courts you came to the centre, wherein you might behold the **constable** himself in his own lodgings, which had windows fronting to each avenue, and ports to **sally** out upon all occasions of prey or defence. In this mansion he had for some time dwelt in peace and plenty, without danger to his person by swallows from above, or to his palace by brooms from below; when it was the pleasure of fortune to conduct thither a wandering bee, to whose curiosity a broken pane in the glass had discovered itself, and in he went, where, **expatiating** a while, he at last happened to **alight** upon one of the outward walls of the spider's **citadel**; which, yielding to the unequal weight, sunk down to the very foundation. Thrice he endeavoured to force his passage, and thrice the centre shook. The spider within, feeling the terrible **convulsion**, supposed at first that nature was approaching to her final dissolution, or else that Beelzebub, with all his legions, was come to revenge the death of many thousands of his subjects whom his enemy had slain and devoured. However, he at length **valiantly** resolved to issue forth and meet his fate. Meanwhile the bee had **acquitted** himself of his toils, and, posted securely at some distance, was employed in cleansing his wings, and **disengaging** them from the ragged remnants of the cobweb. By this time the spider was adventured out, when,

---

1 The text is taken from Swift's *The Battle of Books*.

beholding the chasms, the ruins, and **dilapidations** of his fortress, he was very near at his wit's end; he stormed and swore like a madman, and swelled till he was ready to burst. At length, casting his eye upon the bee, and wisely gathering causes from events (for they know each other by sight), "A plague split you," said he; "is it you, with a vengeance, that have made this litter here; could not you look before you, and be d-d? Do you think I have nothing else to do (in the devil's name) but to mend and repair after you?" "Good words, friend," said the bee, having now pruned himself, and being disposed to droll; "I'll give you my hand and word to come near your kennel no more; I was never in such a confounded pickle since I was born." "Sirrah," replied the spider, "if it were not for breaking an old custom in our family, never to stir abroad against an enemy, I should come and teach you better manners." "I pray have patience," said the bee, "or you'll spend your substance, and, for aught I see, you may stand in need of it all, towards the repair of your house." "Rogue, rogue," replied the spider, "yet me thinks you should have more respect to a person whom all the world allows to be so much your betters." "By my troth," said the bee, "the comparison will amount to a very good jest, and you will do me a favour to let me know the reasons that all the world is pleased to use in so hopeful a dispute." At this the spider, having swelled himself into the size and posture of a disputant, began his argument in the true spirit of controversy, with resolution to be heartily **scurrilous** and angry, to urge on his own reasons without the least regard to the answers or objections of his opposite, and fully predetermined in his mind against all conviction.

"Not to disparage myself," said he, "by the comparison with such a rascal, what art thou but a vagabond without house or home, without stock or inheritance? born to no possession of your own, but a pair of wings and a drone-pipe. Your livelihood is a universal plunder upon nature; a freebooter over fields and gardens; and, for the sake of stealing, will rob a nettle as easily as a violet. Whereas I am a domestic animal, furnished with a native stock within myself. This large castle (to show my improvements in the mathematics) is all built with my own hands, and the materials extracted

Chapter 2
Jonathan Swift
乔纳森·斯威夫特

altogether out of my own person."

"I am glad," answered the bee, "to hear you grant at least that I am come honestly by my wings and my voice; for then, it seems, I am obliged to Heaven alone for my flights and my music; and **Providence** would never have bestowed on me two such gifts without designing them for the noblest ends. I visit, indeed, all the flowers and blossoms of the field and garden, but whatever I collect thence enriches myself without the least injury to their beauty, their smell, or their taste. Now, for you and your skill in architecture and other mathematics, I have little to say: in that building of yours there might, for aught I know, have been labour and method enough; but, by woeful experience for us both, it is too plain the materials are naught; and I hope you will henceforth take warning, and consider duration and matter, as well as method and art. You boast, indeed, of being obliged to no other creature, but of drawing and spinning out all from yourself; that is to say, if we may judge of the liquor in the vessel by what issues out, you possess a good plentiful store of dirt and poison in your breast; and, though I would by no means lesson or disparage your genuine stock of either, yet I doubt you are somewhat obliged, for an increase of both, to a little foreign assistance. Your inherent portion of dirt does not fall of acquisitions, by sweepings exhaled from below; and one insect furnishes you with a share of poison to destroy another. So that, in short, the question comes all to this: whether is the nobler being of the two, that which, by a lazy contemplation of four inches round, by an **overweening** pride, feeding, and engendering on itself, turns all into excrement and venom, producing nothing at all but flybane and a cobweb; or that which, by a universal range, with long search, much study, true judgment, and distinction of things, brings home honey and wax."

This dispute was managed with such eagerness, clamour, and warmth, that the two parties of books, in arms below, stood silent a while, waiting in suspense what would be the issue; which was not long undetermined: for the bee, grown impatient at so much loss of time, fled straight away to a bed of roses, without looking for a reply, and left the spider, like an orator, collected in himself, and just prepared to burst out.

It happened upon this emergency that Aesop[1] broke silence first. He had been of late most barbarously treated by a strange effect of the regent's humanity, who had torn off his title-page, sorely defaced one half of his leaves, and chained him fast among a shelf of Moderns. Where, soon discovering how high the quarrel was likely to proceed, he tried all his arts, and turned himself to a thousand forms. At length, in the borrowed shape of an ass, the regent mistook him for a Modern; by which means he had time and opportunity to escape to the Ancients, just when the spider and the bee were entering into their contest; to which he gave his attention with a world of pleasure, and, when it was ended, swore in the loudest key that in all his life he had never known two cases, so parallel and adapt to each other as that in the window and this upon the shelves. "The disputants," said he, "have admirably managed the dispute between them, have taken in the full strength of all that is to be said on both sides, and exhausted the substance of every argument PRO and CON. It is but to adjust the reasonings of both to the present quarrel, then to compare and apply the labours and fruits of each, as the bee has learnedly deduced them, and we shall find the conclusion fall plain and close upon the Moderns and us. For pray, gentlemen, was ever anything so modern as the spider in his air, his turns, and his paradoxes? He argues in the behalf of you, his **brethren**, and himself, with many boastings of his native stock and great genius; that he spins and spits wholly from himself, and scorns to own any obligation or assistance from without. Then he displays to you his great skill in architecture and improvement in the mathematics. To all this the bee, as an advocate retained by us, the Ancients, thinks fit to answer, that, if one may judge of the great genius or inventions of the Moderns by what they have produced, you will hardly have countenance to bear you out in boasting of either. Erect your schemes with as much method and skill as you please; yet, if the materials be nothing but dirt, spun out of your own entrails (the guts of modern brains), the **edifice** will conclude at last in a cobweb; the duration of which, like that of other spiders' webs, may be imputed to their

---

1 Aesop: the Greek fabulist 伊索

Chapter 2
Jonathan Swift
乔纳森·斯威夫特

being forgotten, or neglected, or hid in a corner. For anything else of genuine that the Moderns may pretend to, I cannot recollect; unless it be a large vein of wrangling and satire, much of a nature and substance with the spiders' poison; which, however they pretend to spit wholly out of themselves, is improved by the same arts, by feeding upon the insects and vermin of the age. As for us, the Ancients, we are content with the bee, to pretend to nothing of our own beyond our wings and our voice: that is to say, our flights and our language. For the rest, whatever we have got has been by infinite labour and search, and ranging through every corner of nature; the difference is, that, instead of dirt and poison, we have rather chosen to till our hives with honey and wax; thus furnishing mankind with the two noblest of things, which are sweetness and light."

I Words and Phrases

turnpike ['tɜːnpaɪk]	n.	gates set across a road to prevent passage until a toll had been paid 收税关卡
palisade [pælɪ'seɪd]	n.	fortification consisting of a strong fence made of stakes driven into the ground 栅栏，篱笆
constable ['kʌnstəbl]	n.	a police officer of the lowest rank 治安官，巡官
sally ['sælɪ]	v.	set out in a sudden 出发，冲出
expatiate [ɪk'speɪʃɪeɪt]	v.	clarify the meaning of and discourse in a learned way 详述
alight [ə'laɪt]	v.	stop on the surface of somthing 停在，落在
citadel ['sɪtədəl]	n.	a stronghold into which people could go for shelter during a battle 城堡，要塞
convulsion [kən'vʌlʃn]	n.	a sudden uncontrollable attack 骚乱
valiantly ['vælɪəntlɪ]	adv.	bravely 英勇地
acquit [ə'kwɪt]	v.	state officially that sb is not guilty of the crime they were accused of 开释
disengage [ˌdɪsɪn'geɪdʒ]	v.	release from something that holds fast, connects, or entangles 解除，使脱离

dilapidation [dɪˌlæpɪ'deɪʃn]	n.	a state of deterioration due to old age or long use 荒废，破损
scurrilous ['skɜːrələs]	adj.	expressing offensive reproach 说话粗鄙恶劣的，无礼的
Providence ['prɒvɪdəns]	n.	a manifestation of God's foresightful care for his creatures 天意；上帝
overweening [ˌəʊvər'wiːnɪŋ]	adj.	unrestrained, especially with regard to feelings 过分的
brethren ['breðrən] (plural)	n.	the lay members of a male religious order <旧> 同胞；同党，同会
edifice ['edɪfɪs]	n.	a structure that has a roof and walls and stands more or less permanently in one place 大厦，大建筑物；大型支柱

II Reading Comprehension Questions

1. According to the essay, what is the argument between the spider and the bee?
2. Why does the spider think he is far better than the bee?
3. How does the bee refute the spider's argument?
4. According to Aesop, what are the common features between bees and Ancients?
5. What are the common features between spiders and Moderns?

Chapter 2
Jonathan Swift
乔纳森·斯威夫特

Quotes of the Author

Ambition often puts men upon doing the meanest offices; so climbing is performed in the same posture with creeping.

The power of fortune is confessed only by the miserable, for the happy impute all their success to prudence or merit.

Vision is the art of seeing things invisible.

We have just enough religion to make us hate, but not enough to make us love one another.

When a true genius appears in the world, you may know him by this sign that the dunces are all in confederacy against him.

Joseph Addison 约瑟夫·艾迪生 (1672—1719) & Richard Steele 理查德·斯梯尔 (1672—1729)

本章导读

在英国文学史上，尤其是散文史上，约瑟夫·艾迪生与理查德·斯梯尔为英国散文的发展做出了极大的贡献。他们继承培根的散文风格的同时，又顺应英国社会的发展状况，发展出了适应于资本主义社会要求的散文风格。

约瑟夫·艾迪生是英国著名的散文家，出生于英国维尔特郡的教区，他的父亲是当地的乡村牧师。在卡特公学，艾迪生遇见了他的一生好友理查德·斯梯尔。理查德·斯梯尔是爱尔兰著名的作家和政治家，同时也是与约瑟夫·艾迪生齐名的散文家。斯梯尔出生于爱尔兰的都柏林地区，作为清教徒的一员，他早年与艾迪生一同在卡特公学接受教育，后来又同时进入牛津大学。1708年，他创办了著名的《闲话报》（the *Tatler*），后来又与艾迪生合办著名的《旁观者报》（the *Spectator*）。

《旁观者报》可以说是期刊文学的创始者，今日杂志和报纸特写文章的鼻祖。这份刊物每期只登一篇文章，涉及世态时尚、道德风貌、文学评论、欣赏趣味等许多方面，融新闻、随感、学术、娱乐等内容为一炉，寓教于乐，让读者在娱乐的同时培养良好的情趣，其幽默自然清纯，亦不乏批评性和哲理性，和咖啡馆、沙龙等场所构成了在政治上抗衡宫廷文化的文学公共领域。其文章清新秀雅、轻捷流畅的文体成为后人模仿的典范，具有较深远的启蒙意义。

艾迪生的散文以幽雅、明晰著称。他观察细致，文笔流畅，并且具有独特的幽默感。散文在其手中变成完美的文体，对后世影响深远。艾迪生善于说理，他的风格被认为是简练、自然、口语化的散文典范。斯梯尔的作品不如艾迪生的作品那样优美，但是因其丰富的想象力和即兴之作而著名。理查德·斯梯尔和约瑟夫·艾迪生两人被认为是现代散文的先驱，是新古典主义时期杰出的启蒙主义文学家。

Chapter 3

Joseph Addison 约瑟夫·艾迪生 &
Richard Steele 理查德·斯梯尔

About the Author

Joseph Addison (1672–1719) is a leading English essayist and prose stylist. Addison's simple and unembellished prose style marked the end of the mannerisms and conventional classical images of the 17th century. Son of a country clergyman in Lichfield, Addison was educated first at Charterhouse and then at Oxford, where he received a good classical education. Addison had a long career in English politics as a committed Whig and in which he held many offices, including Secretary of Ireland and Secretary of State. He died in London at the age of forty-seven. Addison's fame rest with his contributions to two periodicals, the *Talter* and the *Spectator*.

Richard Steele, Addison's chief collaborator of the *Talter* and the *Spectator*, was born in Dublin by his English father and an Irish mother. He made Addison's acquaintance at school, and they were at Oxford together. Steele left the university to enter the army, and opened his literary career, while still a soldier, with *The Christian Hero*. In 1702 he began to write for the stage, and was of notable influence in redeeming the English drama from the indecency which had marked much of it since the Restoration. Like Addison, he combined politics with literature, and in 1715 was knighted as a reward for his services to the Hanoverian party.

Addison and Steele are most remembered for their contribution to periodical essays. The era of Queen Anne was epoch-making in the development of English prose, because pamphlets, newspapers, and magazines spread among the people a good standard style. From April 12, 1709, three times a week for two years, the *Tatler*, edited by Richard Steele, appeared with its political news, gossip of the clubs and coffee-houses, and essays on the manners of the age. March 1, 1711, the first number of the *Spectator* came out. The *Spectator* was a popular periodical Addison founded with Richard Steele. Being an extremely innovative publication, the *Spectator* was enormously influential, not only in the content of its speculations on aesthetics, literary style, and urban life, but also as a medium of education. Addison and Steele used these light and often gently satirical essays to educate the merchants and tradesmen of the emerging English middle class—what he termed the "middle condition"—in the manners and morals needful for their stability and legitimacy in English social structure.

The *Spectator* papers of Addison and Steele served a fourfold purpose: they presented the first excellent characterization outside of the drama and thus advanced the art of the novel; they gave birth to the modern essay; they vernacularized English prose style. As Samuel Johnson wrote, "Whoever wishes to attain an English style, familiar but not coarse, and elegant but not ostentatious, must give his days and nights to the study of Addison." In the fourth place, the *Spectator* has given us the most vivid picture of eighteenth century life and manners.

The playful humor, the vivid pictures of the times, the fund of information, the smoothness and elegance of style, the lofty moral sentiment, the shrewd characterizations, the pointed comments on life and manners, the delicate satire, the kindly spirit, the gossipy tone, the inexhaustible run of thoughts, the manliness and human sympathy—these are a few of the qualities that have endeared the *Spectator* to readers.

In this chapter, the first text is written by Joseph Addison and the second text is by Richard Steele.

Chapter 3

Joseph Addison 约瑟夫·艾迪生 &
Richard Steele 理查德·斯梯尔

The Spectator's Account of Himself

Spectator No. 1, March 1, 1711

  I have observed, that a reader seldom **peruses** a book with pleasure, till he knows whether the writer of it be a black or a fair man, of a mild or **choleric** disposition, married or a bachelor, with other **particulars** of the like nature, that **conduce** very much to the right understanding of an author. To **gratify** this curiosity, which is so natural to a reader, I design this paper and my next as **prefatory** discourses to my following writings, and shall give some account in them of the several persons that are engaged in this work. As the chief trouble of **compiling**, digesting, and correcting will fall to my share, I must do myself the justice to open the work with my own history.

  I was born to a small hereditary estate, which, according to the tradition of the village where it lies, was bounded by the same hedges and ditches in William the Conqueror's time that it is at present, and has been delivered down from father to son whole and entire, without the loss or acquisition of a single field or meadow, during the space of six hundred years. There runs a story in the family, that when my mother **was gone with child** of me about three months she dreamt that she was brought to bed of a judge whether this might **proceed from** a law-suit which was then depending in the family, or my father's being a **justice of the peace**, I cannot determine; for I am not so **vain** as to think it **presaged** any dignity that I should arrive at in my future life, though that was the interpretation which the neighbourhood put upon it.

  The **gravity** of my behaviour at my very first appearance in the world, and all the time that I sucked, seemed to favour my mother's dream: for, as she has often told me, I threw away my **rattle** before I was two months old, and would not make use of my coral till they had taken away the bells from it.

As for the rest of my infancy, there being nothing in it remarkable, I shall pass it over in silence. I find that, during my non-age, I had the reputation of a very **sullen** youth, but was always a favourite of my school-master, who used to say, that my parts were solid, and would wear well. I had not been long at the university, before I distinguished myself by a most profound silence; for during the space of eight years, excepting in the public exercises of the college, I scarce uttered the quantity of an hundred words; and indeed do not remember that I ever spoke three sentences together in my whole life. Whilst I was in this learned body, I **applied myself** with so much diligence **to** my studies, that there are very few **celebrated** books, either in the learned or modern tongues, which I am not acquainted with.

Upon the death of my father, I was resolved to travel into foreign countries, and therefore left the university with the character of an odd, unaccountable fellow, that had a great deal of learning, if I would but show it. An insatiable thirst after knowledge carried me into all the countries of Europe in which there was anything new or strange to be seen: nay, to such a degree was my curiosity raised, that having read the controversies of some great men concerning the antiquities of Egypt, I made a voyage to Grand Cairo, on purpose to take the measure of a pyramid;[1] and as soon as I had set myself right in that particular, returned to my native country with great satisfaction.

I have passed my latter years in this city, where I am frequently seen in most public places, though there are not above half a dozen of my select friends that know me; of whom my next paper shall give a more particular account. There is no place of general **resort**, wherein I do not often make my appearance; sometimes I am seen thrusting my head into a round of politicians at Will's,[2] and listening with great attention to the narratives

---

1 on purpose to take the measure of a pyramid: This is said to allude to a description of the pyramids of Egypt, by John Greaves, a Persian scholar and Savilian Professor of Astronomy at Oxford, who studied the principle of weights and measures in the Roman Foot and the Denarius, and whose visit to the Pyramids in 1638, by aid of his patron Laud, was described in his *Pyramidographia*. That work had been published in 1646, sixty-five years before the appearance of the *Spectator*, and Greaves died in 1652. 波斯人约翰·格里夫斯是牛津大学的天文学教授，曾于1638年亲自测量金字塔并在1646年将其测量结果出版。

2 Will's: Will's Coffee House 威尔咖啡馆

Chapter 3

Joseph Addison 约瑟夫·艾迪生 &
Richard Steele 理查德·斯梯尔

that are made in those little circular audiences. Sometimes I smoke a pipe at Child's[1], and whilst I seem attentive to nothing but *The Post-Man*[2], overhear the conversation of every table in the room. I appear on Sunday nights at St. James's Coffee-house, and sometimes join the little committee of politics in the inner room, as one who comes there to hear and improve. My face is likewise very well known at the Grecian[3], the Cocoa-Tree[4], and in the theatres both of Drury Lane and the Hay-market. I have been taken for a merchant upon the Exchange for above these ten years, and sometimes **pass for** a Jew in the assembly of stock-jobbers at Jonathan's[5]: in short, wherever I see a cluster of people, I always mix with them, though I never open my lips but in my own club.

  Thus I live in the world rather as a spectator of mankind than as one of the species; by which means I have made myself a **speculative** statesman, soldier, merchant, and **artisan**, without ever meddling with any practical part in life. I am very well **versed** in the theory of a husband or a father, and can **discern** the errors in the economy, business, and diversion of others, better than those who are engaged in them; as standers-by discover plots, which are apt to escape those who are in the game. I never **espoused** any part with violence, and am resolved to observe an exact neutrality between the Whigs and Tories, unless I shall be forced to declare myself by the hostilities of either side. In short I have acted in all the parts of my life as a looker-on, which is the character I intend to preserve in this paper.

  I have given the reader just so much of my history and character, as to let him see I am not altogether unqualified for the business I have undertaken. As for other particulars in my life and adventures, I shall insert them in following papers, as I shall see occasion. In the meantime, when I consider how much I

---

1. Child's: Child's refers to Child's Coffee House which was in St. Paul's Churchyard. 蔡尔德咖啡馆
2. *The Post-Man*: It was a penny paper in the highest repute at that time. 《信使报》，当时有名的便士报。
3. the Grecian: It refers to the The Grecian. 希腊人咖啡馆
4. the Cocoa-Tree: It refers to the Cocoa Tree Coffee House. 可可树咖啡馆
5. Jonathan's: Jonathan's Coffee House, in Change Alley, was the place of resort for stock-jobbers. 约拿单咖啡馆，当时的股票商交易中心。

have seen, read, and heard, I begin to blame my own **taciturnity**; and since I have neither time nor inclination to communicate the fulness of my heart in speech, I am resolved to do it in writing, and to print myself out, if possible, before I die. I have been often told by my friends, that it is pity so many useful discoveries which I have made should be in the possession of a silent man. For this reason, therefore, I shall publish a sheet-full of thoughts every morning, for the benefit of my contemporaries; and if I can any way contribute to the diversion or improvement of the country in which I live, I shall leave it, when I am summoned out of it, with the secret satisfaction of thinking that I have not lived in vain.

There are three very material points which I have not spoken to in this paper; and which, for several important reasons, I must keep to myself, at least for some time: I mean an account of my name, my age, and my lodgings. I must confess, I would gratify my reader in anything that is reasonable; but as for these three particulars, though I am sensible they might tend very much to the **embellishment** of my paper, I cannot yet come to a resolution of communicating them to the public. They would indeed draw me out of that obscurity which I have enjoyed for many years, and expose me in public places to several salutes and civilities, which have been always very disagreeable to me; for the greatest pain I can suffer is the being talked to, and being stared at. It is for this reason likewise, that I keep my complexion and dress as very great secrets; though it is not impossible, but I may make discoveries of both in the progress of the work I have undertaken. After having been thus particular upon myself, I shall in tomorrow's paper give an account of those gentlemen who are concerned with me in this work; for, as I have before **intimated**, a plan of it is **laid** and **concerted** (as all other matters of importance are) in a club. However, as my friends have engaged me to stand in the front, those who have a mind to correspond with me, may direct their letters to the SPECTATOR, at Mr. Buckley's, in Little Britain[1]. For I must further acquaint the reader, that though our club meets only on Tuesdays and Thursdays, we have appointed

---

1   Little Britain: a part of London 小不列颠，伦敦地名

Chapter 3

Joseph Addison 约瑟夫·艾迪生 &
Richard Steele 理查德·斯梯尔

a Committee to sit every night, for the inspection of all such papers as may contribute to the advancement of the public **weal**.

I Words and Phrases

peruse [pə'ruːz]	v.	to read sth. in a careful way 细读，精读
choleric ['kɒlərɪk]	adj.	easily moved to anger 易怒的，暴躁的
particular [pə'tɪkjʊlə(r)]	n.	detail, fact 详细说明
conduce [kən'djuːs]	v.	to lead or contribute to (a result) 导致或有助于（结果）
gratify ['grætɪfaɪ]	v.	to please or satisfy 使满意，使满足
prefatory ['prefətərɪ]	adj.	serving as an introduction or preface 前言的，序言的
compile [kəm'paɪl]	v.	to collect and edit into a volume 编辑，编撰
be gone with child		pregnant 怀孕
proceed from		result from 产生于
justice of the peace		a local magistrate with limited powers 治安法官
vain [veɪn]	adj.	conceited 自负的
presage ['presɪdʒ]	v.	to foretell 预言，预示
gravity ['grævɪtɪ]	n.	solemnity or seriousness 庄严，严肃性
rattle ['ræt(ə)l]	n.	a baby's toy that makes percussive noises when shaken 拨浪鼓
sullen ['sʌlən]	adj.	used to describe an angry or unhappy person who does not want to talk, smile, etc. 愤懑的；不高兴的
apply oneself to		devote oneself to 专心致力于
celebrated ['selɪbreɪtɪd]	adj.	famous 著名的
resort [rɪ'zɔːt]	n.	a frequently visited place 常去之地
pass for		be mistaken for 被错当成
speculative ['spekjʊlətɪv]	adj.	suppositional 推测的
artisan [ˌɑːtɪ'zæn]	n.	craftsman 工匠

versed [vɜːst]	adj.	skilled, proficient 熟练的；精通的
discern [dɪˈsɜːn]	v.	to detect with senses other than vision 辨别
espouse [ɪˈspaʊz]	v.	to support 支持，赞成
taciturnity [tæsɪˈtɜːnətɪ]	n.	the trait of being uncommunicative 沉默寡言
embellishment [ɪmˈbelɪʃmənt]	n.	elaboration of an interpretation by the use of decorative detail 修饰，润色
intimate [ˈɪntɪmeɪt]	v.	to hint or imply 暗示
lay [leɪ]	v.	to set down according to a plan 安排
concert [kənˈsɜːt]	v.	to contrive a plan by mutual agreement 协同安排，使协调
weal [wiːl]	n.	prosperity or well-being 福利；幸福

II Reading Comprehension Questions

1. This is the first number of The *Spectator*. What do you think is the function of it?
2. What kind of story runs in the author's family? What's its influence left on the author?
3. How do you understand the meaning of the author's schoolmaster's words?
4. What are the author's qualifications for the business he has undertaken?
5. According to this essay, what is the purpose of the *Spectator*?

III Questions on Writing Style and Language

1. Have you noticed any stylistic features of Addison's writing? Are his sentences long or short? What particular effect is produced by these sentences?
2. Can you sense the gentle humor of Addison in the essay? Please identify some humorous sentences and expressions in the essay.
3. The author used first person point of view in this essay. What is the advantage of this point of view?

Chapter 3

Joseph Addison 约瑟夫·艾迪生 &
Richard Steele 理查德·斯梯尔

4. How does the author account his experiences? Do you see the logic between the parts?
5. According to some critics, Addison's prose is the model of "the middle style", "on grave subjects not formal, on light occasion not groveling; pure without scrupulosity, and exact without apparent elaboration; always equable, and always easy, without glowing words or pointed sentences". Do you agree with this point of view? What are some examples or evidence you can give to support it?

Quotes of the Author

A misery is not to be measured from the nature of the evil, but from the temper of the sufferer.

An ostentatious man will rather relate a blunder or an absurdity he has committed, than be debarred from talking of his own dear person.

Arguments out of a pretty mouth are unanswerable.

How beautiful is death, when earned by virtue!

If men would consider not so much wherein they differ, as wherein they agree, there would be far less of uncharitableness and angry feeling.

The Spectator Club

Spectator, Friday, March 2, 1711

The first of our society is a gentleman of Worcestershire, of an ancient descent, a baronet, his name Sir Roger de Coverley. His great-grandfather was inventor of that famous country-dance which is called after him. All who know that shire are very well acquainted with the parts and merits of Sir Roger. He is a gentleman that is very **singular** in his behaviour, but his singularities proceed from his good sense, and are contradictions to the manners of the world, only as he thinks the world is in the wrong. However, this humour creates him no enemies, for he does nothing with sourness or **obstinacy**; and his being unconfined to modes and forms makes him but the readier and more capable to please and oblige all who know him. When he is in town he lives in Soho Square. It is said he keeps himself a bachelor by reason he **was crossed in love by a perverse** beautiful widow of the next county to him. Before this disappointment, Sir Roger was what you call a fine gentleman, had often supped with my Lord Rochester[1] and Sir George Etherege[2], fought a duel upon his first coming to town, and kicked Bully Dawson[3] in a public coffee-house for calling him youngster. But being ill-used by the above-mentioned widow, he was very serious for a year and a half; and though, his temper being naturally **jovial**, he at last got over it, he grew careless of himself and never dressed afterwards. He continues to wear a coat and doublet of the same cut that were in fashion at the time of his repulse, which, in his merry humours, he tells

---

1. Lord Rochester: 约翰·维尔莫特（John Wilmot），罗契斯特伯爵（Earl of Rochester, 1647—1680），当时深得查理二世宠幸。
2. Sir George Etherege: 乔治·艾塞利基爵士（1636—1694），也是查理二世的宠臣。当时以其三部喜剧作品（*The Comical Revenge, She Would If She Could,* and *The Man of Mode,* or *Sir Fopling Flutter*）闻名。
3. Bully Dawson: a swaggering sharper of Whitefriars 当时有名的一个赌棍

Chapter 3

Joseph Addison 约瑟夫·艾迪生 &
Richard Steele 理查德·斯梯尔

us, has been in and out twelve times since he first wore it. It is said Sir Roger grew humble in his desires after he had forgot his cruel beauty, insomuch that it is reported he has frequently offended with beggars and gypsies; but this is looked upon, by his friends, rather as matter of **raillery** than truth. He is now in his fifty-sixth year, cheerful, gay, and hearty; keeps a good house both in town and country; a great lover of mankind; but there is such a mirthful cast in his behaviours, that he is rather beloved than esteemed. His tenants grow rich, his servants look satisfied, all the young women profess love to him, and the young men are glad of his company. When he comes into a house, he calls the servants by their names, and talks all the way upstairs to a visit. I must not omit that Sir Roger is a justice of the quorum; that he fills the chair at a quarter-session with great abilities, and three months ago gained universal applause, by explaining a passage in the Game Act.

The gentleman next in esteem and authority among us is another bachelor, who is a member of the Inner Temple, a man of great **probity**, wit, and understanding; but he has chosen his place of residence rather to obey the direction of an old **humoursome** father than **in pursuit of** his own inclinations. He was placed there to study the laws of the land, and is the most learned of any of the house in those of the stage. Aristotle and Longinus are much better understood by him than Littleton or Coke. The father sends up every post questions relating to marriage-articles, leases, and tenures, in the neighbourhood; all which questions he agrees with an attorney to answer and take care of **in the lump**. He is studying the passions themselves, when he should be inquiring into the debates among men which arise from them. He knows the argument of each of the orations of Demosthenes and Tully, but not one case in the reports of our own courts. No one ever took him for a fool; but none, except his intimate friends, know he has a great deal of wit. This turn makes him at once both **disinterested** and agreeable. As few of his thoughts are drawn from business, they are most of them fit for conversation. His taste for books is a little too just for the age he lives in; he has read all, but approves of very few. His familiarity with the customs, manners, actions, and writings of the ancients, makes him a very delicate observer of what occurs to him in the present world. He is an excellent critic, and the time of the play is his hour of business; exactly at five he passes through New-inn, crosses through Russell-court, and takes a turn at Will's till the play begins; he has his shoes rubbed and his periwig powdered at the barber's as you go into the Rose. It is for the good of the audience when he is at the play, for the actors have an ambition to please him.

The person of next consideration is Sir Andrew Freeport, a merchant of great eminence in the city of London; a person of **indefatigable** industry, strong reason, and great experience. His notions of trade are noble and generous, and (as every rich man has usually some sly way of **jesting**, which would make no great figure were he not a rich man) he calls the sea the British Common. He is acquainted with commerce in all its parts, and will tell you that it is a stupid and barbarous way to extend dominion by arms; for true power is to be got by arts and industry. He will often argue that, if this part of our trade were well cultivated, we should gain from one nation; and if another, from another. I have heard him prove that diligence makes more lasting acquisitions than **valour**, and that sloth has ruined more nations than the sword. He abounds in several frugal maxims, amongst which the greatest favourite is, "A penny saved is a penny got." A general trader of good sense is pleasanter company than a general scholar; and Sir Andrew having a natural unaffected eloquence, the **perspicuity** of his discourse gives the same pleasure that wit would in another man. He has made his fortune himself; and says that England may be richer than other kingdoms by as plain methods as he himself is richer than other men; though at the same time I can say this of him, that there is not a point in the compass but blows home a ship in which he is an owner.

Next to Sir Andrew in the clubroom sits Captain Sentry, a gentleman of great courage, good understanding, but **invincible** modesty. He is one of those that deserve very well, but are very awkward at putting their talents within the observation of such as should take notice of them. He was some years a captain, and behaved himself with great **gallantry** in several engagements and at several sieges; but having a small estate of his own, and being next heir to Sir Roger, he has quitted a way of life in which no man can rise suitably to his merit, who is not something of a courtier as well as a soldier. I have heard

Chapter 3

Joseph Addison 约瑟夫·艾迪生 &
Richard Steele 理查德·斯梯尔

him often lament that, in a profession where merit is placed in so conspicuous a view, **impudence** should get the better of modesty. When he has talked to this purpose, I never heard him **make a sour expression**, but frankly confess that he left the world because he was not fit for it. A strict honesty and an even regular behaviour are in themselves obstacles to him that must press through crowds, who endeavour at the same end with himself, the favour of a commander. He will, however, in his way of talk excuse generals for not disposing according to men's dessert, or inquiring into it; for, says he, that great man who has a mind to help me has as many to break through to come to me as I have to come at him: therefore he will conclude that the man who would make a figure, especially in a military way, must get over all false modesty, and assist his patron against the **importunity** of other pretenders, by a proper assurance in his own vindication. He says it is a civil cowardice to be backward in asserting what you ought to expect, as it is a military fear to be slow in attacking when it is your duty. With this candour does the gentleman speak of himself and others. The same frankness runs through all his conversation. The military part of his life has furnished him with many adventures, in the relation of which he is very agreeable to the company; for he is never **overbearing**, though accustomed to command men in the utmost degree below him; nor ever too **obsequious**, from an habit of obeying men highly above him.

But that our society may not appear a set of humorists, unacquainted with the gallantries and pleasures of the age, we have amongst us the gallant Will Honeycomb, a gentleman who, according to his years, should be in the decline of his life; but having ever been very careful of his person, and always had a very easy fortune, time has made but a very little impression either by wrinkles on his forehead, or traces on his brain. His person is well turned, and of a good height. He is very ready at that sort of discourse with which men usually entertain women. He has all his life dressed very well, and remembers habits as others do men. He can smile when one speaks to him, and laughs easily. He knows the history of every mode, and can inform you from which of the French king's wenches our wives and daughters had this manner of curling their hair, that way of placing their hoods; whose frailty was covered by such a sort of a petticoat, and whose vanity to show her foot made that part of the dress so short in such a year. In a word, all his conversation and knowledge have been in the female world. As other men of his age will take notice to you what such a minister said upon such and such an occasion, he will tell you when the Duke of Monmouth danced at court, such a woman was then smitten, another was taken with him at the head of his troop in the park. In all these important relations, he has ever about the same time received a kind glance, or a blow of a fan from some celebrated beauty, mother of the present Lord Such-a-one. If you speak of a young commoner that said a lively thing in the House, he starts up, "He has good blood in his veins; Tom Mirable begot him; the rogue cheated me in that affair; that young fellow's mother used me more like a dog than any woman I ever made advances to." This way of talking of his very much enlivens the conversation among us of a more sedate turn, and I find there is not one of the company, but myself, who rarely speak at all, but speaks of him as of that sort of a man who is usually called a well-bred fine gentleman. To conclude his character, where women are not concerned, he is an honest worthy man.

I cannot tell whether I am to account him, whom I am next to speak of, as one of our company; for he visits us but seldom, but when he does, it adds to every man else a new enjoyment of himself. He is a clergyman, a very philosophic man, of general learning, great **sanctity** of life, and the most exact good breeding. He has the misfortune to **be of a very weak constitution**, and consequently cannot accept of such cares and business as **preferments** in his function would oblige him to; he is therefore among divines what a chamber-counsellor is among lawyers. The probity of his mind, and the integrity of his life, create him followers, as being eloquent or loud advances others. He seldom introduces the subject he speaks upon; but we are so far gone in years that he observes, when he is among us, an earnestness to have him fall on some divine topic, which he always treats with much authority, as one who has no interest in this world, as one who is hastening to the object of all his wishes, and conceives hope from his decays and infirmities. These are my ordinary companions.

Joseph Addison 约瑟夫·艾迪生 &
Richard Steele 理查德·斯梯尔

1 Words and Phrases

singular [ˈsɪŋgjʊlə]	*adj.*	beyond or deviating from the usual or expected 奇怪的，异常的
obstinacy [ˈɒbstɪnəsɪ]	*n.*	resolute adherence to your own ideas or desires, stubbornness 顽固，固执
be crossed in love by sb.		be disappointed in love/out of love 爱情受挫；失恋
perverse [pəˈvɜːs]	*adj.*	marked by a disposition to oppose and contradict 不通情理的；任性的
jovial [ˈdʒəʊvɪəl]	*adj.*	full of or showing high-spirited merriment 天性快活的
raillery [ˈreɪlərɪ]	*n.*	light teasing repartee 善意的玩笑；戏谑
probity [ˈprəʊbɪtɪ]	*n.*	complete and confirmed integrity 正直；诚实
humoursome [ˈhjuːməsəm]	*adj.*	capricious and odd 情绪不稳定的；易怒的；古怪的
be in pursuit of		go after 追求
in the lump		altogether, in total 总共；完全地
disinterested [dɪsˈɪntrɪstɪd]	*adj.*	unaffected by self-interest 恬静淡泊的
indefatigable [ˌɪndɪˈfætɪgəbəl]	*adj.*	showing sustained enthusiastic action with unflagging vitality 不知疲倦的；不屈不挠的
jesting [ˈdʒestɪŋ]	*n.*	joking 玩笑；戏谑
valour [ˈvælə]	*n.*	the qualities of a hero or heroine; exceptional or heroic courage when facing danger 勇猛，刚勇
perspicuity [ˌpɜːspɪˈkjuːɪtɪ]	*n.*	clarity as a consequence of being perspicuous 简明
invincible [ɪnˈvɪnsɪb(ə)l]	*adj.*	incapable of being overcome or subdued 无敌的；不能征服的
gallantry [ˈgæləntrɪ]	*n.*	valour 英勇
impudence [ˈɪmpjʊd(ə)ns]	*n.*	the trait of being rude and impertinent; inclined to take liberties 厚颜无耻；放肆，无视
make a sour expression		make some harsh remarks 说一些刺耳的话

importunity [ˌɪmpɔːˈtjuːnɪtɪ]	n.	insistent solicitation and entreaty 强求，硬要
overbearing [əʊvəˈbeərɪŋ]	adj.	expecting unquestioning obedience 盛气凌人的
obsequious [əbˈsiːkwɪəs]	adj.	attempting to win favor from influential people by flattery 谄媚的，奉承的
sanctity [ˈsæŋ(k)tɪtɪ]	n.	holiness 神圣，圣洁
be of a very weak constitution		not strong enough, fragile 体质虚弱
preferment [prɪˈfɜːm(ə)nt]	n.	the act of being given a better and more important job in an organization 晋升，升迁

II Reading Comprehension Questions

1. How many people are depicted in this essay? Can you tell their names and professions one by one?
2. Do you see Sir Roger de Coverley as an interesting character? Please characterize him.
3. Please characterize Sir Andrew Freeport and Will Honeycomb.
4. Why is Captain Sentry not suitable for the world he's in?
5. The members of the spectator club have different professions and characters, but they belong to a new social class as a whole. Do you know what the class is?

III Questions on Writing Style and Language

1. Please paraphrase the following sentence. "However, this humour creates him no enemies, for he does nothing with sourness or obstinacy; and his being unconfined to modes and forms makes him but the readier and more capable to please and oblige all who know him."
2. At the end of the second paragraph, why is that "It is for the good of the audience when he is at the play, for the actors have an ambition to please him"?
3. How do you understand the sentence "There is not a point in the compass but blows home a ship in which he is an owner"? What figure of speech is

Chapter 3

Joseph Addison 约瑟夫·艾迪生 &
Richard Steele 理查德·斯梯尔

used here?

4. Read the following comment and discuss the difference of style between Addison and Steele.

"Steele wrote as he spoke, in rapid, careless fashion. He would not stay for careful elaboration or tedious correction; Addison, on the contrary, was careful, even finicky, in all matters of expression. However, his efforts emerged in a style that was simple, suave, and urbane. He succeeded in combining idiomatic turns with polished, elegant phrases as no other writer of his time could do, and very few have done since."

—C. T. Winchester

Quotes of the Author

Fire and swords are slow engines of destruction, compared to the tongue of a Gossip.

Nothing can atone for the lack of modesty; without which beauty is ungraceful and wit detestable.

Reading is to the mind what exercise is to the body.

That man never grows old who keeps a child in his heart.

Whenever you commend, add your reasons for doing so; it is this which distinguishes the approbation of a man of sense from the flattery of sycophants and admiration of fools.

Samuel Johnson
萨缪尔·约翰逊
(1709—1784)

Chapter 4

本章导读

　　萨缪尔·约翰逊，又被称为"约翰逊博士"，是英国文学史上重要的作家、词汇学家、评论家，以及词典编撰者，是18世纪后半期英国文学界的权威。

　　约翰逊于1709年出生在英国斯塔福德郡的利奇菲尔德，父亲是一个穷书商。约翰逊自小就被认为是天才，在中学的时候就学习了拉丁文。16岁的时候，大概是因为要跟随父亲学习如何经商，他离开学校，在家待了整整两年。但是，他却利用这段时间读了很多书。这段离开学校的时期成为了他奠定知识基础的重要时期。但好景不长，他父亲的生意陷入了困境，之后的几年，约翰逊贫病交加。父亲曾祈求约翰逊接管他的生意，但是被约翰逊拒绝了。后来约翰逊进入了牛津大学。在这里，他不光拓宽了视野，更结识了一些好朋友。1737年，身无分文的约翰逊前往伦敦。1738年，讽刺诗《伦敦》（London）的发表使他一举成名，奠定了他在英国文坛的诗人地位。之后的几年中，他写了无数的传记、诗歌、散文、议会报道，但是他的生活依旧十分贫困。1762年，约翰逊获得了每年300镑的政府津贴。至此，他的经济状况才彻底改善。约翰逊在1765年被授予都柏林三一学院的名誉博士学位，十年后又获得了牛津大学的名誉博士学位。

　　1747年，在几个出版商的建议下，约翰逊开始编写《英语词典》。在当时，保护人制度十分普遍。富有的贵族给文人以经济上的援助，而文人则把作品奉献给自己的保护人。约翰逊怀着希望，登门拜访喜与文人交好、在当时颇有美誉的切斯特菲尔德伯爵，希望能获其赞助，不料被拒之门外。他只好独力着手编辞典，费时七年之久，期间饱受贫困折磨，又逢丧妻之痛，可谓历尽艰辛。约翰逊编撰的词典是英语史上第一部权威词典，是史无前例的恢弘著作。词典出版后，切斯特菲尔德却在报章上发表文章，对该词典大加赞美，约翰逊对此感到气愤，随后便写成《致切斯特菲尔德伯爵书》（*A Letter to Lord Chesterfield*），公开发表。在信中，他用辛辣和反讽的笔调，对切斯特菲尔德冷漠自私和沽名钓誉的行为进行了痛快淋漓的揭露。这篇短信风格典雅、文笔犀利，句法匀称整齐，语气庄重诚恳，语调不卑不亢，表现了一个文人在人生困境和世态炎凉面前不卑不亢的人格魅力。本章节选的另一篇文章《论懒散》（*On Idleness*）源自他主编的散文期刊《懒散者》（*Idler*），是一篇典雅幽默的小品文。

About the Author

Often referred to as Dr. Johnson in the history of English literature, Samuel Johnson (1709–1784) is a famous English poet, essayist, literary critic, and dictionary compiler. Next only to William Shakespeare, Samuel Johnson is perhaps the most quoted English writer. Samuel Johnson is such an important English writer in the 18th century that the latter part of the 18th century is often (in English-speaking countries, of course) called, simply, the Age of Johnson. He was equally celebrated for his brilliant and witty conversation. His rather gross appearance and manners were viewed tolerantly, if not with a certain admiration.

Johnson's first work of lasting importance, and the one that permanently established his reputation in his own time, was his *Dictionary of the English Language* (1755), the first comprehensive lexicographical work on English ever undertaken. At that time, literati without strong family background needed distinguished personnel's guide and support. In 1747, Johnson gave his plan to compile *A Dictionary of the English Language* to his patron Chesterfield for help. Unfortunately, Chesterfield ignored him and never gave him any point of view of this plan. Having no alternative, Johnson had to finish the work by himself, pushing his way through many difficulties and hardships over a period of seven years. After the accomplishment of this dictionary in 1755, Chesterfield published two recommendation articles in the newspaper. Johnson at once wrote "A Letter to Lord Chesterfield" as a response. The letter is perhaps the most famous letter in English Literature, which openly denied Chesterfield's patronage, and attacked him outright for his hypocritical behavior.

The letter is a must read for English majors. The balanced syntax, the refined

Chapter 4
Samuel Johnson
萨缪尔·约翰逊

language, the seemingly peaceful expression, the controlled rhythms, combined with a bitter undertone of defiance and anger, achieved a most desirable satiric effect. It expresses explicitly the author's assertion of his independence, signifying the opening of a new era in the development of literature. Patronage system gradually disappear in Europe since the publication of this letter.

A Letter to Lord Chesterfield[1]

To The Right Honorable, The **Earl** Of Chesterfield
7th February, 1755.

My Lord,

I have been lately informed, by the **proprietor** of *The World*[2], which two papers, in which my Dictionary is recommended to the public, were written by your lordship. To be so distinguished is an honor which, being very little accustomed to favors from the great, I know not well how to receive, or in what terms to acknowledge.

When, upon some slight encouragement, I first visited your lordship, I was **overpowered**, like the rest of mankind, by the **enchantment** of your address, and could not **forbear** to wish that I might boast myself Le vainqueur du vainqueur de la terre[3];—that I might obtain that regard for which I saw the world contending; but I found my attendance so little encouraged, that neither pride nor modesty would suffer me to continue it. When I had once addressed your Lordship in public, I had exhausted all the art of pleasing which a retired and **uncourtly** scholar can possess. I had done all that I could; and no man is well pleased to have his all neglected, be it ever so little.

Seven years, my lord, have now passed, since I waited in your outward rooms, or was repulsed from your door; during which time I have been pushing on my work through difficulties, of which it is useless to complain,

---

1. Lord Chesterfield: Philip Dorner Stanhope（1694—1773）切斯特菲尔德第四位伯爵，也是一位书简家，其信件被编成《切斯特菲尔德书信集》。
2. *The World*: a weekly paper sponsored by Lord Chesterfield at the time《世界报》，周刊，切斯特菲尔德伯爵是其资助者之一。该报于1753—1757年间在伦敦发行，风格与当时的著名刊物《漫谈者》相近。
3. Le vainqueur du vainqueur de la terre: This is a French expression which means "the conqueror of the conqueror of the world". 世界征服者的征服者

Chapter 4
Samuel Johnson
萨缪尔·约翰逊

and have brought it, at last, to the verge of publication, without one act of assistance, one word of encouragement, or one smile of favor. Such treatment I did not expect, for I never had a patron before.

The shepherd in Virgil grew at last acquainted with Love, and found him a native of the rocks.[1]

Is not a patron my lord, one who looks with unconcern on a man struggling for life in the water, and, when he has reached ground, **encumbers** him with help? The notice which you have been pleased to take of my labours, had it been early, had been kind; but it has been delayed till I am indifferent, and cannot enjoy it: till I am solitary[2], and cannot **impart** it; till I am known, and do not want it. I hope it is no very cynical **asperity** not to confess obligations where no benefit has been received, or to be unwilling that the public should consider me as owing that to a patron, which **providence** has enabled me to do for myself.

Having carried on my work thus far with so little obligation to any favourer of learning, I shall not be disappointed though I should conclude it, if less be possible, with less; for I have been long wakened from that dream of hope, in which I once boasted myself with so much exultation, My Lord,

Your lordship's most humble,
most obedient servant,
Sam Johnoson

I Words and Phrases

earl [ɜːl]　　　　　　　　n.　a British peer ranking below a marquess and above a viscount (英) 伯爵

1　The shepherd in Virgil grew at last acquainted with Love, and found him a native of the rocks: This is alluding to Virgil's Eclogue. 典出古罗马诗人维吉尔的长诗《牧歌》。维吉尔诗中的牧羊人终于和爱神相识，却发现爱神如山居野人一般残酷。

2　till I am solitary: Johnson's wife died in 1752, three years before the publication of the dictionary. 约翰逊的妻子 1752 年去世，三年后词典方得出版。

proprietor [prə'praɪətə] *n.* (law) someone who owns (is legal possessor of) a business 业主；经营者

overpower [əʊvə'paʊə] *v.* overcome, as with emotions or perceptual stimuli 压倒；制服

enchantment [ɪn'tʃɑːntm(ə)nt] *n.* a feeling of great liking for something wonderful and unusual 魅力

forbear [fɔː'beə] *v.* refrain from doing 忍耐，克制

uncourtly [ʌn'kɔːtlɪ] *adj.* rude; offensive 无礼的；不典雅的

encumber [ɪn'kʌmbə] *v.* hold back 妨害；拖累

impart [ɪm'pɑːt] *v.* tell or deposit (information) knowledge 告知；透露

asperity [æ'sperətɪ] *n.* harshness of manner (性格的) 粗暴

providence ['prɒvɪd(ə)ns] *n.* the guardianship and control exercised by a deity 天意

II Reading Comprehension Questions

1. According to the first paragraph, why did the author write this letter to Lord Chesterfield?
2. What kind of person do you think Lord Chesterfield is? Why?
3. Why doesn't Samuel Johnson want Lord Chesterfield's help now?
4. Judging by this letter, what kind of person do you think Samuel Johnson is?
5. What is the importance of this letter in the history of English Literature?

III Questions on Writing Style and Language

1. Have you noticed that Johnson adopted a very polite tone in the letter? Where can you see the politeness?
2. Can you sense the indignation of the author in the essay? Please identify the sentences and expressions in the essay.
3. A rhetorical question is a figure of speech in the form of a question that is

Chapter 4
Samuel Johnson
萨缪尔·约翰逊

asked in order to make a point, rather than to elicit an answer. Where can you find the use of it in this letter? What is the stylistic effect?

4. Many critics think that Johnson is a master stylist who is very skilled at handling sentences. Do you agree with this point of view? What are some examples or evidences you can give to support it?

5. What rhetorical device is used in the sentence "The shepherd in Virgil grew at last acquainted with Love, and found him a native of the rocks"? What is the effect?

Text B

On Idleness

Idler 31, Saturday, 18 November 1758

Many moralists have remarked, that pride has of all human vices the widest dominion, appears in the greatest multiplicity of forms, and lies hid under the greatest variety of disguises; of disguises, which, like the moon's veil of brightness, are both its luster and its shade, and betray it to others, though they hide it from ourselves.

It is not my intention to degrade pride from this pre-eminence of mischief, yet I know not whether idleness may not maintain a very doubtful and obstinate competition.

There are some that profess idleness in its full dignity, who call themselves the Idle, as Busiris in the play calls himself the Proud; who boast that they do nothing, and thank their stars that they have nothing to do; who sleep every night till they can sleep no longer, and rise only that exercise may enable them to sleep again; who prolong the reign of darkness by double curtains, and never see the sun but to tell him how they hate his beams; whose whole labour is to vary the postures of indulgence, and whose day differs from their night but as a couch or chair differs from a bed.

These are the true and open **votaries** of idleness, for whom she weaves the **garlands** of poppies, and into whose cup she pours the waters of **oblivion**; who exist in a state of **unruffled** stupidity, forgetting and forgotten; who have long ceased to live, and at whose death the survivors can only say, that they have ceased to breathe.

But idleness predominates in many lives where it is not suspected, for being a vice which terminates in itself, it may be enjoyed without injury to others, and is therefore not watched like fraud, which endangers property, or like pride which naturally seeks its **gratifications** in another's inferiority.

Chapter 4

Samuel Johnson
萨缪尔·约翰逊

Idleness is a silent and peaceful quality, that neither raises envy by ostentation, nor hatred by opposition; and therefore no body is busy to censure or detect it.

As pride sometimes is hid under humility, idleness is often covered by turbulence and hurry. He that neglects his known duty and real employment, naturally endeavours to crowd his mind with something that may bar out the remembrance of his own folly, and does any thing but what he ought to do with eager diligence, that he may keep himself in his own favour.

Some are always in a state of preparation, occupied in previous measures, forming plans, accumulating materials, and providing for the main affair. These are certainly under the secret power of idleness. Nothing is to be expected from the workman whose tools are for ever to be sought. I was once told by a great master, that no man ever excelled in painting, who was eminently curious about pencils and colours.

There are others to whom idleness dictates another expedient, by which life may be passed unprofitably away without the **tediousness** of many vacant hours. The art is, to fill the day with petty business, to have always something in hand which may raise curiosity, but not **solicitude**, and keep the mind in a state of action, but not of labour.

This art has for many years been practised by my old friend Sober, with wonderful success. Sober is a man of strong desires and quick imagination, so exactly balanced by the love of ease, that they can seldom stimulate him to any difficult undertaking; they have, however, so much power, that they will not suffer him to lie quite at rest, and though they do not make him sufficiently useful to others, they make him at least weary of himself.

Mr. Sober's chief pleasure is conversation; there is no end of his talk or his attention; to speak or to hear is equally pleasing; for he still fancies that he is teaching or learning something, and is free for the time from his own **reproaches**.

But there is one time at night when he must go home, that his friends may sleep; and another time in the morning, when all the world agrees to shut out interruption. These are the moments of which poor Sober trembles at the thought. But the misery of these tiresome intervals, he has many means of alleviating. He has persuaded himself that the manual arts are undeservedly overlooked; he has observed in many trades the effects of close thought, and just ratiocination. From speculation he proceeded to practice, and supplied himself with the tools of a carpenter, with which he mended his coal-box very successfully, and which he still continues to employ, as he finds occasion.

He has attempted at other times the crafts of the shoemaker, tinman, plumber, and potter; in all these arts he has failed, and resolves to qualify himself for them by better information. But his daily amusement is chemistry. He has a small **furnace**, which he employs in distillation, and which has long been the solace of his life. He draws oils and waters, and essences and spirits, which he knows to be of no use; sits and counts the drops as they come from his **retort**, and forgets that, while a drop is falling, a moment flies away.

Poor Sober! I have often teased him with (reproof), and he has often promised reformation; for no man is so much open to conviction as the idler, but there is none on whom it operates so little. What will be the effect of this paper I know not; perhaps he will read it and laugh, and light the fire in his furnace; but my hope is that he will quit his trifles, and betake himself to rational and useful diligence.

Words and Phrases

votary ['vəʊt(ə)rɪ]	n.	a devoted (almost religiously so) adherent of a cause or person or activity 崇拜者
garland ['gɑːlənd]	n.	flower arrangement consisting of a circular band of foliage or flowers for ornamental purposes 花环
oblivion [ə'blɪvɪən]	n.	total forgetfulness 遗忘；赦免
unruffled [ʌn'rʌf(ə)ld]	adj.	free from emotional agitation or nervous tension 平静的；镇定的
gratification [grætɪfɪ'keɪʃn]	n.	state of being gratified; great satisfaction 满意；喜悦
tediousness ['tiːdɪəsnɪs]	n.	dullness owing to length or slowness 沉闷；乏味

Chapter 4
Samuel Johnson
萨缪尔·约翰逊

solicitude [sə'lɪsɪtjuːd]	*n.*	a feeling of excessive concern 焦虑；担心
reproach [rɪ'prəʊtʃ]	*n.*	a mild rebuke or criticism 责备，责怪
furnace ['fɜːnɪs]	*n.*	an enclosed chamber in which heat is produced to heat buildings 火炉，熔炉
retort [rɪ'tɔːt]	*n.*	a quick reply to a question or remark (especially a witty or critical one) 反驳，顶嘴

II Reading Comprehension Questions

1. Why do you think the author begins the essay with a discussion of pride?
2. What's the similarities and differences between "pride" and "idleness"?
3. In the author's point of view, why is turbulence and hurry a disguise of idleness?
4. What's Mr. Sober's art to avoid the tediousness of life?
5. Does the author's idle friend Sober remind you of somebody you know?

Quotes of the Author

Few things are impossible to diligence and skill. Great works are performed not by strength, but perseverance.

Hope is itself a species of happiness, and, perhaps, the chief happiness which this world affords.

Hope is necessary in every condition.

Of all noises, I think music is the least disagreeable.

Self-confidence is the first requisite to great undertakings.

Charles Lamb
查尔斯·兰姆
(1775—1834)

Chapter 5

本章导读

查尔斯·兰姆（Charles Lamb，1775—1834），英国文学史上著名的随笔作家。兰姆在有生之年涉猎不同文体的文学创作，包括诗歌、传奇、剧本、评论、散文等，其中取得最大成就的是在随笔领域，是与蒙田并列具有世界声誉的大家。

查尔斯·兰姆生于伦敦一个下层职员家庭。7 岁时进入为贫寒子弟开设的基督慈幼学校读书，与诗人柯勒律治成为同学并结下终生友谊。兰姆因口吃于 15 岁辍学，未能进入大学。17 岁起就在东印度公司当小职员，工作了 33 年。业余时间从事文学创作。1796 年，兰姆的家庭遭遇了一个重大悲剧：他的姐姐玛丽因遗传的精神病突发竟用刀子刺死了自己的母亲。由于姐姐的精神病经常周期性地发作，兰姆便承担起了照顾姐姐的义务，并为此终身未娶。同样，姐姐也用自己的体贴和关照来回报兰姆。兰姆本人也有短期（1795—1796 年）的精神错乱，可怕的精神错乱是他终生的阴影。值得一提的是，他的姐姐玛丽其实是一个极有灵性的女子，姐弟俩合作编写的少儿读物《莎士比亚戏剧故事集》，至今仍广泛流传于世界各地。

经历过如此多的苦难，兰姆在文学上取得的巨大成就显得格外耀眼。兰姆写过诗歌、传奇、剧本、莎剧论文、美术评论，出了两卷《文集》。兰姆最重要的代表作是《伊利亚随笔》（1823）和《伊利亚续笔》（1833）。从 1820 年开始，兰姆借用一位老同事的名字"伊利亚"作为笔名在《伦敦杂志》陆陆续续发表了大小 60 多篇随笔散文，之后汇集为两本书出版，即在世界文学宝库中独领风骚的两集《伊利亚随笔》。

我国 30 年代研究介绍兰姆的梁遇春曾如此评价兰姆的作品，它们"……是止血的灵药。兰姆一生逢着好多不顺意的事，可是他能用飘逸的想头，轻快的文字，把很沉重的苦痛拨开了。什么事情他都取了一种特别的观察点，所以可给普通人许多愁闷的事情，他随随便便不当一回事地过去了。"刘炳善教授评论说兰姆创作的这种既不同于古人、也不同于当代作家的作品有着强烈的个人印记：首先，它是个性毕露、披肝沥胆的，兰姆在他的随笔里以伦敦的城市生活为描写对象，赋予日常生活中的平凡小事以浪漫的异彩，从芸芸众生中的苦难与悲伤中寻找诗意。其次，他的作品的总情调是怀旧的，笔法则是亦庄亦谐，寓庄于谐，在谐谑之中暗含着个人的辛酸。他的散文中抒情、记事、议论相互穿插；文言、白话、简古交互使用，怎么方便怎么写；有话即长，无话则短，跌宕多姿，妙趣横生。尽管一生孤苦，兰姆奉献给大家的却是最单纯美丽的心灵所能感悟到的人生，而这给予人们的恰恰是灵魂深处的净化。他说过，他的随笔集，不需要序言来介绍，因为他的每篇随笔都是自己的"序言"。他的随笔乃是一颗善良的心里所发出的含泪微笑。

About the Author

Charles Lamb was an English writer and essayist, best known for his *Essays of Elia*, a series of miscellaneous（多方面的，多角度的）articles which appeared in *The London Magazine* between 1820 and 1823.

Lamb was born in London on February 10, 1775. He studied at Christ's Hospital where he formed a lifelong friendship with Samuel Taylor Coleridge. When he was 20 years old, Lamb suffered a period of insanity. His sister, Mary Ann Lamb, had similar problems and in 1796 murdered her mother in a fit of madness. Mary was confined to an asylum（精神病院）but was eventually released into the care of her brother. *Tales from Shakespeare* (1807) which Lamb wrote in collaboration with his sister and *The Adventures of Ulysses* (1808) were valuable retellings of classic works for children. Lamb's critical comments in *Specimens of English Dramatic Poets Who Lived about the Time of Shakespeare* (1808) are among the classics of English criticism.

The subjects of Lamb's essays were often drawn from the richness of London life. He also wrote a number of poems, and was part of a literary circle in England, along with Samuel Taylor Coleridge and William Wordsworth, whom he befriended. He has been referred to by E. V. Lucas, his principal biographer, as "the most lovable figure in English literature". Lamb's essays are as much an expression of the Romantic Movement, but he is

Chapter 5

Charles Lamb
查尔斯·兰姆

quite different from the romantic poets of his day, he felt more at home in the city than in the wild nature.

As a writer, Lamb may not be called as "great", but as an essayist, he owns a worldwide reputation which still remains side by side with Montaigne. Lamb's style is peculiarly his own. Writing in the genre of "the personal essay", again and again Lamb made literary delightfulness of the things that tormented him most—including his resentments and drunkenness. In so doing, Charles Lamb brought a new kind of warmth to English prose. His beautiful sentences can be intense, they can sneer, they can scream, but they always have a kind of rounded glow, like a welcoming, slightly melancholy fireplace. His close-knit, subtle organization, his self-revealing observations on life, and his humor, fantasy, and pathos（悲怆，痛苦）combine to make him one of the great masters of the English essays.

Text A

Dream-Children

A Reverie

Charles Lamb

Childern love to listen to stories about their elders, when they were children; to stretch their imagination to the conception of a traditionary great-uncle or **grandame**, whom they never saw. It was in this spirit that my little ones crept about me the other evening to hear about their great-grandmother Field, who lived in a great house in Norfolk (a hundred times bigger than that in which they and papa lived) which had been the scene—so at least it was generally believed in that part of the country—of the tragic incidents which they had lately become familiar with from the ballad of the *Children in the Wood*[1]. Certain it is that the whole story of the children and their cruel uncle was to be seen fairly carved out in wood upon the **chimney-piece** of the great hall, the whole story down to the Robin Redbreasts, till a foolish rich person pulled it down to set up a marble one of modern invention in its stead, with no story upon it. Here Alice put out one of her dear mother's looks, too tender to be called **upbraiding**. Then I went on to say, how religious and how good their great-grandmother Field was, how beloved and respected by everybody, though she was not indeed the mistress of this great house, but had only the charge of it (and yet in some respects she might be said to be the mistress of it too) committed to her by the owner, who preferred living in a newer and more fashionable mansion which he had purchased somewhere in the **adjoining** county; but still she lived in it in a manner as if it had been her own, and kept

---

1 *Children in the Wood*: a famous ballad in English culture 《林中幼子》是英国文化中有名的歌谣。歌谣叙述一富绅临终前将其幼子幼女二人及全部家私托给他的弟弟照管。但孩子们的叔叔本是个凶残的人，于是蓄意杀死他的侄子侄女而独吞财产。他雇了两名恶汉带孩子去一树林当中，准备在那里处死孩子。恶汉中一人忽生悔心，于是杀了另一恶汉而逃走，结果两个孩子遂被活活冻死在林中。事泄，这个凶残的叔父被拘下狱。

Chapter 5
Charles Lamb
查尔斯·兰姆

up the dignity of the great house in a sort while she lived, which afterward came to decay, and was nearly pulled down, and all its old ornaments stripped and carried away to the owner's other house, where they were set up, and looked as awkward as if some one were to carry away the old tombs they had seen lately at the Abbey, and stick them up in Lady C.'s **tawdry** gilt drawing-room. Here John smiled, as much as to say, "that would be foolish indeed." And then I told how, when she came to die, her funeral was attended by a **concourse** of all the poor, and some of the **gentry** too, of the neighbourhood for many miles round, to show their respect for her memory, because she had been such a good and religious woman; so good indeed that she knew all the **Psaltery** by heart, aye, and a great part of the **Testament** besides. Here little Alice spread her hands. Then I told what a tall, upright, graceful person their great-grandmother Field once was; and how in her youth she was esteemed the best dancer—here Alice's little right foot played an involuntary movement, till upon my looking grave, it **desisted**—the best dancer, I was saying, in the county, till a cruel disease, called a cancer, came, and bowed her down with pain; but it could never bend her good spirits, or make them **stoop**, but they were still upright, because she was so good and religious. Then I told how she was used to sleep by herself in a lone chamber of the great lone house; and how she believed that an **apparition** of two infants was to be seen at midnight gliding up and down the great staircase near where she slept, but she said "those innocents would do her no harm"; and how frightened I used to be, though in those days I had my maid to sleep with me, because I was never half so good or religious as she—and yet I never saw the infants. Here John expanded all his eyebrows and tried to look courageous. Then I told how good she was to all her grand-children, having us to the great house in the holidays, where I in particular used to spend many hours by myself, in gazing upon the old **busts** of the Twelve Cæsars, that had been Emperors of Rome, till the old marble heads would seem to live again, or I to be turned into marble with them; how I never could be tired with **roaming** about that huge mansion, with its vast empty rooms, with their **worn-out** hangings, **fluttering tapestry**, and carved **oaken** panels, with the gilding almost rubbed out—sometimes in the spacious old-fashioned gardens, which I had almost to myself, unless when now and then a solitary gardening man would cross me—and how the **nectarines** and peaches hung upon the walls, without my ever offering to **pluck** them, because they were forbidden fruit, unless now and then,—and because I had more pleasure in **strolling** about among the old melancholy-looking yew trees, or the firs, and picking up the red berries, and the **fir** apples, which were good for nothing but to look at—or in lying about upon the fresh grass, with all the fine garden smells around me—or **basking** in the **orangery**, till I could almost fancy myself ripening, too, along with the oranges and the **limes** in that grateful warmth—or in watching the **dace** that **darted** to and fro in the fish pond, at the bottom of the garden, with here and there a great **sulky pike** hanging midway down the water in silent state, as if it mocked at their **impertinent friskings**,—I had more pleasure in these busy-idle diversions than in all the sweet flavours of peaches, nectarines, oranges, and such like common **baits** of children. Here John **slyly** deposited back upon the plate a bunch of grapes, which, not unobserved by Alice, he had mediated dividing with her, and both seemed willing to **relinquish** them for the present as irrelevant. Then, in somewhat a more heightened tone, I told how, though their great-grandmother Field loved all her grand-children, yet in an especial manner she might be said to love their uncle, John L—, because he was so handsome and spirited a youth, and a king to the rest of us; and, instead of **moping** about in solitary corners, like some of us, he would mount the most **mettlesome** horse he could get, when but an **imp** no bigger than themselves, and make it carry him half over the county in a morning, and join the hunters when there were any out—and yet he loved the old great house and gardens too, but had too much spirit to be always **pent** up within their boundaries—and how their uncle grew up to man's estate as brave as he was handsome, to the admiration of everybody, but of their great-grandmother Field most especially; and how he used to carry me upon his back when I was a lame-footed boy—for he was a good bit older than me—many a mile when I could not walk for pain;—and how in after life he became lame-footed too, and I did not always (I fear) make allowances enough for him when he was impatient,

Chapter 5
Charles Lamb
查尔斯·兰姆

and in pain, nor remember sufficiently how considerate he had been to me when I was lame-footed; and how when he died, though he had not been dead an hour, it seemed as if he had died a great while ago, such a distance there is **betwixt** life and death; and how I bore his death as I thought pretty well at first, but afterward it haunted and haunted me; and though I did not cry or take it to heart as some do, and as I think he would have done if I had died, yet I missed him all day long, and knew not till then how much I had loved him. I missed his kindness, and I missed his crossness, and wished him to be alive again, to be quarreling with him (for we quarreled sometimes), rather than not have him again, and was as uneasy without him, as he their poor uncle must have been when the doctor took off his limb. Here the children fell a crying, and asked if their little mourning which they had on was not for uncle John, and they looked up and prayed me not to go on about their uncle, but to tell them some stories about their pretty, dead mother. Then I told them how for seven long years, in hope sometimes, sometimes in despair, yet persisting ever, I courted the fair Alice W—n; and, as much as children could understand, I explained to them what **coyness**, and difficulty, and denial meant in maidens—when suddenly, turning to Alice, the soul of the first Alice looked out at her eyes with such a reality of re-presentment, that I became in doubt which of them stood there before me, or whose that bright hair was; and while I stood gazing, both the children gradually grew fainter to my view, receding, and still receding till nothing at last but two mournful features were seen in the uttermost distance, which, without speech, strangely impressed upon me the effects of speech: "We are not of Alice, nor of thee, nor are we children at all. The children of Alice call Bartrum father. We are nothing; less than nothing, and dreams. We are only what might have been, and must wait upon the tedious shores of Lethe[1] millions of ages before we have existence, and a name"—and immediately awaking, I found myself quietly seated in my

---

1　Lethe: one of the five rivers in Hades 希腊神话中的忘川，也叫遗忘之河，是冥府中五条河流之一。亡魂须饮此河之水以忘掉人间事。冥府中其他四条河流分别是：Styx（悔恨之河）、Acheron（苦难之河）、Cocytus（悲叹之河）和 Phlegethon（熔岩之河）。

bachelor armchair, where I had fallen asleep, with the faithful Bridget[1] unchanged by my side—but John L.[2] (or James Elia) was gone forever.

I Words and Phrases

grandame ['grændæm]	n.	grandmother 祖母；外祖母
chimney-piece ['tʃɪmnɪpɪs]	n.	a place in which wood can be burned to keep warm 壁炉架
upbraiding [ʌp'breɪdɪŋ]	n.	a severe scolding 谴责
adjoining [ə'dʒɔɪnɪŋ]	adj.	close in distance 相连的，毗邻的
tawdry ['tɒdrɪ]	adj.	cheap and vulgar 低劣俗艳的
concourse ['kɒŋkɔːs]	n.	a large gathering of people 群众；集合
gentry ['dʒentrɪ]	n.	upper class and noble class 绅士们；贵族们；上层阶级
Psaltery ['sɔːltərɪ]	n.	赞美诗
Testament ['testəmənt]	n.	pledge, a biblical book（基督教）圣约书；确实的证明；誓约
desist [dɪ'zɪst]	v.	to choose not to consume 停止；断念
stoop [stuːp]	v.	to debase oneself morally, act in an undignified, unworthy, or dishonorable way 屈服；堕落
apparition [ˌæpə'rɪʃən]	n.	a ghostly appearing figure 幽灵；幻影
bust [bʌst]	n.	a half of statue 半身雕塑像
roam [rəʊm]	v.	wander about 漫步，漫游
worn-out ['wɔːn'aʊt]	adj.	can not use any more and shabby 破旧；不能再用或穿的
flutter ['flʌtə(r)]	v.	move up and down to the wind 飘动，（旗帜）飘扬
tapestry ['tæpɪstrɪ]	n.	a wall hanging of heavy handwoven fabric with pictorial designs 挂毯

---

1 Bridget: a penname for Mary Charels 作者姐姐的化名
2 John L.: John Lamb 约翰·兰，即约翰·兰姆，兰姆之兄

Chapter 5
Charles Lamb
查尔斯·兰姆

oaken ['əʊkən]	adj.	made of oak 橡木制的
nectarine ['nektərɪn]	n.	油桃
pluck [plʌk]	v.	pick it up 拔掉；采
stroll [strəʊl]	v.	wander about 漫步；闲逛
fir [fɜː]	n.	a kind of plant 冷杉；<植>枞木
bask [bɑːsk]	v.	be exposed to the sun 晒太阳
orangery ['ɔːrɪndʒərɪ]	n.	a garden to plant orange 橘园，橘子的温室
lime [laɪm]	n.	酸橙；椴树
dace [deɪs]	n.	a kind of fish 鲦鱼
dart [dɑːt]	v.	to move suddenly and quickly in a particular direction 猛冲，飞奔
sulky ['sʌlkɪ]	adj.	looked angry and gloomy 愠怒的，生闷气的
pike [paɪk]	n.	梭子鱼；长矛
impertinent [ɪm'pɜːtɪnənt]	adj.	impolite and with no courtesy 无礼的；莽撞的
frisking [frɪskɪŋ]	n.	the act of moving lively and energetically（动物）活蹦乱跳
bait [beɪt]	n.	food which you put on a hook or in a trap in order to catch fish or animals 饵，诱饵；置诱饵于……
slyly ['slaɪlɪ]	adv.	in an artful manner 狡猾地；俏皮地
relinquish [rɪ'lɪŋkwɪʃ]	v.	give it up 放弃，让出（权利，财产等）
mope [məʊp]	adj.	be apathetic, gloomy, or dazed 忧郁；百无聊赖
mettlesome ['metls(ə)m]	adj.	having a proud and unbroken spirit 精神饱满的
imp [ɪmp]	n.	little monster in the story 小恶魔，小淘气，顽童
pent [pent]	adj.	be shut down or closed 被关闭的
betwixt [bɪ'twɪkst]	prep.	in the middle of something <旧>在其间，在……中间
coyness [kɔɪnəs]	n.	be shy of 怕羞，羞怯

II　Reading Comprehension Questions

1. How do you understand the meaning of the title and subtitle? What is this essay about?
2. According to the narrator, what kind of person is Grandmother Field?
3. According to the narrator, what kind of person is Uncle John?
4. According to the narrator, what kind of personality the author had when he was a young boy? Where can you see it?
5. As far as subject matter is concerned, "Dream Children" is a perfect example of mixture of fiction and reality. Can you tell which part of the content is fiction and which part is reality?

III　Questions on Writing Style and Language

1. Have you noticed any stylistic features of Lamb's writings? Are his sentences long or short? What particular effect is produced by these sentences?
2. Can you sense the gentle humor of Lamb from this essay? Please identify some humorous sentences and expressions in the essay.
3. The author did not divide the essay into paragraphs but it is still close-knit. Do you see the logic of its organization?
4. The author described the "little ones" with great vividness. Please find out the techniques the author used to achieve such vividness.
5. Transferred epithet is a figure of speech where an epithet (an adjective or descriptive phrase) is transferred from the noun it should rightly modify to another to which it does not really belong. Can you identify the use of transferred epithet in Lamb's sentence "… or basking in the orangery, till I could almost fancy myself ripening, too, along with the oranges and the limes in that grateful warmth"?

Charles Lamb
查尔斯·兰姆

New Year's Eve

Charles Lamb

Every man hath two birth-days: two days, at least, in every year, which set him upon revolving the **lapse** of time, as it affects his mortal duration. The one is that which in an especial manner he termth his. In the gradual **desuetude** of old observances, this custom of solemnizing our proper birth-day hath nearly passed away, or is left to children, who reflect nothing at all about the matter, nor understand anything in it beyond cake and orange. But the birth of a New Year is of an interest too wide to be **pretermitted** by king or **cobbler**. No one ever regarded the First of January with indifference. It is that from which all date their time, and count upon what is left. It is the **nativity** of our common Adam.

Of all sounds of all bells—(bells, the music nighest bordering upon heaven)—most solemn and touching is the peal which rings out the Old Year. I never hear it without a gathering-up of my mind to a concentration of all the images that have been **diffused** over the past twelve month; all I have done or suffered, performed or neglected—in that regretted time. I begin to know its worth, as when a person dies. It takes a personal colour; nor was it a poetical flight in a contemporary, when he exclaimed

I saw the skirts of the departing Year.

It is no more than what in sober sadness every one of us seems to be conscious of, in that awful **leave-taking**. I am sure I felt it, and all felt it with me, last night; though some of my companions affected rather to manifest an exhilaration at the birth of the coming year, than any very tender regrets for the decease of its predecessor. But I am none of those who—

Welcome the coming, speed the parting guest.

I am naturally, beforehand, shy of **novelties**; new books, new faces, new years, from some mental twist which makes it difficult in me to face the prospective. I have almost ceased to hope; and am **sanguine** only in the prospects of other (former) years. I plunge into foregone visions and conclusions. I encounter pell-mell with past disappointments. I am armour-proof against old discouragements. I forgive, or overcome in fancy, old adversaries. I play over again for love, as the **gamesters** phrase it, games, for which I once paid so dear. I would scarce now have any of those **untoward** accidents and events of my life reversed. I would no more alter them than the incidents of some well-contrived novel. Methinks, it is better that I should have pined away seven of my goldenest years, when I was thrall to the fair hair, and fairer eyes, of Alice W—n, than that so passionate a love-adventure should be lost. It was better that our family should have missed that legacy, which old Dorrell cheated us of, than that I should have at this moment two thousand pounds in banco, and be without the idea of that specious old **rogue**.

In a degree beneath manhood, it is my infirmity to look back upon those early days. Do I advance a paradox, when I say, that, skipping over the intervention of forty years, a man may have leave to love himself, without the **imputation** of self-love?

If I know **aught** of myself, no one whose mind is **introspective**—and mine is painfully so—can have a less respect for his present identity, than I have for the man Elia. I know him to be light, and vain, and humorsome; a notorious ***; addicted to ***: averse from counsel, neither taking it, nor offering it; —*** besides; a **stammering** buffoon; what you will; lay it on, and spare not; I subscribe to it all, and much more, than thou canst be willing to lay at his door—but for the child Elia—that "other me," there, in the back-ground—I must take leave to cherish the remembrance of that young master—with as little reference, I protest, to this stupid **changeling** of five-and-forty, as if it had been a child of some other house, and not of my parents. I can cry over its patient small-pox at five, and rougher medicaments. I can lay its poor fevered head upon the sick pillow at Christ's, and wake with it in surprise at the gentle posture of maternal tenderness hanging over it, that unknown had watched its sleep. I know how it shrank from any the least colour of

Chapter 5

Charles Lamb
查尔斯·兰姆

falsehood. God help thee, Elia, how art thou changed! Thou art sophisticated. I know how honest, how courageous (for a weakling) it was—how religious, how imaginative, how hopeful! From what have I not fallen, if the child I remember was indeed myself, and not some dissembling guardian, presenting a false identity, to give the rule to my unpractised steps, and regulate the tone of my moral being!

That I am fond of indulging, beyond a hope of sympathy, in such **retrospection**, may be the symptom of some sickly **idiosyncrasy**. Or is it owing to another cause; simply, that being without wife or family, I have not learned to project myself enough out of myself; and having no offspring of my own to dally with, I turn back upon memory and adopt my own early idea, as my heir and favourite? If these speculations seem fantastical to thee, reader (a busy man, perchance), if I tread out of the way of thy sympathy, and am singularly-conceited only, I retire, impenetrable to ridicule, under the phantom cloud of Elia.

The elders, with whom I was brought up, were of a character not likely to let slip the sacred observance of any old institution; and the ringing out of the Old Year was kept by them with circumstances of peculiar ceremony. In those days the sound of those midnight **chimes**, though it seemed to raise hilarity in all around me, never failed to bring a train of **pensive** imagery into my fancy. Yet I then scarce conceived what it meant, or thought of it as a reckoning that concerned me. Not childhood alone, but the young man till thirty, never feels practically that he is mortal. He knows it indeed, and, if need were, he could preach a homily on the fragility of life; but he brings it not home to himself, any more than in a hot June we can appropriate to our imagination the freezing days of December. But now, shall I confess a truth? I feel these audits but too powerfully. I begin to count the probabilities of my duration, and to **grudge** at the expenditure of moments and shortest periods, like **miser's** farthings. In proportion as the years both lessen and shorten, I set more count upon their periods, and would **fain** lay my ineffectual finger upon the spoke of the great wheel. I am not content to pass away "like a weaver's shuttle". Those metaphors solace me not, nor sweeten the **unpalatable** draught of mortality. I care not to be carried with the tide, that smoothly bears human life to eternity; and reluct at the inevitable course of destiny. I am in love with this green earth; the face of town and country; the unspeakable rural solitudes, and the sweet security of streets. I would set up my tabernacle here. I am content to stand still at the age to which I am arrived; I, and my friends: to be no younger, no richer, no handsomer. I do not want to be weaned by age; or drop, like mellow fruit, as they say, into the grave. Any alteration, on this earth of mine, in diet or in lodging, puzzles and discomposes me. My household-gods plant a terrible fixed foot, and are not rooted up without blood. They do not willingly seek Lavinian shores. A new state of being staggers me.

Sun, and sky, and breeze, and solitary walks, and summer holidays, and the greenness of fields, and the delicious juices of meats and fishes, and society, and the cheerful glass, and candle-light, and fire-side conversations, and innocent vanities, and **jests**, and irony itself—do these things go out with life?

Can a ghost laugh, or shake his **gaunt** sides, when you are pleasant with him?

And you, my midnight darlings, my **Folios**! must I part with the intense delight of having you (huge armfuls) in my embraces? Must knowledge come to me, if it come at all, by some awkward experiment of intuition, and no longer by this familiar process of reading?

Shall I enjoy friendships there, wanting the smiling indications which point me to them here,—the recognisable face—the "sweet assurance of a look"—?

In winter this intolerable disinclination to dying—to give it its mildest name—does more especially haunt and beset me. In a **genial** August noon, beneath a sweltering sky, death is almost problematic. At those times do such poor snakes as myself enjoy an immortality. Then we expand and burgeon. Then are we as strong again, as valiant again, as wise again, and a great deal taller. The blast that nips and shrinks me, puts me in thoughts of death. All things allied to the insubstantial, wait upon that master feeling; cold, numbness, dreams, perplexity; moonlight itself, with its shadowy and spectral appearances,—that cold ghost of the sun, or Phoebus' sickly sister, like that innutritious one denounced in the Canticles:—I am none of her minions—I

Chapter 5
Charles Lamb
查尔斯·兰姆

hold with the Persian.

Whatsoever thwarts, or puts me out of my way, brings death into my mind. All partial evils, like humours, run into that capital plague-sore. I have heard some profess an indifference to life. Such hail the end of their existence as a port of refuge; and speak of the grave as of some soft arms, in which they may slumber as on a pillow. Some have wooed death—but out upon thee, I say, thou foul, ugly phantom! I detest, abhor, execrate, and (with Friar John) give thee to six-score thousand devils, as in no instance to be excused or tolerated, but shunned as a universal viper; to be branded, proscribed, and spoken evil of! In no way can I be brought to digest thee, thou thin, melancholy Privation, or more frightful and confounding Positive!

Those antidotes, prescribed against the fear of thee, are altogether frigid and insulting, like thyself. For what satisfaction hath a man, that he shall "lie down with kings and emperors in death," who in his life-time never greatly coveted the society of such bed-fellows?—or, forsooth, that "so shall the fairest face appear?"—why, to comfort me, must Alice W—n be a goblin? More than all, I conceive disgust at those impertinent and misbecoming familiarities, inscribed upon your ordinary tombstones. Every dead man must take upon himself to be lecturing me with his odious truism, that "such as he now is, I must shortly be." Not so shortly, friend, perhaps, as thou imaginest. In the meantime I am alive. I move about. I am worth twenty of thee. Know thy betters! Thy New Years' Days are past. I survive, a jolly candidate for 1821. Another cup of wine—and while that turn-coat bell, that just now mournfully chanted the obsequies of 1820 departed, with changed notes lustily rings in a successor, let us attune to its peal the song made on a like occasion, by hearty, cheerful Mr. Cotton.—

THE NEW YEAR
Hark, the cock crows, and yon bright star
Tells us, the day himself's not far;
And see where, breaking from the night,
He gilds the western hills with light.

With him old Janus doth appear,
Peeping into the future year,
With such a look as seems to say,
The prospect is not good that way.
Thus do we rise ill sights to see,
And 'gainst ourselves to prophesy;
When the prophetic fear of things
A more tormenting mischief brings,
More full of soul-tormenting gall,
Than direst mischiefs can befall.
But stay! but stay! methinks my sight,
Better inform'd by clearer light,
Discerns sereneness in that brow,
That all contracted seem'd but now.
His revers'd face may show distaste,
And frown upon the ills are past;
But that which this way looks is clear,
And smiles upon the New-born Year.
He looks too from a place so high,
The Year lies open to his eye;
And all the moments open are
To the exact discoverer.
Yet more and more he smiles upon
The happy revolution.
Why should we then suspect or fear
The influences of a year,
So smiles upon us the first morn,
And speaks us good so soon as born?
Plague on't! the last was ill enough,
This cannot but make better proof;
Or, at the worst, as we brush'd through
The last, why so we may this too;

Chapter 5

Charles Lamb
查尔斯·兰姆

And then the next in reason shou'd
Be superexcellently good:
For the worst ills (we daily see)
Have no more perpetuity,
Than the best fortunes that do fall;
Which also bring us wherewithal
Longer their being to support,
Than those do of the other sort:
And who has one good year in three,
And yet repines at destiny,
Appears ungrateful in the case,
And merits not the good he has.
Then let us welcome the New Guest
With lusty brimmers of the best;
Mirth always should Good Fortune meet,
And renders e'en Disaster sweet:
And though the Princess turn her back,
Let us but line ourselves with sack,
We better shall by far hold out,
Till the next Year she face about.

How say you, reader—do not these verses smack of the rough magnanimity of the old English vein? Do they not fortify like a cordial; enlarging the heart, and productive of sweet blood, and generous spirits, in the concoction? Where be those puling fears of death, just now expressed or affected? Passed like a cloud—absorbed in the purging sunlight of clear poetry—clean washed away by a wave of genuine Helicon, your only *Spa* for these hypochondries—And now another cup of the generous! and a merry New Year, and many of them, to you all, my masters!

I. Words and Phrases

lapse [læps]	v.	to glide along 流逝
desuetude ['deswɪtjʊd]	n.	in a state of disuse 废止，不用
pretermit [ˌpriːtə'mɪt]	v.	to disregard intentionally or let pass 忽略；对……置之不问
cobbler ['kɒblə]	n.	a person whose job is to make or mend shoes 鞋匠
nativity [nə'tɪvɪtɪ]	n.	birth or origin, esp in relation to the circumstances surrounding it 出生；起源
diffuse [dɪ'fjuːz]	v.	made known over a wide area or to a lot of people 传播（知识、消息等）；散布
leave-taking		the act of departing politely 告辞，告别；告别语
novelty ['nɒv(ə)ltɪ]	n.	something that is new and therefore interesting 新奇的事物
sanguine ['sæŋgwɪn]	adj.	confidently optimistic and cheerful 乐观的
gamester ['geɪmstə]	n.	a person who habitually plays games for money; gambler 赌徒
untoward [ˌʌntə'wɔːd]	adj.	unexpected and causing difficulties 困难的；不幸的
rogue [rəʊg]	n.	a man who behaves in a dishonest or criminal way 流氓，无赖
imputation [ˌɪmpjuː'teɪʃən]	n.	a statement attributing something dishonest 归罪
aught [ɔːt]	n.	anything at all; anything whatever 任何事物
introspective [ˌɪntrə'spektɪv]	adj.	(people) spending a lot of time examining their own thoughts, ideas, and feelings 反省的，内省的
stammering ['stæmərɪŋ]	adj.	speaking with difficulty, hesitating and repeating words or sounds 结结巴巴地说，口吃
changeling ['tʃeɪn(d)ʒlɪŋ]	n.	a child who was put in the place of another child when they were both babies 调包婴儿

Chapter 5

Charles Lamb
查尔斯·兰姆

retrospection [ˌretrə'spekʃən]	n.	reference to things past 回顾	
idiosyncrasy [ˌɪdɪə(ʊ)'sɪŋkrəsɪ]	n.	unusual personal habits or characteristics 习性；癖好；特性	
chime [tʃaɪm]	v.	when a bell or a clock chimes, it makes ringing sounds 鸣响	
pensive ['pensɪv]	adj.	persistently or morbidly thoughtful 沉思的，忧郁的；悲伤的	
grudge [grʌdʒ]	v.	bear unfriendly feelings toward others because of something they did in the past 积怨	
miser ['maɪzə]	n.	a stingy hoarder of money and possessions (often living miserably) 守财奴，吝啬鬼	
fain [feɪn]	adj.	in a willing manner 不得不的；乐意的	
unpalatable [ʌn'pælətəb(ə)l]	adj.	not pleasant or acceptable to the taste or mind 味道差的，难吃的；讨人厌的	
jest [dʒest]	n.	something said or done to amuse people 玩笑	
gaunt [gɔːnt]	adj.	look very thin and worried 憔悴的	
folio ['fəʊlɪəʊ]	n.	a book (or manuscript) consisting of large sheets of paper folded in the middle to make two leaves or four pages 对开的书	
genial ['dʒiːnɪəl]	adj.	diffusing warmth and friendliness 适宜的	

II Reading Comprehension Questions

1. According to the author, when are the two birthdays in every man's life? What do the two birthdays have to do with the theme?
2. How does the author describe his present identity and the "Child Elia"? What is revealed to you by this contrast?
3. On hearing the midnight chime, what does the author want to confess? How is it different from his younger days?
4. What are some of the things that the author cherishes in his life?
5. How does the poem at the end of the essay back up the author's ideas?

Quotes of the Author

I am determined that my children shall be brought up in their father's religion, if they can find out what it is.

Lawyers, I suppose, were children once.

There is nothing so nice as doing good by stealth and being found out by accident.

Nothing to me is more distasteful than that entire complacency and satisfaction which beam in the countenances of a newly married couple.

My motto is: Contented with little, yet wishing for more.

William Hazlitt
威廉·哈兹里特
(1778—1830)

本章导读

威廉·哈兹里特是一位极具时代性的散文家和文学评论家,他凭借独到的评论和平易的小品文在英国文学浪漫主义时期占有一席之地。

威廉·哈兹里特出生于牧师家庭,在爱尔兰和美国度过童年时代,曾就读于哈克尼神学院;去过巴黎学习绘画,早期生活以作画为主;当过记者,之后转向文学和戏剧评论;1805年后,潜心研究过哲学,结识著名诗人柯勒律治和华兹华斯,与查尔斯·兰姆更是一生的挚友。他同情法国大革命,积极主张民主共和;崇尚个人主义,反对权威和习俗,以观点鲜明、思想激进和喜好论争而闻名于文坛。

哈兹里特一生作品众多,以散文为主。其散文以内容为标准大体归为两类:一类是文学评论;另一类是小品文。哈兹里特的文学评论作品主要包括:《莎士比亚剧中的人物》(*Characters of Shakespeare's Plays*),《英国诗人论集》(*Lectures on the English Poets*),《英国戏剧作家论集》(*Lectures on the English Comic Writers*,1819),以及《时代精神》(*The Spirit of the Age*)等。哈兹里特另一文学成就在于其小品文。比起文学评论,他的小品文更出名,大都首先登载在各种报章杂志上,然后汇集成册出版。主要有《圆桌》(*The Round Table*,1817),《闲谈集》(*Table Talk*),《直言者》(*The Plain Speaker*),以及他去世后才得以出版的《随笔与散文》(*Sketches and Essays*)等。

哈兹里特的全集于1902—1906年出版,共13卷,达6000页之多。一位评论家说,"他的勤奋是惊人的……也许没有任何一位写得这么多的英国作家能像他这样写出这么多上乘的作品。"哈兹里特一生坦率直言,无所畏惧。1830年,他在孤独中死去,年仅52岁。他临终前兰姆在他的身旁,这给了他安慰,他最后对兰姆说:"好,我度过了美好的一生。"

哈兹里特文笔犀利、风趣，语言准确流畅，文章既充满生活气息，又富于哲理，多机智的警句和通俗的类比，爱广征博引，寓精练于浩瀚之中。哈兹里特主张平易通俗的风格，因而用词简易，句子接近口语，行文流畅，气势不凡，夹有大量的典故和引语，其中不乏隽永妙句，令人应接不暇。他认为平易通俗的风格是一种既不故示艰深，也不庸俗媚众的形式。他主张使用最恰当的词语来表达自己的思想。他特别善于使用形容词，往往会出人意料地遣词造句，新颖奇特，使人印象分外深刻，如亲临其境。人们常说的"诗中有画"，哈兹里特的文章就大有这种意境。19世纪末著名作家斯蒂文森（Stevenson, 1850—1894）曾评论说："虽然今天我们都是好手，却写不出像哈兹里特那样的文章。"

About the Author

William Hazlitt was a journalist, parliamentary reporter, dramatist critic and essayist. He was born in Maidstone, Kent, and his father was an Irish Unitarian minister. His mother, Grace Loftus, was from an English dissenting family who were friendly with Godwin's family, so Hazlitt's writings draw strongly on the culture of radical dissent in Britain and Ireland. As an ardent supporter of the French Revolution, he was also deeply concerned about the social ills of his own country.

Hazlitt was the first writer to make a large part of his livelihood from descriptive criticism. His most famous works include *Characters of Shakespear's Plays* (1817), *English Comic Writers* (1819), and *Table Talk*, etc.

William Hazlitt is one of the great masters of English prose style. He is a major literary critic and radical polemicist whose intellect is both analytical and sensuously particular. Keats worshipped him, and his poems and letters are shaped by Hazlitt's influence—his sentences are like "a whale's back in the sea of prose", Keats commented. Many of his essays are like conversation poems—witty, profound and eagerly alive to the surfaces of the work of art he is appreciating. No study of the Romantic movement can be complete without a reading of his essays. For too long he has been regarded as a marginal figure, instead of being seen as the supreme genius of Romantic prose. A radical republican, like Milton, he possessed an epic imagination which he chose to embody in an eloquent stream of reviews and critical essays.

William Hazlitt
威廉·哈兹里特

On Familiar Style
(Excerpt)

The proper force of words lies not in the words themselves, but in their application. A word may be a fine-sounding word, of an unusual length, and a very imposing from its learning and novelty, and yet in the connection in which it is introduced may be quite pointless and irrelevant. It is not **pomp** or **pretension**, but the adaptation of the expression to the idea, that **clinches** a writer's meaning:—as it is not the size of **glossiness** of the materials, but their being fitted each to its place, that gives strength to the arch; or as the pegs and nails are as necessary to the support of the building as the larger timber, and more so than the mere showy, unsubstantial ornaments. I hate anything that occupies more space than it is worth. I hate to see a load of band-boxes go along the street, and I hate to see a parcel of big words without anything in them. A person who does not deliberately dispose of all his thoughts alike in **cumbrous** draperies and **flimsy** disguises, may strike out twenty varieties of familiar every-day language, each coming somewhat nearer to the feeling he wants to convey, and at last not hit upon that particular and only one which may be said to be identical with the exact impression in his mind. This would seem to show that Mr Cobbet is hardly right in saying that the first word that occurs is always the best. It may be a very good one; and yet a better may present itself on reflection or from time to time. It should be suggested naturally, however, and spontaneously, from a fresh and lively conception of the subject. We seldom succeed by trying at improvement, or by merely substituting one word for another that we are not satisfied with, as we cannot recollect the name of a place or person by merely **plaguing** ourselves about it. We wander farther from the point by persisting in a wrong scent; but it start up accidentally in the memory when we least expect it, by touching some link in the chain of previous association.

There are those who **hoard** up and make a cautious display of nothing but rich and rare **phraseology**—ancient medals, obscure coins, and Spanish pieces of eight. They are very curious to inspect, but I myself would neither offer not take them in the course of exchange. A sprinkling of archaisms is not amiss, but a tissue of obsolete expressions is more fit for keep than wear. I do not say I would not use any phrase that had been brought into fashion before the middle or the end of the last century, but I should be shy of using any that had not been employed by any approved author during the whole of that time. Words, like clothes, get old-fashioned, or mean and ridiculous, when they have been for some time laid aside. Mr. Lamb is the only imitator of old English style I can read with pleasure; and he is so thoroughly **imbued** with the spirit of his authors that the idea of imitation is almost done away. There is an inward unction, a marrowy vein, both in the thought and feeling, an intuition, deep and lively, of his subject, that carries off any **quaintness** or awkwardness arising from an **antiquated** style and dress. The matter is completely his own, though the manner is assumed. Perhaps his ideas are altogether so marked and individual as to require their point and **pungency** to be neutralised by the affectation of a singular but traditional form of conveyance. Tricked out in the prevailing costume, they would probably seem more startling and out of the way. The old English authors, Burton, Fuller, Coryate, Sir Thomas Browne, are a kind of mediators between us and the more eccentric and whimsical modern, reconciling us to his peculiarities. I do not, however, know how far this is the case or not, till he **condescends** to write like one of us. I must confess that what I like best of his papers under the signature of Elia (still I do no presume amidst such excellence, to decide what is most excellent) is the account of "Mrs Battle's Opinions on Whist," which is also the most free from obsolete allusions and turns of expression—

"A well of native English **undefiled**."

Chapter 6
William Hazlitt
威廉·哈兹里特

I Words and Phrases

pomp [pɒmp]	n.	cheap or pretentious or vain display 盛况；浮华；夸耀
pretension [prɪ'tenʃən]	n.	the quality of being pretentious 自负；骄傲
clinch [klɪntʃ]	v.	hold in a tight grasp 扭住，揪住
glossiness ['glɒsɪnɪs]	n.	the property of being smooth and shiny 光泽度，有光泽
cumbrous ['kʌmbrəs]	adj.	difficult to handle or use especially because of size or weight 累赘的，成负担的
flimsy ['flɪmzɪ]	adj.	having little substance or significance 不厚实的；不重要的
plague [pleɪg]	v.	to cause to suffer a blight 折磨；使苦恼
hoard [hɔːd]	v.	save up as for future use 贮藏
phraseology [ˌfreɪzɪ'ɒlədʒɪ]	n.	the manner in which something is expressed in words 措辞；语法；词组
imbue [ɪm'bjuː]	v.	spread or diffuse through 灌输；使渗透
quaintness [kweɪntnəs]	n.	strangeness as a consequence of being old fashioned 离奇有趣
antiquated ['æntɪkweɪtɪd]	adj.	obsolete or old-fashioned 过时的，旧式的
pungency ['pʌndʒənsɪ]	n.	wit, having a sharp and caustic quality 辛辣；尖刻
condescend [kɒndɪ'send]	v.	do something that one considers to be below one's dignity 屈尊
undefiled [ʌndɪ'faɪld]	adj.	free from stain or blemish; (of language) not having its purity or excellence debased 洁净的，纯粹的

II Reading Comprehension Questions

1. What is a familiar style in Hazlitt's opinion?
2. What do you think of the words by Mr Cobbet that "the first word that occurs is always the best"?
3. What is Hazlitt's opinion on Charles Lamb's style?
4. What does the author think of Burton, Fuller, Sir Thomas Browne?
5. Are archaisms to be discarded altogether in writing? What do you think of "a sprinkling of archaisms" in writing?

III Questions on Writing Style and Language

1. Have you noticed any stylistic features of Hazlitt's writing? What particular effect is produced by these sentences?
2. Paradox is a figure of speech consisting of a statement or proposition which on the face of it seems self-contradictory, absurd or contrary to established fact or practice, but which on further thinking and study may prove to be true, well-founded, and even to contain a succinct point. For example: More haste, less speed. Can you find the uses of paradoxes in the essay? What is the stylistic effect created by it?
3. To Hazlitt, quotation is a good device. He likes to interweave quotations from literature, old and new, in his writing. What do you think is the stylistic effect of it?
4. How do you understand this sentence "Mr. Lamb is the only imitator of old English style I can read with pleasure; and he is so thoroughly imbued with the spirit of his authors that the idea of imitation is almost done away"? Do you agree with Hazlitt?
5. What do you think Hazlitt's Style of "On Familiar Style"? Do you think the essay itself a typical demonstration of the so-called familiar style?

William Hazlitt
威廉·哈兹里特

Text B

On Going a Journey
(Excerpt)

One of the pleasantest things in the world is going a journey; but I like to go by myself. I can enjoy society in a room; but out of doors, Nature is company enough for me. I am then never less alone than when alone.

"The fields his study, Nature was his book."

I cannot see the wit of walking and talking at the same time. When I am in the country I wish to vegetate like the country. I am not for criticising hedgerows and black cattle. I go out of town in order to forget the town and all that is in it.

There are those who for this purpose go to **watering-places**, and carry the metropolis with them. I like more **elbow-room** and fewer **encumbrances**. I like solitude, when I give myself up to it for the sake of solitude; nor do I ask for —"a friend in my **retreat**,

Whom I may whisper solitude is sweet."

The soul of a journey is liberty, perfect liberty, to think, feel, do, just as one pleases. We go a journey chiefly to be free of all impediments and of all inconveniences; to leave ourselves behind much more than to get rid of others. It is because I want a little breathing-space to muse on indifferent matters, where Contemplation

"May **plume** her feathers and let grow her wings,

That in the various bustle of resort

Were all too ruffled, and sometimes impair'd,"

that I absent myself from the town for a while, without feeling at a loss the moment I am left by myself. Instead of a friend in a postchaise or in a **tilbury**, to exchange good things with, and vary the same **stale** topics over again, for once let me have a truce with impertinence. Give me the clear blue sky over my head, and the green **turf** beneath my feet, a winding road before me, and a three hours' march to dinner—and then to thinking! It is hard if I cannot start some game on these lone heaths. I laugh, I run, I leap, I sing for joy. From the point of **yonder** rolling cloud I plunge into my past being, and **revel** there as the sun-burnt Indian plunges headlong into the wave that **wafts** him to his native shore. Then long-forgotten things, like "sunken wrack and sumless treasuries," burst upon my eager sight, and I begin to feel, think, and be myself again. Instead of an awkward silence, broken by attempts at wit or dull common-places, mine is that undisturbed silence of the heart which alone is perfect eloquence. No one likes puns, alliterations, antitheses, argument, and analysis better than I do; but I sometimes had rather be without them. "Leave, oh, leave me to my repose!" I have just now other business in hand, which would seem idle to you, but is with me "the very stuff o' the conscience." Is not this wild rose sweet without a comment? Does not this daisy leap to my heart set in its coat of **emerald**? Yet if I were to explain to you the circumstance that has so endeared it to me you would only smile. Had I not better then keep it to myself, and let it serve me to **brood** over, from here to yonder **craggy** point, and from thence onward to the far-distant horizon? I should be but bad company all that way, and therefore prefer being alone. I have heard it said that you may, when the moody fit comes on, walk or ride on by yourself, and indulge your **reveries**. But this looks like a **breach** of manners, a neglect of others, and you are thinking all the time that you ought to rejoin your party. "Out upon such half-faced fellowship," say I. I like to be either entirely to myself, or entirely at the disposal of others; to talk or be silent, to walk or sit still, to be sociable or solitary. I was pleased with an observation of Mr. Cobbett's, that "he thought it a bad French custom to drink our wine with our meals, and that an Englishman ought to do only one thing at a time." So I cannot talk and think, or indulge in melancholy musing and lively conversation **by fits and starts**. "Let me have a companion of my way," says Sterne, "were it but to remark how the shadows lengthen as the sun declines." It is beautifully said: but, in my opinion, this continual comparing of notes interferes with the involuntary impression of things upon

Chapter 6
William Hazlitt
威廉·哈兹里特

the mind, and hurts the sentiment. If you only hint what you feel in a kind of dumb show, it is insipid: if you have to explain it, it is making a toil of a pleasure. You cannot read the book of Nature without being perpetually put to the trouble of translating it for the benefit of others. I am for the synthetical method on a journey in preference to the analytical. I am content to lay in a stock of ideas then, and to examine and **anatomise** them afterwards. I want to see my vague notions float like the down of the thistle before the breeze, and not to have them entangled in the briars and thorns of controversy. For once, I like to have it all my own way; and this is impossible unless you are alone, or in such company as I do not covet.

I have no objection to argue a point with any one for twenty miles of measured road, but not for pleasure. If you remark the scent of a bean-field crossing the road, perhaps your fellow-traveller has no smell. If you point to a distant object, perhaps he is short-sighted and has to take out his glass to look at it. There is a feeling in the air, a tone in the colour of a cloud, which hits your fancy, but the effect of which you are unable to account for.

There is then no sympathy, but an uneasy craving after it, and a dissatisfaction which pursues you on the way, and in the end probably produces ill-humour. Now I never quarrel with myself, and take all my own conclusions for granted till I find it necessary to defend them against objections. It is not merely that you may not be of accord on the objects and circumstances that present themselves before you—they may recall a number of ideas, and lead to associations too delicate and refined to be possibly communicated to others. Yet these I love to cherish, and sometimes still fondly clutch them, when I can escape from the throng to do so. To give way to our feelings before company, seems extravagance or affectation; on the other hand, to have to **unravel** this mystery of our being at every turn, and to make others take an equal interest in it (otherwise the end is not answered) is a task to which few are competent. We must "give it an understanding, but no tongue." My old friend C— [Samuel Taylor Coleridge], however, could do both.

He could go on in the most delightful explanatory way over hill and dale, a summer's day, and convert a landscape into a didactic poem or a

Pindaric ode. "He talked far above singing." If I could so clothe my ideas in sounding and flowing words, I might perhaps wish to have some one with me to admire the swelling theme; or I could be more content, were it possible for me still to bear his echoing voice in the woods of All-Foxden. They had "that fine madness in them which our first poets had"; and if they could have been caught by some rare instrument, would have breathed such strains as the following

"Here be woods as green
As any, air likewise as fresh and sweet
As when smooth Zephyrus plays on the fleet
Face of the curled streams, with flow'rs as many
As the young spring gives, and as choice as any;
Here be all new delights, cool streams and wells,
Arbours o'ergrown with woodbines, caves and dells:
Choose where thou wilt, whilst I sit by and sing,
Or gather rushes to make many a ring
For thy long fingers; tell thee tales of love,
How the pale Phoebe, hunting in a grove,
First saw the boy Endymion, from whose eyes
She took eternal fire that never dies;
How she convey'd him softly in a sleep,
His temples bound with poppy, to the steep
Head of old Latmos, where she stoops each night,
Gilding the mountain with her brother's light,
To kiss her sweetest."

Had I words and images at command like these, I would attempt to wake the thoughts that lie **slumbering** on golden ridges in the evening clouds: but at the sight of Nature my fancy, poor as it is, droops and closes up its leaves, like flowers at sunset. I can make nothing out on the spot: I must have time to collect myself.

In general, a good thing spoils out-of-door prospects: it should be reserved for Table-talk. L—[Charles Lamb] is for this reason, I take it, the worst

Chapter 6
William Hazlitt
威廉·哈兹里特

company in the world out of doors; because he is the best within. I grant, there is one subject on which it is pleasant to talk on a journey; and that is, what one shall have for supper when we get to our inn at night. The open air improves this sort of conversation or friendly **altercation**, by setting a keener edge on appetite. Every mile of the road heightens the flavour of the viands we expect at the end of it. How fine it is to enter some old town, walled and turreted, just at approach of nightfall, or to come to some **straggling** village, with the lights streaming through the surrounding gloom; and then, after inquiring for the best entertainment that the place affords, to "take one's ease at one's inn!" These eventful moments in our lives are in fact too precious, too full of solid, heart-felt happiness to be frittered and dribbled away in imperfect sympathy. I would have them all to myself, and drain them to the last drop: they will do to talk of or to write about afterwards. What a delicate speculation it is, after drinking whole **goblets** of tea,

"The cups that cheer, but not inebriate"

and letting the fumes ascend into the brain, to sit considering what we shall have for supper—eggs and a rasher, a rabbit smothered in onions, or an excellent veal-cutlet! Sancho in such a situation once fixed on cow heel; and his choice, though he could not help it, is not to be **disparaged**. Then, in the intervals of pictured scenery and Shandean contemplation, to catch the preparation and the stir in the kitchen—Procul, O procul este profani! These hours are sacred to silence and to musing, to be treasured up in the memory, and to feed the source of smiling thoughts hereafter. I would not waste them in idle talk; or if I must have the integrity of fancy broken in upon, I would rather it were by a stranger than a friend. A stranger takes his **hue** and character from the time and place: his is a part of the furniture and costume of an inn. If he is a Quaker, or from the West Riding of Yorkshire, so much the better. I do not even try to sympathise with him, and he **breaks no squares**. I associate nothing with my travelling companion but present objects and passing events. In his ignorance of me and my affairs, I in a manner forget myself. But a friend reminds one of other things, **rips up old grievances**, and destroys the abstraction of the scene. He comes in ungraciously between us and our imaginary character. Something is dropped in the course of conversation that gives a hint of your profession and pursuits; or from having some one with you that knows the less sublime portions of your history, it seems that other people do. You are no longer a citizen of the world; but your "unhoused free condition is put into **circumspection** and confine."

The incognito of an inn is one of its striking privileges—"lord of one's self, uncumbered with a name." Oh! it is great to shake off the trammels of the world and of public opinion—to lose our **importunate**, tormenting, everlasting personal identity in the elements of nature, and become the creature of the moment, clear of all ties—to hold to the universe only by a dish of sweet-breads, and to owe nothing but the score of the evening—and no longer seeking for applause and meeting with contempt, to be known by no other title than the Gentleman in the parlour!

One may take one's choice of all characters in this romantic state of uncertainty as to one's real pretensions, and become indefinitely respectable and negatively right-worshipful. We baffle prejudice and disappoint conjecture; and from being so to others, begin to be objects of curiosity and wonder even to ourselves. We are no more those hackneyed commonplaces that we appear in the world; an inn restores us to the level of Nature, and quits scores with society! I have certainly spent some enviable hours at inns—sometimes when I have been left entirely to myself and have tried to solve some metaphysical problem, as once at Witham-common, where I found out the proof that likeness is not a case of the association of ideas—at other times, when there have been pictures in the room, as at St Neot's (I think it was) where I first met with Gribelin's engravings of the Cartoons, into which I entered at once; and at a little inn on the borders of Wales, where there happened to be hanging some of Westall's drawings, which I compared triumphantly (for a theory that I had, not for the admired artist) with the figure of a girl who had ferried me over the Severn, standing up in a boat between me and the fading twilight—at other times I might mention luxuriating in books, with a peculiar interest in this way, as I remember sitting up half the night to read Paul and Virginia, which I picked up at an inn at Bridgewater, after being drenched in the rain all day; and at the

Chapter 6
William Hazlitt
威廉·哈兹里特

same place I got through two volumes of Madam D'Arblay's Camilla.

It was on the 10th of April, 1798, that I sat down to a volume of the New Eloise, at the inn at Llangollen, over a bottle of sherry and cold chicken. The letter I chose was that in which St. Preux describes his feelings as he first caught a glimpse from the heights of the Jura of the Pays de Vaud, which I had brought with me as a bon bouche to crown the evening with. It was my birthday, and I had for the first time come from a place in the neighbourhood to visit this delightful spot. The road to Llangollen turns off between Chirk and Wrexham; and on passing a certain point you come all at once upon the valley, which opens like an amphitheatre, broad, barren hills rising in majestic state on either side, with "green upland swells that echo to the bleat of flocks" below, and the river Dee babbling over its stony bed in the midst of them. The valley at this time "glittered green with sunny showers," and a budding ash-tree dipped its tender branches in the chiding stream. How proud, how glad I was to walk along the high road that overlooks the delicious prospect, repeating the lines which I have just quoted from Mr Coleridge's poems! But besides the prospect which opened beneath my feet, another also opened to my inward sight, a heavenly vision, on which were written, in letters large as Hope could make them, these four words, Liberty, Genius, Love, Virtue; which have since faded in the light of common day, or mock my idle gaze.

"The Beautiful is vanished, and returns not."

Still I would return some time or other to this enchanted spot; but I would return to it alone. What other self could I find to share that influx of thoughts, of regret, and delight, the traces of which I could hardly **conjure** up myself, so much have they been broken and defaced! I could stand on some tall rock and overlook the precipice of years that separates me from what I then was. I was at that time going shortly to visit the poet whom I have above named. Where is he now? Not only I myself have changed; the world, which was then new to me, has become old and incorrigible. Yet will I turn to thee in thought, O sylvan Dee, as then thou wert, in joy, in youth and gladness; and thou shalt always be to me the river of Paradise, where I will drink the waters of life freely!

1 Words and Phrases

watering-place	n.	a health resort near a spring or at the seaside 矿泉疗养地；饮水池
elbow-room	n.	space for movement 可自由活动的场所
encumbrance [ɪnˈkʌmbrəns]	n.	any obstruction that impedes or is burdensome 妨害；累赘物
retreat [rɪˈtriːt]	n.	a quiet, isolated place for rest in private 隐居处；休养处
plume [pluːm]	v.	dress or groom with elaborate care 打扮；装饰（羽毛）
tilbury [ˈtɪlb(ə)rɪ]	n.	a light two-wheeled horse-drawn open carriage, seating two people 无顶双轮轻便马车
stale [steɪl]	adj.	not interesting or new, boring（地方、活动、主意）缺乏新鲜感的；陈腐的
turf [tɜːf]	n.	surface layer of ground containing a mat of grass and grass roots 草皮，草地
yonder [ˈjɒndə]	n.	an old-fashioned or dialect word for "over there"（古语或方言中的）那里，那边
revel [ˈrev(ə)l]	v.	enjoy very much 陶醉，沉湎；狂欢
waft [wɑːft]	v.	blow gently 吹送；使飘荡
emerald [ˈem(ə)r(ə)ld]	n.	an emerald is a precious stone that is clear and bright green 翡翠
brood [bruːd]	v.	to think about something usually in an unhappy way 计较（尤指愤恨不满）；郁闷地沉思
craggy [ˈkrægɪ]	adj.	steep and rocky 陡峭的；多岩石的
reverie [ˈrev(ə)rɪ]	n.	a state of imagining or thinking about pleasant things, as if you are dreaming 幻想；白日梦
breach [briːtʃ]	n.	an act of breaking 违反
by fits and starts		间歇地，一阵阵地；不规则地；发作性地
anatomise [əˈnætəmaɪz]	v.	dissect in order to analyze 解剖；解析

Chapter 6
William Hazlitt
威廉·哈兹里特

unravel [ʌnˈrævl]	v.	disentangle 解开；阐明
slumber [ˈslʌmbə]	v.	be asleep 睡眠；睡着度过
altercation [ˌɒltəˈkeɪʃ(ə)n]	n.	noisy quarrel 争执
straggling [ˈstræglɪŋ]	adj.	spreading out carelessly (as if wandering) in different directions 离散的
goblet [ˈgɒblɪt]	n.	a drinking glass with a base and stem 酒杯；高脚杯
disparage [dɪˈspærɪdʒ]	v.	express a negative opinion of 蔑视；毁谤
hue [hjuː]	n.	the quality of a color as determined by its dominant wavelength 色彩；色度
break no squares		无关紧要
rip up old grievances		重提旧怨，翻出老账
circumspection [ˌsəːkəmˈspekʃən]	n.	the trait of being circumspect and prudent 慎重；细心
importunate [ɪmˈpɔːtjunət]	adj.	expressing earnest entreaty 急切的；纠缠不休的
conjure [ˈkʌndʒə]	v.	(often as if by magic) summon into action or bring into existence 念咒召唤；用魔法驱赶

II Reading Comprehension Questions

1. According to the author, what is the soul of a journey?
2. Why does the author mention Mr. Cobbet and Stern? Do the two quotes have the same function?
3. According to Hazlitt, What is a synthetical method on a journey? And what is the analytical? Why does he prefer the latter?
4. Which are the examples given to show that the feelings are unable to account for? Do you find them humorous?
5. As Robert Louis Stevenson observed in his essay *Walking Tours*, Hazlitt's "On Going a Journey" is "so good that there should be a tax levied on all who have not read it." Do you agree with this point of view? Why or why not?

Quotes of the Author

If you think you can win, you can win. Faith is necessary to victory.

Man is the only animal that laughs and weeps, for he is the only animal that is struck with the difference between what things are and what they ought to be.

The love of liberty is the love of others; the love of power is the love of ourselves.

We could pass our lives in Oxford without having or wanting any other idea—that of the place is enough. We imbibe the air of thought; we stand in the presence of learning.

When a thing ceases to be a subject of controversy, it ceases to be a subject of interest.

Thomas De Quincey
托马斯·德·昆西
(1785—1859)

本章导读

托马斯·德·昆西（1785—1859）是英国著名散文家和文学批评家。他出生于曼彻斯特的一个商人家庭。早在中学时期他就擅长希腊文和拉丁文。16岁时逃离就读的文法学校，漫游威尔士；17岁时在伦敦流浪了一个严冬。早年风餐露宿的经历令他成为一个生活阴暗面的深刻洞察者，也使他罹患终生未愈的胃病和牙痛。1804年，德·昆西进入牛津大学，着重学习英国文学和德国文学，对英国新兴的浪漫主义文学非常向往。为了缓解神经痛，他开始吸食鸦片，成为终生的瘾君子。这也给他的创作带来很多奇异的灵感。他于1821年在《伦敦杂志》发表的著名作品《一个英国吸食鸦片者的自白》就是他以吸食鸦片的亲身体验，描写了主人公的心理和潜意识活动。从1853年起直至去世，德·昆西致力于编辑他自己的全集，共14卷，出版于1853年至1860年之间，文章涉及历史、政治经济学、哲学和文艺理论。

他把文学分为两大类——知识的文学和力量的文学。这是他文艺理论的重要组成部分。在这一划分中，他更倾向于动之以情的力量文学，认为知识文学属于低层次，其提供的信息要诉诸纯然推演之思辨；而力量文学则高于知识文学，其功能更高级，由怡情悦性、同气交感而发生作用。在知识的文学方面，他写有经济著作《三位法学家的对话》，哲学著作《论康德》，教育著作《致失学青年的信》，历史著作《贞德》（1847），文学批评著作《论〈麦克白〉剧中的敲门声》（1823）、《论风格》（1840）等。在力量的文学方面，德·昆西写了《自传》（1834—1853）、《来自深处的叹息》（1845）、《英国邮车》（1849）和《被看成是一种艺术的谋杀》（1827）等。

德·昆西蜚声文坛还因为其对散文诗化的探索和对潜意识领域的开拓。他对散文诗化的探索不仅体现在他作品中富有幻想和感情的内容，还有他在词汇的选择上十分注重音乐性。其作华美与瑰奇兼具，激情与疏缓并蓄，常常有意识地模仿17世纪早期英国散文家的风格。伍尔芙在《书与画像》中这样谈到："德·昆西是一位刻意求工的艺术家，他能那样细致而优美地安排句子里的音调、调整语言的节奏。"德·昆西对潜意识领域的开拓在其著作《一个英国吸食鸦片者的自白》中体现得尤其明显。在"鸦片之苦"和"鸦片之乐"这两个部分中，作者不想争辩、不想改变别人的信仰，甚至不想说故事，只是梳理自己的记忆，娓娓道来。尤其是在"鸦片之苦"的部分，德·昆西通过对梦境和幻想的刻画影射他潜意识的内容，他的理智在鸦片酊中迷醉，潜意识的大门打开，鳄鱼、猴子、鹦鹉、宝塔、木乃伊还有僧侣等光怪陆离的动物、人物和场景涌现而出，让读者目不暇接。他所有的梦境和幻觉是由心灵深处记忆的碎片拼接而成，这与其对伦敦悲惨生活的亲身经历有着不可割舍的关系。

　　本章所选第一篇《论〈麦克白〉中的敲门声》是莎学研究中的一篇经典之作。莎士比亚最有名的四大悲剧之一——《麦克白》，历来是研究者关注的对象。这部以描写阴谋、凶杀而著称的悲剧，其在表现悲剧主人公心理方面的深度令人震惊，所昭示的人生哲理也常常让读者感到难以理解。德·昆西在这篇文章中选择了一个极好的切入角度：从分析麦克白夫妇刺杀邓肯的阴谋成功后，忽然听到的敲门声这个细节开始。他的问题是：莎士比亚为何要在此时设计这样一次敲门声？敲门声为什么对德·昆西产生了多少年以后还无法消失的心理上一种说不清楚的影响？从这样一个细节开始，德·昆西带领我们走进莎士比亚的世界。一个小小的戏剧动作，一个不引人注目的细节，经过德·昆西的分析，竟然使我们发现蕴含有如此丰富的内涵。这使我们在惊叹莎士比亚的戏剧天分之余，也不由得对德·昆西的天才分析感到由衷地佩服。

About the Author

　　Thomas Penson De Quincey (15 August, 1785—8, December, 1859) was an English essayist, best known for his *Confessions of an English Opium-Eater* (1821). Full of psychological insight and colorful descriptive writing, the book surprised and fascinated De Quincey's contemporaries and has continued to exert its powerful and eccentric appeal ever since. Many scholars suggested that in publishing this work De Quincey inaugurated the tradition of addiction literature in the West.

Chapter 7

Thomas De Quincey
托马斯·德·昆西

De Quincey was born in Manchester in 1785, in a rich family. In 1802, at 17, Quincey ran away from school and spent five harrowing months penniless and hungry on the streets of London, and he began to take opium. In 1804, he entered Oxford, but left four years later without taking his degree. In 1809, he moved to the English Lake District, a place near William Wordsworth and Samuel Taylor Coleridge. In 1813, he became dependent on opium again, and over the next few years he slid deeper into debt and addiction. In 1816, he married Margaret Simpson. They had eight children. In 1819, penury forced him to join *Blackwood's Edinburgh Magazine* at the urging of his close friend John Wilson. In 1818, he was for a short time the editor of the *Westmorland Gazette*. Instead of printing news of the day and political articles, as the proprietors wished, he filled his columns with long reports of lurid crimes collected from all over the country. Four years later, he published his most famous piece of literary criticism, a short essay "On the Knocking at the Gate in Macbeth" in *The London Magazine*. De Quincey died in Edinburgh on 8 December, 1859.

The major characteristic of De Quincey's essays lies on its poetic sense which reveals in his other representative works including *Sighs from the Depth* (1845), *The English Mail Coach* (1849) and *Autobiographical Sketches* (1853) etc. The quality of dreamlike fantasy and color integrated with musical feature impressed his readers. However, discursiveness is often pointed out to be one of the flaws in his works for the large amount of ornate descriptions of his fantasies and dreams coming from his subconsciousness. His essays have influenced many other famous writers like Edgar Allan Poe, Fitz Hugh Ludlow, Charles Baudelaire and Nikolai Gogo.

Text A

On the Knocking at the Gate in *Macbeth*

Thomas De Quincey

From my boyish days I had always felt a great perplexity on one point in *Macbeth*. It was this: the knocking at the gate, which succeeds to the murder of Duncan, produced to my feelings an effect for which I never could account. The effect was, that it reflected back upon the murderer a peculiar awfulness and a depth of **solemnity**; yet, however **obstinately** I endeavoured with my understanding to comprehend this, for many years I never could see why it should produce such an effect.

Here I pause for one moment, to **exhort** the reader never to pay any attention to his understanding, when it stands in opposition to any other faculty of his mind. The mere understanding, however useful and indispensable, is the meanest faculty in the human mind, and the most to be distrusted; and yet the great majority of people trust to nothing else, which may do for ordinary life, but not for philosophical purposes. Of this out of ten thousand instances that I might produce, I will cite one. Ask of any person whatsoever, who is not previously prepared for the demand by a knowledge of the perspective, to draw in the rudest way the commonest appearance which depends upon the laws of that science; as, for instance, to represent the effect of two walls standing at right angles to each other, or the appearance of the houses on each side of a street, as seen by a person looking down the street from one extremity. Now in all cases, unless the person has happened to observe in pictures how it is that artists produce these effects, he will be utterly unable to make the smallest approximation to it. Yet why? For he has actually seen the effect every day of his life. The reason is—that he allows his understanding to overrule his eyes. His understanding, which includes no

Chapter 7

Thomas De Quincey
托马斯·德·昆西

intuitive knowledge of the laws of vision, can furnish him with no reason why a line which is known and can be proved to be a horizontal line, should not appear a horizontal line; a line that made any angle with the **perpendicular**, less than a right angle, would seem to him to indicate that his houses were all tumbling down together. Accordingly, he makes the line of his houses a horizontal line, and fails, of course, to produce the effect demanded. Here, then, is one instance out of many, in which not only the understanding is allowed to overrule the eyes, but where the understanding is positively allowed to **obliterate** the eyes, as it were; for not only does the man believe the evidence of his understanding in opposition to that of his eyes, but (what is monstrous!) the idiot is not aware that his eyes ever gave such evidence. He does not know that he has seen (and therefore quoad[1] his consciousness has not seen) that which he has seen every day of his life.

But to return from this digression, my understanding could furnish no reason why the knocking at the gate in *Macbeth* should produce any effect, direct or reflected. In fact, my understanding said positively that it could not produce any effect. But I knew better; I felt that it did; and I waited and clung to the problem until further knowledge should enable me to solve it. At length, in 1812, Mr. Williams[2] made his debut on the stage of Ratcliff Highway, and executed those unparalleled murders which have procured for him such a brilliant and undying reputation. On which murders, by the way, I must observe, that in one respect they have had an ill effect, by making the **connoisseur** in murder very **fastidious** in his taste, and dissatisfied by anything that has been since done in that line. All other murders look pale by the deep crimson of his; and, as an amateur once said to me in a **querulous** tone, 'There has been absolutely nothing doing since his time, or nothing that's worth speaking of.' But this is wrong; for it is unreasonable to expect all men to be great artists, and born with the genius of Mr. Williams. Now it will

---

1 quoda: Lantin word which means "as far as" in English 拉丁语，等于英语的 as far as。
2 Mr. Williams: 指 John Williams，1811 年 12 月伦敦拉特克利夫大道谋杀案（The Ratcliff Highway Murder）的凶手，在相隔 12 天的两起谋杀案中，杀害了马尔和威廉逊两家及相关人员共 7 人，整个伦敦为之震惊。作者记为 1812 年，系笔误。

be remembered, that in the first of these murders (that of the Marrs)¹, the same incident (of a knocking at the door) soon after the work of **extermination** was complete, did actually occur, which the genius of Shakespeare has invented; and all good judges, and the most eminent **dilettanti**, acknowledged the felicity of Shakespeare's suggestion, as soon as it was actually realized. Here, then, was a fresh proof that I was right in relying on my own feeling, in opposition to my understanding; and I again set myself to study the problem; at length I solved it to my own satisfaction, and my solution is this. Murder, in ordinary cases, where the sympathy is wholly directed to the case of the murdered person, is an incident of coarse and vulgar horror; and for this reason, that it flings the interest exclusively upon the natural but ignoble instinct by which we **cleave** to life; an instinct which, as being indispensable to the primal law of self-preservation, is the same in kind (though different in degree) amongst all living creatures: this instinct, therefore, because it **annihilates** all distinctions, and degrades the greatest of men to the level of "the poor **beetle** that we tread on"², exhibits human nature in its most abject and humiliating attitude. Such an attitude would little suit the purposes of the poet. What then must he do? He must throw the interest on the murderer. Our sympathy must be with him (of course I mean a sympathy of comprehension, a sympathy by which we enter into his feelings, and are made to understand them, —not a sympathy of pity or **approbation**). In the murdered person, all strife of thought, all flux and reflux of passion and of purpose, are crushed by one overwhelming panic; the fear of instant death smites him "with its petrific mace"³. But in the murderer, such a murderer as a poet will **condescend** to, there must be raging some great storm of passion—jealousy, ambition, vengeance, hatred—which will create a hell within him; and into this hell we are to look.

---

1 the marrs: 敦拉特克利夫大道谋杀案的第一个受害家庭。布商马尔一家三口以及一名店员被凶手 John Williams 所杀。

2 the poor beetle that we tread on: 典出莎士比亚《一报还一报》，三幕一场，86 行。

3 the fear... "with its petrific mace": 对迫在眉睫的死亡的恐惧使他犹如泥塑木雕一般。"with its petrific mace" 典出弥尔顿《失乐园》第十章，293 行。petrific 意为有石化能力的；mace 意为钉头槌（中古武器）。

Chapter 7

Thomas De Quincey
托马斯·德·昆西

In *Macbeth*, for the sake of gratifying his own enormous and teeming faculty of creation, Shakespeare has introduced two murderers: and, as usual in his hands, they are remarkably discriminated: but, though in Macbeth the strife of mind is greater than in his wife, the tiger spirit not so awake, and his feelings caught chiefly by **contagion** from her, —yet, as both were finally involved in the guilt of murder, the murderous mind of necessity is finally to be presumed in both. This was to be expressed; and on its own account, as well as to make it a more proportionable antagonist to the unoffending nature of their victim, "the gracious Duncan", and adequately to expound "the deep **damnation** of his taking off", this was to be expressed with peculiar energy. We were to be made to feel that the human nature, i.e. the divine nature of love and mercy, spread through the hearts of all creatures, and seldom utterly withdrawn from man—was gone, vanished, extinct, and that the **fiendish** nature had taken its place. And, as this effect is marvellously accomplished in the dialogues and soliloquies themselves, so it is finally consummated by the expedient under consideration; and it is to this that I now **solicit** the reader's attention. If the reader has ever witnessed a wife, daughter, or sister in a fainting fit, he may chance to have observed that the most affecting moment in such a spectacle is that in which a sigh and a stirring announce the recommencement of suspended life. Or, if the reader has ever been present in a vast metropolis, on the day when some great national idol was carried in funeral pomp to his grave, and chancing to walk near the course through which it passed, has felt powerfully in the silence and desertion of the streets, and in the **stagnation** of ordinary business, the deep interest which at that moment was possessing the heart of man—if all at once he should hear the death-like stillness broken up by the sound of wheels rattling away from the scene, and making known that the transitory vision was dissolved, he will be aware that at no moment was his sense of the complete suspension and pause in ordinary human concerns so full and affecting, as at that moment when the suspension ceases, and the goings-on of human life are suddenly resumed. All action in any direction is best expounded, measured, and made apprehensible, by reaction. Now apply this to the case in *Macbeth*. Here, as I have said, the retiring of the human heart, and the entrance of the fiendish heart was to be expressed and made sensible. Another world has stept in; and the murderers are taken out of the region of human things, human purposes, human desires. They are transfigured: Lady Macbeth is "unsexed"; Macbeth has forgot that he was born of woman; both are conformed to the image of devils; and the world of devils is suddenly revealed. But how shall this be conveyed and made palpable? In order that a new world may step in, this world must for a time disappear. The murderers, and the murder must be insulated—cut off by an immeasurable gulf from the ordinary tide and succession of human affairs—locked up and sequestered in some deep recess; we must be made sensible that the world of ordinary life is suddenly arrested—laid asleep—tranced—racked into a dread armistice; time must be annihilated; relation to things without abolished; and all must pass self-withdrawn into a deep syncope and suspension of earthly passion. Hence it is, that when the deed is done, when the work of darkness is perfect, then the world of darkness passes away like a pageantry in the clouds: the knocking at the gate is heard; and it makes known audibly that the reaction has commenced; the human has made its reflux upon the fiendish; the pulses of life are beginning to beat again; and the re-establishment of the goings-on of the world in which we live, first makes us profoundly sensible of the awful parenthesis that had suspended them.

O mighty poet! Thy works are not as those of other men, simply and merely great works of art; but are also like the phenomena of nature, like the sun and the sea, the stars and the flowers; like frost and snow, rain and dew, hail-storm and thunder, which are to be studied with entire submission of our own faculties, and in the perfect faith that in them there can be no too much or too little, nothing useless or inert—but that, the farther we press in our discoveries, the more we shall see proofs of design and self-supporting arrangement where the careless eye had seen nothing but accident!

Chapter 7

Thomas De Quincey
托马斯·德·昆西

I Words and Phrases

solemnity [sə'lemnɪtɪ]	*n.*	a trait of dignified seriousness 庄严，严肃
obstinately ['ɒbstənɪtlɪ]	*adv.*	in a stubborn unregenerate manner 顽固地，固执地
exhort [ɪg'zɔːt]	*v.*	force or impel in an indicated direction. 劝告；忠告
perpendicular [ˌpɜːpən'dɪkjʊlə]	*adj.*	at right angles to the plane of the horizon or a base line 垂直的；正交的
obliterate [ə'blɪtəreɪt]	*v.*	remove completely from recognition or memory 消除；忘掉
connoisseur [kɑːnə'sɜː]	*n.*	an expert able to appreciate a field; especially in the fine arts 鉴赏家；内行
fastidious [fæ'stɪdɪəs]	*adj.*	giving careful attention to detail; hard to please 挑剔的，苛求的；难取悦的
querulous ['kwerʊləs]	*adj.*	habitually complaining 抱怨的；爱挑剔的
extermination [ɪkˌstɜːmɪ'neɪʃn]	*n.*	complete annihilation 消灭；根除
dilettanti [dɪlɪ'tæntɪ]	*n.*	a person whose interest in an area of knowledge is not very deep or serious 业余爱好者；一知半解者
cleave [kliːv]	*v.*	continue to believe in or be loyal to sth. 坚信；信守；忠于
annihilate [ə'naɪəleɪt]	*v.*	kill in large numbers 歼灭
beetle ['biːt(ə)l]	*n.*	an insect with a hard covering to its body 甲虫
approbation [ˌæprə'beʃən]	*n.*	official approval 认可；批准
condescend [kɒndɪ'send]	*v.*	behave in a patronizing and condescending manner 屈尊；谦逊
contagion [kən'tedʒən]	*n.*	speading of a disease or idea 传染
damnation [dæm'neʃən]	*n.*	the act of damning 诅咒；非难
fiendish ['fiːndɪʃ]	*adj.*	extremely evil or cruel; expressive of cruelty or befitting hell 恶魔似的；残忍的；极坏的

solicit [sə'lɪsɪt]　　　　　v.　make an entreaty for something; request urgently or persistently 请求；祈求

stagnation [stæg'neɪʃən]　　n.　a state of inactivity (in business or art etc) 停滞，滞止

II Reading Comprehension Questions

1. What effect was produced on the author by the knocking at the Gate in *Macbeth*?
2. Why did the author exhort the reader not to pay any attention to his understanding, when it stands in opposition to any other faculty of his mind?
3. What is the author's intention to refer to Mr. Williams?
4. What is the most striking artistic effect of the knocking you've observed?
5. How do you understand the last sentence "the farther we press in our discoveries, the more we shall see proofs of design and self-supporting arrangement where the careless eye had seen nothing but accident"?

III Questions on Writing Style and Language

1. Have you noticed any stylistic features of De Quincey's writing? Are his sentences long or short? What particular effect is produced by these sentences?
2. Many criticisms have been written on Shakespeare's art of creation. In what way is this text distinguished as a piece of criticism? What can you learn from it from the perspective of writing?
3. What is the function of the second paragraph from the perspective of text organization?
4. In expounding on the effect produced by the knocking at the gate in *Macbeth*, why did the author mention the case of Mr. Williams's murder on the Ratcliffe Highway in 1812?
5. According to the author, what are the artistic effect of the knocking at the gate in *Macbeth*? Do you think this is a natural conclusion of what he said

Chapter 7
Thomas De Quincey
托马斯·德·昆西

before?

Text B

A Happy Home

Thomas De Quincey

I have said already that, on a subject so important to us all as happiness, we should listen with pleasure to any man's experience or experiments, even though he were but a ploughboy, who cannot be supposed to have ploughed very deep in such an **intractable** soil as that of human pains and pleasures, or to have conducted his researches upon any very enlightened principles. But I, who have taken happiness, both in a solid and a liquid shape, both boiled and unboiled, both East Indian and Turkish—who have conducted my experiments upon this interesting subject with a sort of **galvanic** battery, and have, for the general benefit of the world, inoculated myself, as it were, with the poison of eight thousand drops of **laudanum** per day (and for the same reason as a French surgeon **inoculated** himself lately with a cancer, an English one, twenty years ago, with plague, and a third, who was also English, with hydrophobia), I, it will be admitted, must surely now know what happiness is, if anybody does.

And therefore I will here lay down an analysis of happiness; and, as the most interesting mode of communicating it, I will give it, not didactically, but wrapped up and involved in a picture of one evening, as I spent every evening during the **intercalary** year, when laudanum, though taken daily, was to me no more than the elixir of pleasure.

Let there be a cottage, standing in a valley, eighteen miles from any town; no spacious valley, but about two miles long by three-quarters-of-a-mile in average width—the benefit of which provision is, that all the families resident within its circuit will compose, as it were, one larger household, personally familiar to your eye, and more or less interesting to your affections. Let the mountains be real mountains, between three and four thousand feet high, and the cottage a real cottage, not (as a witty author has it) "a cottage with a double coachhouse"; let it be, in fact (for I must abide by the actual scene), a white cottage, **embowered** with flowering shrubs, so chosen as to unfold a succession of flowers upon the 25 walls and clustering around the windows, through all the months of spring, summer, and autumn; beginning, in fact, with May roses, and ending with jasmine. Let it, however, not be spring, nor summer, nor autumn; but winter, in its sternest shape. This is a most important point in the science of happiness. And I am surprised to see people overlook it, as if it were actually matter of congratulation that winter is going, or, if coming, is not likely to be a severe one. On the contrary, I put up a petition, annually, for as much snow, hail, frost, or storm of one kind or other, as the skies can possibly afford. Surely everybody is aware of the divine pleasures which attend a winter fireside—candles at four o'clock, warm hearth-rugs, tea, a fair tea-maker, shutters closed, curtains flowing in ample draperies on the floor, whilst the wind and rain are raging audibly without,

And at the doors and windows seem to call, As heaven and earth they would together mell; Yet the least entrance find they none at all; Whence sweeter grows our rest secure in massy hall. (Castle of Indolence)

All these are items in the description of a winter evening which must surely be familiar to everybody born in a high latitude. And it is evident that most of these delicacies cannot be ripened, without weather stormy or **inclement** in some way or other. I am not "particular" whether it be snow, or black frost, or wind so strong that (as Mr. Anti-slavery [Thomas] Clarkson says) "you may lean your back against it like a post." I can put up even with rain, provided that it rains cats and dogs, or, as sailors say, "great guns and marlinespikes"; but something of the sort I must have; and if I have it not, I think myself in a manner ill-used; for why am I called on to pay so heavily for winter in coals, candles, etc., if I am not to have the article good of its kind! No: a Canadian winter for my money, or a Russian one, where every man is but a co-proprietor with the north wind in the fee-simple of his own ears.

Chapter 7

Thomas De Quincey
托马斯·德·昆西

Indeed, so great an **epicure** am I in this matter that I cannot relish a winter night fully, if it be much past St. Thomas's Day [December 21st], and have degenerated into disgusting tendencies towards **vernal** indications: in fact, it must be divided by a thick wall of black nights from all return of light and sunshine. Start, therefore, at the first week of November: thence to the end of January, Christmas Eve being the meridian line, you may compute the period when happiness is in season, which in my judgment, enters the room with the tea-tray. For tea, though ridiculed by those who are naturally coarse in their nervous sensibilities, or are become so from wine-drinking, and are not **susceptible** of influence from so refined a stimulant, will always be the favorite beverage of the intellectual; and, for my part, I would have joined Dr. Johnson in a bellum internecinum [mutually destructive war] against Jonas Hanway, or any other impious person who should have presumed to disparage it. But here, to save myself the trouble of too much verbal description, I will introduce a painter, and give him directions for the rest of the picture. Painters do not like white cottages, unless a good deal **weather-stained**; but, as the reader now understands that it is a winter night, his services will not be required except for the inside of the house.

Paint me, then, a room seventeen feet by twelve, and not more than seven and a half feet high. This, reader, is somewhat ambitiously styled, in my family, the drawing room; but, being contrived, "a double debt to pay," it is also, and more justly, termed the library; for it happens that books are the only article of property in which I am richer than my neighbors. Of these I have about five thousand, collected gradually since my eighteenth year.

Therefore, painter, put as many as you can into this room. Make it populous with books; and, furthermore, paint me a good fire; and furniture plain and modest, befitting the unpretending cottage of a scholar. And near the fire paint me a tea-table; and (as it is clear that no creature can come to see one on such a stormy night) place only two cups and saucers on the tea-tray; and, if you know how to paint such a thing, symbolically or otherwise, paint me an eternal tea-pot—eternal a parte ante, and a parte post [from the part before and the part after]; for I usually drink tea from eight o'clock at night to four in the morning. And, as it is very unpleasant to make tea, or to pour it out for one's self, paint me a lovely young woman sitting at the table. Paint her arms like Aurora's and her smiles like Hebe's; but no, dear M—— [De Quincey's wife, Margaret]! not even in jest let me **insinuate** that thy power to illuminate my cottage rests upon a tenure so perishable as mere personal beauty; or that the witchcraft of angelic smiles lies within the empire of any earthly pencil.

Pass, then, my good painter, to something more within its power; and the next article brought forward should naturally be myself—a picture of the Opium-eater, with his "little golden **receptacle** of the **pernicious** drug" lying beside him on the table. As to the opium, I have no objection to see a picture of that; you may paint it, if you choose; but I **apprise** you that no "little" receptacle would, even in 1816, answer my purpose, who was at a distance from the "stately **Pantheon**" and all druggists (mortal or otherwise). No: you may as well paint the real receptacle, which was not of gold, but of glass, and as much like a **sublunary** wine-**decanter** as possible. In fact, one day, by a series of happily-conceived experiments, I discovered that it was a decanter. Into this you may put a quart of ruby-colored laudanum; that, and a book of German metaphysics placed by its side, will sufficiently attest my being in the neighborhood; but, as to myself, there I demur. I admit that, naturally, I ought to occupy the foreground of the picture; that, being the hero of the piece, or (if you choose) the criminal at the bar, my body should be had into court. This seems reasonable; but why should I confess on this point to a painter? or why confess it at all? If the public (into whose private ear I am confidentially whispering my Confessions, and not into any painter's) should chance to have framed some agreeable picture for itself of the Opium-eater's exterior—should have ascribed to him, romantically, an elegant person or a handsome face— why should I barbarously tear from it so pleasing a delusion?—pleasing both to the public and to me. No: paint me, if at all, according to your own fancy; and since a painter's fancy should teem with beautiful creations, I cannot fail, in that way, to be a gainer. And now, reader, we have run through all the ten categories of my condition, as it stood about 1816-17, up to the middle 20 of

Chapter 7

Thomas De Quincey
托马斯・德・昆西

which latter year I judge myself to have been a happy man; and the elements of that happiness I have endeavored to place before you, in the above sketch of the interior of a scholar's library, in a cottage among the mountains, on a stormy winter evening, rain driving **vindictively** and with malice **aforethought** against the windows, and darkness such that you cannot see your own hand when held up against the sky.

I Words and Phrases

intractable [ɪnˈtræktəbl]	*adj.* difficult to manage or mold 难驾驭的；倔强的
galvanic [gælˈvænɪk]	*adj.* pertaining to or producing electric current by chemical action 电流的；似被电击般的
laudanum [ˈlɔːdənəm]	*n.* narcotic consisting of an alcohol solution of opium or any preparation in which opium is the main ingredient 鸦片酒；鸦片酊
inoculate [ɪˈnɒkjuleɪt]	*v.* introduce a microorganism into 给……注射疫苗
intercalary [ɪnˈtɜːkəˌlerɪ]	*adj.* having a day or month inserted to make the calendar year correspond to the solar year 闰的
embower [emˈbaʊə]	*v.* enclose in lots of trees 隐蔽于树荫中
inclement [ɪnˈklemənt]	*adj.* (of weather or climate) severe 气候严酷的
epicure [ˈepɪkjʊə]	*n.* a person devoted to refined sensuous enjoyment (especially good food and drink) 美食家
vernal [ˈvɜːn(ə)l]	*adj.* suggestive of youth; vigorous and fresh 青春的；春天般清新的
susceptible [səˈseptɪb(ə)l]	*adj.* easily influenced by 易受影响的
weather-stained [ˈweðəˌsteɪnd]	*adj.* marked or dyed or discolored after being exposed to sunshine or rain for certain time 因日晒雨淋而变色的
insinuate [ɪnˈsɪnjueɪt]	*v.* introduce or insert (oneself) in a subtle manner

		暗示；迂回进行
receptacle [rɪ'septəkl]	n.	a container that is used to put or keep things in 容器
pernicious [pə'nɪʃəs]	adj.	exceedingly harmful 有害的；恶性的
apprise [ə'praɪz]	v.	inform (somebody) of something 通知
Pantheon ['pænθɪəːn]	n.	all the gods of a religion 众神
sublunary [sʌb'luːnərɪ]	adj.	of this earth 尘世的
decanter [dɪ'kæntə]	n.	a bottle with a stopper for serving wine or water (用来倾倒的) 玻璃瓶；酒瓶
vindictive [vɪn'dɪktɪv]	adj.	disposed to seek revenge or intended for revenge 怀恨的
aforethought [ə'fɔːθɔːt]	adj.	planned in advance 事先考虑的

II Reading Comprehension Questions

1. Why does the author consider himself a qualified person to talk about happiness?
2. What impresses you most in the author's description of the cottage? Why?
3. According to the author, what is a most important point in the science of happiness? Why?
4. The author imaginatively asked a painter to paint the inside of the house, what is the rhetorical function of this?
5. What will be your description of a happy home?

Chapter 7

Thomas De Quincey
托马斯·德·昆西

Quotes of the Author

Call for the grandest of all earthly spectacles, what is that? It is the sun going to his rest. Call for the grandest of all human sentiments, what is that? It is that man should forget his anger before he lies down to sleep.

It is most absurdly said, in popular language, of any man, that he is disguised in liquor; for, on the contrary, most men are disguised by sobriety.

Books, we are told, propose to instruct or to amuse. Indeed!... The true antithesis to knowledge, in this case, is not pleasure, but power. All that is literature seeks to communicate power; all that is not literature, to communicate knowledge.

If once a man indulges himself in murder, very soon he comes to think little of robbing; and from robbing he comes next to drinking and Sabbath-breaking, and from that to incivility and procrastination. Once begun upon this downward path, you never know where you are to stop. Many a man has dated his ruin from some murder or other that perhaps he thought little of at the time.

Bertrand Russell
伯特兰·罗素
(1872—1970)

本章导读

　　伯特兰·罗素是 20 世纪英国杰出的哲学家、数学家、逻辑学家、历史学家，也是上世纪西方最著名、影响最大的学者和和平主义社会活动家之一，被世人誉为"世纪智者"。从 1896 年出版第一部著作，到 1969 年，共 73 年间，罗素每年都至少会有一部作品问世，另外还有一些随笔、信件等零散创作。在其漫长的一生中，他完成了 40 余部著作，涉及哲学、数学、科学、论理学、社会学、教育、历史、宗教及政治等各个领域，对西方哲学产生了深刻影响。1950 年，罗素获得诺贝尔文学奖，以表彰其"多样且重要的作品，持续不断地追求人道主义理想和思想自由"。伯特兰·罗素一生著述颇丰，享有"百科全书式"思想家的称号。

　　罗素的文学造诣极高，虽是一位"非文学"作家，罗素的散文却具有极高的文学价值，他的散文不仅有大师类作品的清新自然，优美动人；还极具个人风格。他的散文饱含了对大自然的冥想和对真理、正义的追求，带给人思想和心灵的震撼、引人深思。他的散文作品更多的是在探讨自由思想、信仰和人生。罗素的语言平易朴实，不事雕琢，因为他一直追求笛福、斯威夫特以来的平易散文风格。他不浮夸，不卖弄，不用大词、长词，而是力求通俗易懂。哲学是一种抽象思维，哲学家的文章很容易写得苦涩难懂，使人望而生畏，但罗素却不然，他的哲学论文不少都是通俗浅显、清楚明了，读起来十分有趣。他的文章有时格调优雅、富有哲理，有时故意夸张、引人发笑，有时略带幽默，有时讽刺尖锐，但都非常得体，读起来给人以清新之感。

　　总而言之，罗素的散文平易朴实、简洁洗练、行文优美、充满机智。他之所以能写出这样的美文，不仅因为他有着高尚的品味、深邃的智慧、敏锐的洞察力，以及对人类命运的深切关注，而且因为他数学般准确、明晰的语言风格，他以优美的文字、

Chapter 8
Bertrand Russell
伯特兰·罗素

幽默的口吻和极富说服力的论证激励和启发着全世界富有进取精神的读者。

About the Author

Bertrand Russell was a British philosopher, logician, essayist, and social critic, best known for his work in mathematical logic and analytic philosophy.

Bertrand Russell was born on 18 May 1872 at Trellech, Monmouthshire, Wales, into an aristocratic English family. After the early death of his parents, Bertrand was placed chiefly in the care of his grandmother, who influenced tremendously on Russell's outlook on social justice and standing up for principles. Educated at home by a series of tutors, Russell went to Trinity College, Cambridge in 1890 and quickly distinguished himself in mathematics and philosophy. The first of three volumes of *Principia Mathematica* (written with Whitehead) was published in 1910, which (along with the earlier *The Principles of Mathematics*) soon made Russell world famous in his field. His subsequent works were numerous and varied.

Over the course of a long career, Russell also made significant contributions to a broad range of ohter subjects, including ethics, politics, education theory, the history of ideas and religious studies. In addition, generations of general readers have benefited from his many popular writings on a wide variety of topics in both the humanities and the natural sciences. Russell was also a prominent anti-war activist and was imprisoned in World War I for his irreconcilable pacifist position. He remained a prominent public figure until his death at the age of 97.

Text A

What I Have Lived For

Three passions, simple but overwhelmingly strong, have governed my life: the longing for love, the search for knowledge, and unbearable pity for the suffering of mankind. These passions, like great winds, have blown me hither and thither, in a **wayward** course, over a deep ocean of **anguish**, reaching to the very verge of despair.

I have sought love, first, because it brings ecstasy—ecstasy so great that I would often have sacrificed all the rest of life for a few hours of this joy. I have sought it, next, because it relieves loneliness—that terrible loneliness in which one shivering consciousness looks over the rim of the world into the cold **unfathomable** lifeless **abyss**. I have sought it, finally, because in the union of love I have seen, in a mystic **miniature**, the **prefiguring** vision of the heaven that saints and poets have imagined. This is what I sought, and though it might seem too good for human life, this is what—at last—I have found.

With equal passion I have sought knowledge. I have wished to understand the hearts of men. I have wished to know why the stars shine. And I have tried to apprehend the Pythagorean power[1] by which number holds sway above the **flux**. A little of this, but not much, I have achieved.

Love and knowledge, so far as they were possible, led upward toward the heavens. But always pity brought me back to earth. Echoes of cries of pain **reverberate** in my heart. Children in famine, victims tortured by oppressors, helpless old people a hated burden to their sons, and the whole world of loneliness, poverty, and pain make a **mockery** of what human life should be. I long to **alleviate** the evil, but I cannot, and I too suffer.

This has been my life. I have found it worth living, and would gladly live it again if the chance were offered me.

---

1 Pythagorean power: 毕达哥拉斯学说的力量

Chapter 8
Bertrand Russell
伯特兰·罗素

I Words and Phrases

wayward ['weɪwəd]	*adj.*	resistant to guidance or discipline 任性的；不规则的
anguish ['æŋgwɪʃ]	*n.*	extreme mental distress 痛苦，极度痛苦
unfathomable [ʌn'fæðəməbl]	*adj.*	so deep as to be immeasurable 深不可测的，无底的
abyss [ə'bɪs]	*n.*	a bottomless gulf or pit 深渊，深邃，无底洞；地狱
miniature ['mɪnɪtʃə]	*n.*	a copy that reproduces something in greatly reduced size 缩影；微型
prefigure [priː'fɪgə]	*v.*	imagine or consider beforehand 预示；预想
flux [flʌks]	*n.*	a state of uncertainty, a series of changes 变迁；不稳定
reverberate [rɪ'vɜːbəreɪt]	*v.*	to be repeated several times as it is reflected off different surfaces 回荡，回响
mockery ['mɒk(ə)rɪ]	*n.*	showing your contempt by derision 嘲笑
alleviate [ə'liːvɪeɪt]	*v.*	make easier 减轻；缓和

II Reading Comprehension Questions

1. What are the three passions that have governed the author's life?
2. Why did the author seek love first? And did he succeed in finding it?
3. What kind of knowledge do you think the author has searched for?
4. What always brought the author back to earth? Can you understand this profound feeling?

III Questions on Writing Style and Language

1. Have you noticed any stylistic features of the author's writing? What particular effect is produced by these sentences?
2. Can you feel the author's passion in the essay? How does the author

achieve this kind of strong emotional effect?
3. Study the essay carefully, and discuss what kind of figure of speech the author uses in this essay.
4. How does the author organize his ideas into this compact essay? Do you see the logic between the parts?
5. The following sentences are taken from Russell's essay "How to Grow Old." Please analyze the part both from rhetorical level and textual level.

"An individual human existence should be like a river—small at first, narrowly contained within its banks, and rushing passionately past rocks and over waterfalls. Gradually the river grows wider, the banks recede, the waters flow more quietly, and in the end, without any visible break, they become merged in the sea, and painlessly lose their individual being."

Chapter 8

Bertrand Russell
伯特兰·罗素

Text B

On Human Nature and Politics

Undoubtedly the desire for food has been, and still is, one of the main causes of great political events. But man differs from other animals in one very important respect, and that is that he has desires which are, so to speak, infinite, which can never be fully gratified, and which would keep him restless even in Paradise. The **boa constrictor**, when he has had an adequate meal, goes to sleep, and does not wake until he needs another meal. Human beings, for the most part, are not like this. When the Arabs, who had been used to living **sparingly** on a few dates, acquired the riches of the Eastern Roman Empire and dwelt in palaces of almost unbelievable luxury, they did not, on that account, become inactive. Hunger could no longer be a motive, for Greek slaves supplied them with exquisite **viands** at the slightest nod. But other desires kept them active: four in particular, which we can label acquisitiveness, rivalry, vanity and love of power.

Acquisitiveness—the wish to possess as much as possible of goods, or the title to goods—is a motive which, I suppose, has its origin in a combination of fear with the desire for necessaries.

I once **befriended** two little girls from Esthonia, who had narrowly escaped death from starvation in a famine. They lived in my family, and of course had plenty to eat. But they spent all their leisure visiting neighbouring farms and stealing potatoes, which they hoarded. Rockefeller, who in his infancy had experienced great poverty, spent his adult life in a similar manner. Similarly the Arab **chieftains** on their silken Byzantine **divans** could not forget the desert, and hoarded riches far beyond any possible physical need. But whatever the psychoanalysis of acquisitiveness, no one can deny that it is one of the great motives—especially among the more powerful, for, as I said before, it is one of the infinite motives. However much you may acquire you will always wish to acquire more; **satiety** is a dream which will always **elude** you.

But acquisitiveness, although it is the mainspring of the capitalist system, is by no means the most powerful of the motives that survive the conquest of hunger. Rivalry is a much stronger motive. Over and over again in Muhammadan history, dynasties have come to grief because the sons of a **sultan** by different mothers could not agree, and in the resulting civil war universal ruin resulted. The same sort of thing happens in modern Europe. When the British Government very unwisely allowed the **Kaiser** to be present at a naval review at Spithead, the thought which arose in his mind was not the one which we had intended. What he thought was, I must have a Navy as good as Grandmamma's." And from this thought have sprung all our subsequent troubles. The world would be a happier place than it is if acquisitiveness were always stronger than rivalry. But in fact, a great many men will cheerfully face impoverishment if they can thereby secure complete ruin for their rivals. Hence the present level of taxation.

Vanity is a motive of immense potency. Anyone who has much to do with children knows how they are constantly performing some **antic** and saying "Look at me". "Look at me" is one of the most fundamental desires of the human heart. It can take innumerable forms, from **buffoonery** to the pursuit of **posthumous** fame. There was a Renaissance Italian **princeling** who was asked by the priest on his deathbed if he had anything to repent of. "Yes," he said. "There is one thing. On one occasion I had a visit from the Emperor and the Pope simultaneously. I took them to the top of my tower to see the view, and I neglected the opportunity to throw them both down, which would have given me immortal fame." History does not relate whether the priest gave him absolution. One of the troubles about vanity is that it grows with what it feeds on. The more you are talked about, the more you will wish to be talked about. The condemned murderer who is allowed to see the account of his trial in the Press is indignant if he finds about himself in other newspapers, the more indignant he will be with those whose reports are meagre. Politicians and literary men are in the same case. And the more famous they become, the more difficult the presscutting agency finds it to satisfy them. It is scarcely

Chapter 8
Bertrand Russell
伯特兰·罗素

possible to exaggerate the influence of vanity throughout the range of human life, from the child of three to the **potentate** at whose frown the world trembles. Mankind have even committed the impiety of attributing similar desires to the deity, whom they imagine avid for continual praise.

But great as is the influence of the motives we have been considering, there is one which outweighs them all… Power, like vanity, is insatiable. Nothing short of **omnipotence** could satisfy it completely. And as it is especially the vice of energetic men, the casual **efficacy** of love of power is out of all proportion to its frequency. It is, indeed, by far the strongest motive in the lives of important men. Love of power is greatly increased by the experience of power, and this applies to petty power as well as to that of potentates. In the happy days before 1914, when well-to-do ladies could acquire a host of servants, their pleasure in exercising power over the domestics steadily increased with age. Similarly, in any autocratic regime, the holders of power become increasingly tyrannical with experience of the delights that power can afford. Since power over human beings is shown in making them do what they would rather not do, the man who is **actuated** by love of power is more apt to **inflict** pain than to permit pleasure. If you ask your boss for leave of absence from the office on some legitimate occasion, his love of power will derive more satisfaction from refusal than from consent. If you require a building permit, the petty official concerned will obviously get more pleasure from saying "No" than from saying "Yes". It is this sort of thing which makes the love of power such a dangerous motive. But it has other sides which are more desirable. The pursuit of knowledge is, I think, mainly actuated by love of power. And so are all advances in scientific technique. In politics, also, a reformer may have just as strong a love of power as a **despot**. It would be a complete mistake to decry love of power altogether as a motive. Whether you will be led by this motive to actions which are useful, or to actions which are pernicious, depends upon the social system, and upon your capacities.

I come now to other motives which, though in a sense less fundamental than those we have been considering, are still of considerable importance. The first of these is love of excitement. Human beings show their superiority to the brutes by their capacity for boredom, though I have sometimes thought, in examining the apes at the Zoo, that they, perhaps, have the rudiments of this tiresome emotion. However that may be, experience shows that escape from boredom is one of the really powerful desires of almost all human beings.

When white men first effect contact with some unspoilt race of savages, they offer them all kinds of benefits, from the light of the Gospel to pumpkin pie. These, however, much as we may regret it, most savages receive with indifference. What they really value among the gifts that we bring to them is intoxicating liquor, which enables them, for the first time in their lives, to have the illusion, for a few brief moments, that it is better to be alive than dead.

Red Indians, while they were still unaffected by white men, would smoke their pipes, not calmly as we do, but orgiastically, inhaling so deeply that they sank into a faint. And when excitement by means of nicotine failed, a patriotic orator would stir them up to attack a neighbouring tribe, which would give them all the enjoyment that we (according to our temperament), derive from a horse race or a General Election.

With civilized men, as with primitive Red Indian tribes, it is, I think, chiefly love of excitement which makes the populace applaud when war breaks out; the emotion is exactly the same as at a football match, although the results are sometimes somewhat more serious.

It is not altogether easy to decide what is the root cause of the love of excitement. I incline to think that our mental make-up is adapted to the stage when men lived by hunting. When a man spent a long day with very primitive weapons in stalking a deer with the hope of dinner and when, at the end of the day, he dragged the carcase triumphantly to his cave, he sank down in contented weariness, while his wife dressed and cooked the meat. He was sleepy, and his bones ached, and the smell of cooking filled every nook and cranny of his consciousness. At last after eating, he sank into deep sleep. In such a life there was neither time nor energy for boredom. But when he took to agriculture, and made his wife do all the heavy work in the fields, he had time to reflect upon the vanity of human life, to invent mythologies and systems of philosophy, and to ream of the life hereafter in which he would perpetually

Chapter 8

Bertrand Russell
伯特兰·罗素

hunt the wild boar of Valhalla[1].

Our mental make-up is suited to a life of very severe physical labour. I used, when I was younger, to take my holidays walking. I would cover 25 miles a day, and when the evening came I had no need of anything to keep me from boredom, since the delight of sitting amply sufficed. But modern life cannot be conducted on these physically strenuous principles. A great deal of work is sedentary and most manual work exercises only a few specialized muscles. When London crowds assemble in Trafalgar Square to cheer to the echo an announcement that the government has decided to have them killed, they would not do so if they had walked 25 miles that day. This cure for bellicosity is, however, impracticable, and if the human race is to survive—a thing which is, perhaps, undesirable—other means must be found for securing an innocent outlet for the unused physical energy that produces love of excitement.

This is a matter which has been too little considered, both by moralists and by social reformers. The social reformers are of the opinion that they have more serious things to consider. The moralists, on the other hand, are immensely impressed with the seriousness of all the permitted outlets of the love of excitement; the seriousness, however, in their minds is that of Sin. Dance halls, cinemas, this age of jazz are all, if we may believe our ears, gateways to Hell, and we should be better employed sitting at home contemplating our sins. I find myself unable to be in entire agreement with the grave men who utter these warnings. The devil has many forms, some designed to deceive the young, some designed to deceive the old and serious. If it is the devil that tempts the young to enjoy themselves, is it not, perhaps, the same personage that persuades the old to condemn their enjoyment? And is not condemnation perhaps merely a form of excitement appropriate to old age? And is it not, perhaps, a drug which—like opium—has to be taken in continually stronger dose to produce the desired effect? Is it not to be feared that, beginning with the wickedness of the cinema, we should be led step by

---

1   Valhalla: from Germanic mythology, the home of the gods, used in a commendatory sense as roughly the equivalent of heaven 瓦尔哈拉殿堂，德国神话中众神的家园，大致相当于天堂的意思

step to condemn the opposite political party, dagoes, wops, Asiatics, and, in short, everybody except the fellow members of our club? And it is from just such condemnations, when widespread, that wars proceed. I never heard of a war that proceeded from dance halls.

What is serious about excitement is that so many of its forms are destructive. It is destructive in those who cannot resist excess in alcohol or gambling. It is destructive when it takes the form of mob violence. And above all it is destructive when it leads to war. It is so deep a need that it will find harmful outlets of this kind unless innocent outlets are at hand. There are such innocent outlets at present in sport, and in politics so long as it is kept in constitutional bounds. But these are not sufficient, especially as the kind of politics that is most exciting is also the kind that does most harm.

Civilized life has grown altogether too tame, and, if it is to be stable, it must provide harmless outlets for the impulses which our remote ancestors satisfied in hunting. In Australia, where people are few and rabbits are many, I watched a whole populace satisfying the primitive impulse in the primitive manner by the skilful slaughter of many thousands of rabbits. But in London or New York, where people are many and rabbits are few, some other means must be found to gratify primitive impulse. I think every big town should contain artificial waterfalls that people could descend in very fragile canoes, and they should contain bathing pools full of mechanical sharks. Any persons found advocating a preventive war should be condemned to two hours a day with these ingenious monsters.

1 Words and Phrases

boa constrictor ['bəʊə] [kən'strɪktə]   a large snake that kills animals by wrapping itself round their bodies and squeezing them to death 蟒蛇

sparingly ['spɛərɪŋlɪ]   *adv.* to a meager degree or in a meager manner economically 节俭地

Chapter 8
Bertrand Russell
伯特兰·罗素

viand ['vaɪənd]	n.	a type of food, esp a delicacy 食物，尤指美食
befriend [bɪ'frend]	v.	make friends with... 和……交朋友；友好对待
chieftain ['tʃɪftən]	n.	a chieftain is the leader of a tribe（部落）酋长
divan [dɪ'væn]	n.	a long soft seat that has no back or arms 无靠背无扶手的长软凳
satiety [sə'taɪətɪ]	n.	the state of being satisfactorily full and unable to take on more 满足；饱足
elude [ɪ'lud]	v.	fail to be obtained by, fail to be understood by 不为……所获得或理解
sultan ['sʌltən]	n.	a ruler in some Muslim countries 苏丹（某些穆斯林国家的统治者的称法）
Kaiser ['kaɪzə]	n.	the title of the Holy Roman Emperors or the emperors of Austria or of Germany until 1918（德国）皇帝
antic ['æntɪk]	n.	a ludicrous or grotesque act done for fun and amusement 滑稽动作
buffoonery [bə'fʊnərɪ]	n.	foolish behavior intended to make people laugh 插科打诨
posthumous ['pɒstjʊməs]	adj.	happening after a person's death 死后的；身后的
princeling ['prɪnslɪŋ]	n.	a petty or insignificant prince who rules some unimportant principality 幼君
potentate ['pəʊt(ə)nteɪt]	n.	a ruler who has complete power over his people 专制君主
omnipotence [ɒm'nɪpət(ə)ns]	n.	the state of having total authority or power 全能
efficacy ['efɪkəsɪ]	n.	capacity or power to produce a desired effect 功效，效力
actuate ['æktʃueɪt]	v.	give an incentive for action 促使，驱使
inflict [ɪn'flɪkt]	v.	impose something unpleasant 使遭受（损伤、痛苦等）
despot ['despɒt]	n.	a ruler who has a lot of power and who uses it unfairly or cruelly 专制者

II Reading Comprehension Questions

1. According to the author, what are the motives for politics in human nature? Do you agree with the him?
2. What is the prominent method the author uses in supporting his argumentation?
3. In what case will men "cheerfully face impoverishment"? And what's the reason behind that?
4. How do you understand the sentence "The pursuit of knowledge is, mainly actuated by love of power"? Do you agree with the author here?
5. Why does the author say that love of excitement is destructive? And how can we avoid the destruction?

Chapter 8
Bertrand Russell
伯特兰·罗素

Quotes of the Author

A stupid man's report of what a clever man says can never be accurate, because he unconsciously translates what he hears into something he can understand.

Life is nothing but a competition to be the criminal rather than the victim.

Many people would sooner die than think; In fact, they do so.

No one gossips about other people's secret virtues.

Our great democracies still tend to think that a stupid man is more likely to be honest than a clever man.

Edward Morgan Forster
爱德华·摩根·福斯特
(1879—1970)

本章导读

爱德华·摩根·福斯特是20世纪杰出的英国小说家、散文家、随笔作家、小说理论家。他的小说深受其哲学观、社会观、道德观和艺术观的影响，形成了一套独具特色的小说思想体系。他同乔伊斯、劳伦斯和伍尔夫并称为"20世纪英国最伟大的小说家"。此外，他还作有关于社会、政治、哲学方面的大量论文，使他成为20世纪里为数不多的哲人之一。

爱德华·摩根·福斯特生于伦敦建筑师家庭，父亲早亡。少年时就读肯特郡唐布利奇学校的不愉快经历造成了他对英国中上层社会的反感。1897年，福斯特进入剑桥大学国王学院学习，加入了门徒社（The Apostle）。门徒社成员毕业后组成"布鲁姆斯伯里派"（Bloomsbury Group），包括哲学家摩尔、罗素以及伍尔夫夫妇等。这些文人和作家强调爱、同情、敏感、美的创造和享受、追求知识的勇气，实际上是流行在上层知识分子中间的人文主义精神。福斯特在思想上受其影响非常大，使他最终形成了人文主义联接观，而这一观点伴随了他一生，几乎体现在他的每一部作品之中。

20世纪起，福斯特开始游历希腊、意大利、埃及、印度等地，并开始创作小说。他的第一部小说《天使不敢驻足的地方》（Where Angels Fear to Tread）描写一位英国贵妇与一位意大利平民结合后两家对此事的不同感受。同样将场景设定在意大利的小说还有《看得见风景的房间》（A Room with a View），描写一位英国贵族少女在意大利与一位年轻男子邂逅相遇，社会习俗的约束使她不敢表达自己的感情，但最后终于冲破樊篱，挣脱包办婚姻，走向自由。另外，福斯特成就最大的小说之一《印度之行》（A Passage to India）则是根据他本人在印度殖民地的所见所闻创作的。

Chapter 9
Edward Morgan Forster
爱德华·摩根·福斯特

福斯特小说的思想内容正是人文主义在20世纪的反映。他以此为武器，讽刺、批评英国社会，并相信实现了"爱的原则"，社会矛盾就可以和解。作者善于描写人与人之间的微妙关系，往往幽默又微带讽刺。文字优美精练，常用一些象征手法，耐人寻味。

除了小说之外，福斯特所作散文尽管不多，但却独具特色。

无论是福斯特的散文还是小说，又或者是诸如《小说面面观》（*Espects of the Novel*）这类理论作品，他的语言向来都清晰易懂，行文措辞深入浅出，能把一些专业性强、复杂深奥的学术理论化解为明白易懂的语言，简单明了。再者，他在文中随时提供许多通俗、生动而且典型的例子，令人印象格外深刻。举例来说，他在《小说面面观》中阐述"扁平人物"和"圆形人物"的观点时，并非单纯的说教，而是举了大量人们耳熟能详的名作中的人物，其中有《大卫·科波菲尔》中的米考伯太太，有简·奥斯丁笔下的贝特兰夫人，也有夏洛蒂·勃朗特塑造的鲁西·斯诺威等等，以此将要阐述的观点巧妙生动地融入读者的思想中去，使其理论著作也毫无枯燥沉闷之感。

About the Author

Edward Morgan Forster was a noted English novelist, short story writer, essayist and a member of the Bloomsbury group. He was born in London on January 1, 1871 as the son of an architect, who died before his only child was two years old. Forster's years at Tonbridge School as a teenager were difficult—he suffered from the cruelty of his classmates. Forster attended King's College, Cambridge (1897-1901), where he met members of the later formed Bloomsbury Group (writers, artists, and philosophers living in London who helped shape the modernist movement of the first half of this century). Forster was born in London, but was raised in the countryside of Herforshire. While studying at King's College, Cambridge, he became deeply interested in cultures other than his own and later traveled widely. In 1912, he sailed with two friends to India where his observations and experiences provided him with the materials from which he later created his highly acclaimed novel *A Passage to India* (1924), the book to which he refers in the first paragraph of "My Wood."

Forster is known best for his ironic and well-plotted novels examining class difference and hypocrisy and also the attitudes towards gender and homosexuality in early 20th-century British society. Forster's humanistic impulse toward understanding and sympathy may be aptly summed up in the epigraph to his 1910 novel *Howards End*: "Only connect ... ". His 1908 novel, *A Room with a View*, is his most optimistic work, while *A Passage to India* (1924) brought him his greatest success. He was nominated for the Nobel Prize in Literature 13 different years.

"My Wood", one of the essays chosen in this chapter, is part of Forster's 1936 essay, *Abinger Harvest*. In this essay, Forster explains the effects produced by owning property. It encourages us to think about the nature of materialism and the seductive power of our possessions. With wit and humor, Forster suggests that purchasing land may not bring the uncomplicated happiness we might expect.

Forster was also a superb literary critic and his most notable work of literary criticism is *Aspects of the Novel*. Witty and informal, the book is a classic discussion of the techniques of fiction. *Aspects of the Novel* remains a delightful reading for its sharp, penetrating bursts of insight and simple, brisk yet varied style.

Chapter 9

Edward Morgan Forster
爱德华·摩根·福斯特

My Wood

E. M. Forster

A few years ago I wrote a book which dealt in part with the difficulties of the English in India[1]. Feeling that they would have had no difficulties in India themselves, the Americans read the book freely. The more they read it the better it made them feel, and a cheque to the author was the result. I bought a wood with the cheque. It is not a large wood—it contains scarcely any trees, and it is intersected, blast it, by a public footpath. Still, it is the first property that I have owned, so it is right that other people should participate in my shame, and should ask themselves, in accents that will vary in horror, this very important question: What is the effect of property upon the character? Don't let's touch economics; the effect of private ownership upon the community as a whole is another question—a more important question, perhaps, but another one. Let's keep to psychology. If you own things, what's their effect on you? What's the effect on me of my wood?

In the first place, it makes me feel heavy. Property does have this effect. Property produces men of weight, and it was a man of weight who failed to get into the Kingdom of Heaven. He was not wicked, that unfortunate millionaire in the parable, he was only **stout**; he stuck out in front, not to mention behind, and as he **wedged** himself this way and that in the crystalline entrance and bruised his well-fed **flanks**, he saw beneath him a comparatively slim camel

---

[1] I wrote a book which dealt in part with the difficulties of the English in India: The British first came to India in 1608 and remained until 1947 when India was granted independence. The book that Forster is alluding to is *A Passage to India* (1924). 英国人从 1608 年开始统治印度长达 300 多年。此处的书指的是福斯特于 1924 年出版的小说《印度之行》。

passing through the eye of a needle and being woven into the robe of God[1]. The Gospels all through couple stoutness and slowness. They point out what is perfectly obvious, yet seldom realized: that if you have a lot of things you cannot move about a lot, that furniture requires dusting, dusters require servants, servants require insurance stamps, and the whole tangle of them makes you think twice before you accept an invitation to dinner or go for a bathe in the Jordan[2] Sometimes the Gospels proceed further and say with Tolstoy[3] that property is sinful; they approach the difficult ground of **asceticism** here, where I cannot follow them. But as to the immediate effects of property on people, they just show straightforward logic. It produces men of weight. Men of weight cannot, by definition, move like the lightning from the East unto the West, and the ascent of a fourteen-stone[4] bishop into a pulpit is thus the exact antithesis of the coming of the Son of Man. My wood makes me feel heavy.

In the second place, it makes me feel it ought to be larger.

The other day I heard a twig snap in it. I was annoyed at first, for I thought that someone was blackberrying, and depreciating the value of the undergrowth. On coming nearer, I saw it was not a man who had trodden on the twig and snapped it, but a bird, and I felt pleased. My bird. The bird was not equally pleased. Ignoring the relation between us, it took fright as soon as it saw the shape of my face, and flew straight over the boundary hedge into a field, the property of Mrs. Henessy, where it sat down with a loud squawk. It had become Mrs. Henessy's bird. Something seemed grossly amiss here,

---

1　he saw beneath him a comparatively slim camel passing through the eye of a needle and being woven into the robe of God: is a Biblical allusion. Matthew 19:24: "It is easier for a camel to pass through the eye of a needle than for a rich man to enter the kingdom of God." 马太福音 19 章 24 节:"耶稣对门徒说,骆驼穿过针的眼,比财主进神的国还容易呢。"

2　the Jordan: the river in which John the Baptist christened repentant sinners. 在《圣经》中,约旦河是施洗者约翰为忏悔的罪人洗礼的地方。

3　Tolstoy: a Russian writer and philosopher, author of *War and Peace* and *Anna Karenina*. This is an apparent reference to a short story by Tolstoy entitled *How Much Land Does a Man Need?* 托尔斯泰,俄国著名作家、哲学家,著有《战争与和平》和《安娜·卡列尼娜》等作品。托尔斯泰曾写了一篇名为《人需要多大的土地?》的故事来表达"财产是罪恶的"的主题。

4　stone: a British unit of weight; 14 stone equals 196 pounds. 石是英国的重量单位,14 石等于 196 磅。

Chapter 9
Edward Morgan Forster
爱德华·摩根·福斯特

something that would not have occurred had the wood been larger. I could not afford to buy Mrs. Henessy out, I dared not murder her, and limitations of this sort beset me on every side. Ahab[1] did not want that vineyard—he only needed it to round off his property, preparatory to plotting a new curve—and all the land around my wood has become necessary to me in order to round off the wood. A boundary protects. But—poor little thing—the boundary ought in its turn to be protected. Noises on the edge of it. Children throw stones. A little more, and then a little more, until we reach the sea. Happy Canute[2]! Happier Alexander[3]! And after all, why should even the world be the limit of possession? A rocket containing a Union Jack, will, it is hoped, be shortly fired at the moon, Mars, Sirius. Beyond which... But these immensities ended by saddening me. I could not suppose that my wood was the destined nucleus of universal dominion—it is so very small and contains no mineral wealth beyond the blackberries. Nor was I comforted when Mrs. Henessy's bird took alarm for the second time and flew clean away from us all, under the belief that it belonged to itself.

In the third place, property makes its owner feel that he ought to do something to it. Yet he isn't sure what. A restlessness comes over him, a vague sense that he has a personality to express—the same sense which, without any vagueness, leads the artist to an act of creation. Sometimes I think I will cut down such trees as remain in the wood, at other times I want to fill up the gaps between them with new trees. Both impulses are pretentious and empty. They are not honest movements towards money-making or beauty. They spring from a foolish desire to express myself and from an inability to enjoy what I have got. Creation, property, enjoyment form a sinister trinity in the

---

1 Ahab: a 9th century B.C. Pagan king of Israel 亚哈是公元前 9 世纪以色列的国王。此处用了圣经中的典故：亚哈并不想霸占葡萄园。在圣经中，亚哈由于贪婪并受到魔鬼的指使霸占了拿波的葡萄园。

2 Canute: He is known as "the Great King of England (1016-1035), Denmark (1018-1035), and Norway (1028-1035)" whose reign, at first brutal, was later marked by wisdom and temperance. He is the subject of many legends. 克努特大帝，曾统治过英国、丹麦、挪威三国，是很多传奇故事中的主角。

3 Alexander: He is known as "Alexander the Great" (356-323 B.C.). 亚历山大大帝，以领土扩张与占领而闻名于人类历史。

human mind. Creation and enjoyment are both very, very good, yet they are often unattainable without a material basis, and at such moments property pushes itself in as a substitute, saying, "Accept me instead—I'm good enough for all three." It is not enough. It is, as Shakespeare said of lust, "The expense of spirit in a waste of shame": it is "Before, a joy proposed; behind, a dream." Yet we don't know how to shun it. It is forced on us by our economic system as the alternative to starvation. It is also forced on us by an internal defect in the soul, by the feeling that in property may lie the **germs** of self-development and of exquisite or heroic deeds. Our life on earth is, and ought to be, material and **carnal**. But we have not yet learned to manage our materialism and carnality properly; they are sill entangled with the desire for ownership, where (in the words of Dante[1]) "Possession is one with loss."

And this brings us to our fourth and final point: the blackberries.

Blackberries are not plentiful in this meager grove, but they are easily seen from the public footpath which traverses it, and all too easily gathered. Foxgloves, too—people will pull up the foxgloves, and ladies of an educational tendency even **grub** for **toadstools** to show them on the Monday in class. Other ladies, less educated, roll down the bracken in the arms of their gentlemen friends. There is paper, there are tins. Pray, does my wood belong to me or doesn't it? And, if it does, should I not own it best by allowing no one else to walk there? There is a wood near Lyme Regis[2], also cursed by a public footpath, where the owner has not hesitated on this point. He has built high stone walls each side of the path, and has spanned it by bridges, so that the public circulate like **termites** while he **gorges** on the blackberries unseen. He really does own his wood, this able chap. Dives[3] in Hell did pretty well, but

---

1 Dante: the Italian poet (1265-1321) whose masterpiece, *The Divine Comedy* (completed in 1321), details his visionary progress through Hell and Purgatory, escorted by Virgil, and through Heaven, guided by his lifelong idealized love Beatrice 此处指的是意大利诗人但丁,《神曲》的作者

2 Lyme Regis: a resort city in the county of Dorset on the southwest coast of England 莱姆利捷思, 英国多塞特郡的一个休闲度假城市

3 Dives: a man of great wealth in the parable of Lazarus and the rich man in the Bible 戴夫斯, 圣经故事中的一个大财主

Chapter 9
Edward Morgan Forster
爱德华·摩根·福斯特

the gulf dividing him from Lazarus could be traversed by vision, and nothing traverses it here. And perhaps I shall come to this in time. I shall wall in and fence out until I really taste the sweets of property. Enormously stout, endlessly avaricious, pseudo-creative, intensely selfish, I shall weave upon my forehead the quadruple crown of possession until those nasty Bolshies come and take it off again and thrust me aside into the outer darkness.

I Words and Phrases

stout [staʊt]	*adj.*	a stout person is rather fat 肥胖的
wedge [wedʒ]	*v.*	force something to remain in a particular position or by sticking something next to it to prevent it from moving 把……楔住；把……抵牢
flank [flæŋk]	*n.*	the side of anything large can be referred to as its flank（大型物体的）侧面
asceticism [əˈsetɪsɪz(ə)m]	*n.*	a simple, strict way of life with no luxuries or physical pleasures 禁欲主义
germ [dʒɜːm]	*n.*	a germ is a very small organism that causes disease 病菌
carnal [ˈkɑːn(ə)l]	*adj.*	of or relating to the body or flesh 肉体的
grub [grʌb]	*v.*	search for something especially by digging 挖掘；搜寻
toadstool [ˈtəʊdstuːl]	*n.*	common name for an inedible or poisonous agaric (contrasting with the edible mushroom) 毒菌；伞菌
termite [ˈtɜːmaɪt]	*n.*	whitish soft-bodied ant-like social insect that feeds on wood 白蚁
gorge [ɡɔːdʒ]	*v.*	overeat or eat immodestly; make a pig of oneself 拼命吃，狼吞虎咽

II Reading Comprehension Questions

1. In the opening section of the essay, Forster describes the response of

Americans to a book he wrote. Why does he emphasize the reaction of Americans? What relationship does the opening paragraph have to the rest of the essay?

2. What are the four effects Forster describes as resulting from his purchase of the wood? Explain briefly some of the details Forster uses to explain each of these four effects.

3. How are the Gospel of Matthew, 19:24 and Leo Tostoys views on property in the second paragraph related to the central idea of the essay?

4. Why does Forster feel sad when he reflects on the size of the wood?

5. In this essay, Forster uses his own experience with ownership to generalize about society's materialism. Do you consider yourself materialistic? In what ways? Do you consider it a positive or negative trait in yourself or others? Think of something you have purchased after wanting it for a long time. In an essay explain the two or three main ways in which owning this item has affected your life.

III Questions on Writing Style and Language

1. Have you noticed any stylistic features of Forster's writing? Are his sentences long or short? What particular effect is produced by these sentences?

2. Can you sense the gentle humor in the essay? Please identify some humorous sentences and expressions in the essay.

3. Forster uses personal experience as a way to exemplify his general thesis concerning the effects of property. Analyze these personal examples and discuss in what way they are related to the topic being discussed.

4. The writer enumerates the effects property produces on him. How does he arrange his points of view? Are they logically connected?

5. The essay is rich in biblical and literary allusions An allusion is a reference to a person, place, event, or thing that bears an association to the topic of a discourse. This association expands the discourse by drawing in ideas that illustrate the topic, provide a comparison or contrast, suggest consequences,

Chapter 9
Edward Morgan Forster
爱德华·摩根·福斯特

evoke an image, or otherwise enlarge or elucidate the author's ideas. In much "classic" literature, allusions are made to the Bible, to Greek and Roman writers, and to mythology. However, allusions may be made to any field: history, politics, science, Etc. The nature of the allusions affects both the immediate comprehension of the discourse as well as its eventual fate. While allusions enhance the understanding of informed readers, they impede the comprehension of those less knowledgeable. Please try to understand all the allusions used in this essay and think about the stylistic effect of these allusions.

Text B

People[1]

E. M. Forster

We may divide characters into flat and round.

Flat characters were called "humours" in the seventeenth century, and are sometimes called types, and sometimes caricatures. In their purest form, they are constructed round a single idea or quality: when there is more than one factor in them, we get the beginning of the curve towards the round. The really flat character can be expressed in one sentence such as "I never will desert Mr. Micawber". There is Mrs. Micawber[2]—she says she won't desert Mr. Micawber, she doesn't, and there she is. Or: "I must conceal, even by **subterfuges**, the poverty of my master's house." There is Caleb Balderstone in *The Bride of Lammermoor*.[3] He does not use the actual phrase, but it completely describes him; he has no existence outside it, no pleasures, none of the private lusts and aches that must complicate the most consistent of **servitors**. Whatever he does, wherever he goes, whatever lies he tells or plates he breaks, it is to conceal the poverty of his master's house. It is not his idée fixe[4], because there is nothing in him into which the idea can be fixed. He is the idea, and such life as he possesses radiates from its edges and from the **scintillations** it strikes when other elements in the novel impinge. Or take Proust[5]. There are numerous

---

1 The present essay is abridged from *Aspects of the Novel* (1927). 本文节选自福斯特的文论《小说面面观》。

2 Mr. Micawber: a character in Dickens' novel *David Copperfield* 米考伯夫人，狄更斯小说《大卫·科波菲尔》中的人物

3 *The Bride of Lammermoor*: a novel by the Scottish novelist Walter Scott《拉马摩尔的新娘》是苏格兰小说家司各特的小说。

4 idée fixe: French for fixed idea 固定观念；困扰

5 Proust: Marcel Proust (1871-1922), French novelist 普鲁斯特，法国著名小说家

Chapter 9
Edward Morgan Forster
爱德华·摩根·福斯特

flat characters in Proust, such as the Princess of Parma, or Legrandin[1]. Each can be expressed in a single sentence, the Princess's sentence being, "I must be particularly careful to be kind." She does nothing except to be particularly careful, and those of the other characters who are more complex than herself easily see through the kindness, since it is only a **by-product** of the carefulness.

One great advantage of flat characters is that they are easily recognized whenever they come in—recognized by the reader's emotional eye, not by the visual eye, which merely notes the recurrence of a proper name. In Russian novels, where they so seldom occur, they would be a decided help. It is a convenience for an author when he can strike with his full force at once, and flat characters are very useful to him, since they never need reintroducing, never run away, have not to be watched for development, and provide their own atmosphere—little luminous disks of a pre-arranged size, pushed **hither** and **thither** like counters across the void or between the stars; most satisfactory.

A second advantage is that they are easily remembered by the reader afterwards. They remain in his mind as unalterable for the reason that they were not changed by circumstances; they moved through circumstances, which gives them in retrospect a comforting quality, and preserves them when the book that produced them may decay. The Countess in *Evan Harrington*[2] **furnishes** a good little example here. Let us compare our memories of her with our memories of Becky Sharp[3]. We do not remember what the Countess did or what she passed through. What is clear is her figure and the formula that surrounds it, namely, "Proud as we are of dear papa, we must conceal his memory." All her rich humour proceeds from this. She is a flat character. Becky is round. She, too, is on the make, but she cannot be summed up in a single phrase, and we remember her in connection with the great scenes through

---

1 Princess of Parma, or Legrandin: characters in Proust's novel *Remembrance of Things Past* 帕尔玛王妃，普鲁斯特的名著《追忆似水年华》中的人物

2 *Evan Harrington*: a novel by the English novelist and poet George Meredith (1828-1909) 《埃文·哈林顿》，英国小说家、诗人梅瑞德斯的小说

3 Becky Sharp: a main character in *Vanity Fair* by the English novelist William Makepeace Thackeray (1811-1863) 贝奇·夏普，萨克雷小说《名利场》中的人物

which she passed and as modified by those scenes—that is to say, we do not remember her so easily because she waxes and wanes and has facets like a human being. All of us, even the sophisticated, yearn for permanence, and to the unsophisticated permanence is the chief excuse for a work of art. We all want books to endure, to be refuges, and their inhabitants to be always the same, and flat characters tend to justify themselves on this account.

All the same, critics who have their eyes fixed severely upon daily life—as were our eyes last week—have very little patience with such renderings of human nature. Queen Victoria, they argue, cannot be summed up in a single sentence, so what excuse remains for Mrs. Micawber? One of our foremost writers, Mr. Norman Douglas[1], is a critic of this type, and the passage from him which I will quote puts the case against flat characters in a forcible fashion. The passage occurs in an open letter to D. H. Lawrence, with whom he is quarrelling: a **doughty** pair of combatants, the hardness of whose hitting makes the rest of us feel like a lot of ladies up in a pavilion. He complains that Lawrence, in a biography, has falsified the picture by employing "the novelist's touch," and he goes on to define what this is:

It consists, I should say, in a failure to realize the complexities of the ordinary human mind; it selects for literary purposes two or three facets of a man or woman, generally the most spectacular, and therefore useful ingredients of their character and disregards all the others. Whatever fails to fit in with these specially chosen traits is eliminated—must be eliminated, for otherwise the description would not hold water. Such and such are the data: everything incompatible with those data has to **go by the board**. It follows that the novelist's touch argues, often logically, from a wrong premise: it takes what it likes and leaves the rest. The facts may be correct as far as they go but there are too few of them: what the author says may be true and yet by no means the truth. That is the novelist's touch. It falsifies life.

Well, the novelist's touch as thus defined is, of course, bad in biography, for no human being is simple. But in a novel it has its place: a novel that is

---

1 Norman Douglas: an English novelist (1868-1952) 诺曼·道格拉斯，英国小说家

Chapter 9
Edward Morgan Forster
爱德华·摩根·福斯特

at all complex often requires flat people as well as round, and the outcome of their collisions parallels life more accurately than Mr. Douglas implies. The case of Dickens is significant. Dickens' people are nearly all flat (Pip and David Copper-field[1] attempt roundness, but so **diffidently** that they seem more like bubbles than solids). Nearly every one can be summed up in a sentence, and yet there is this wonderful feeling of human depth. Probably the immense vitality of Dickens causes his characters to vibrate a little, so that they borrow his life and appear to lead one of their own. It is a conjuring trick; at any moment we may look at Mr. Pickwick[2] edgeways and find him no thicker than a gramophone record. But we never get the sideway view. Mr. Pickwick is far too **adroit** and well trained. He always has the air of weighing something, and when he is put into the cupboard of the young ladies' school he seems as heavy as Falstaff[3] in the buck-basket at Windsor. Part of the genius of Dickens is that he does use types and caricatures, people whom we recognize the instant they re-enter, and yet achieves effects that are not mechanical and a vision of humanity that is not shallow. Those who dislike Dickens have an excellent case. He ought to be bad. He is actually one of our big writers, and his immense success with types suggests that there may be more in flatness than the severer critics admit.

Or take H. G. Wells. With the possible exceptions of Kipps and the aunt in Tono Bungay, all Wells' characters are as flat as a photograph. But the photographs are agitated with such vigour that we forget their complexities lie on the surface and would disappear if it was scratched or curled up. A Wells character cannot indeed be summed up in a single phrase; he is tethered much more to observation, he does not create types. Nevertheless his people seldom pulsate by their own strength. It is the deft and powerful hands of their maker that shake them and trick the reader into a sense of depth. Good

---

1 Pip: a character in Dicken's novel *Great Expectations*; David Copperfield: a character in a novel of the same name by Dickens 匹普是狄更斯小说《远大前程》中的人物；大卫·科波菲尔，狄更斯同名小说中的人物

2 Mr. Pickwick: a character in Dicken's novel *The Pickwick Papers* 匹克威克，狄更斯小说《匹克威克外传》中的人物

3 Falstaff: a comic character created by William Shakespeare 福斯塔夫，莎士比亚喜剧中的人物

but imperfect novelists, like Wells and Dickens, are very clever at transmitting force. The part of their novel that is alive **galvanizes** the part that is not, and causes the characters to jump about and speak in a convincing way. They are quite different from the perfect novelist who touches all his material directly, who seems to pass the creative finger down every sentence and into every word. Richardson, Defoe, Jane Austen, are perfect in this particular way; their work may not be great but their hands are always upon it; there is not the tiny interval between the touching of the button and the sound of the bell which occurs in novels where the characters are not under direct control.

For we must admit that flat people are not in themselves as big achievements as round ones, and also that they are best when they are comic. A serious or tragic flat character is apt to be a bore. Each time he enters crying "Revenge!" or "My heart bleeds for humanity!" or whatever his formula is, our hearts sink. One of the romances of a popular contemporary writer is constructed round a Sussex farmer who says, "I'll plough up that bit of gorse." There is the farmer, there is the gorse; he says he'll plough it up, he does plough it up, but it is not like saying "I'll never desert Mr. Micawber," because we are so bored by his consistency that we do not care whether he succeeds with the gorse or fails. If his formula was analysed and connected up with the rest of the human outfit, we should not be bored any longer, the formula would cease to be the man and become an obsession in the man; that is to say he would have turned from a flat farmer into a round one. It is only round people who are fit to perform tragically for any length of time and can move us to any feelings except humour and appropriateness.

So now let us desert these two-dimensional people, and by way of transition to the round, let us go to Mansfield Park, and look at Lady Bertram, sitting on her sofa with pug. Pug is flat, like most animals in fiction. He is once represented as straying into a rose-bed in a cardboard kind of way, but that is all, and during most of the book his mistress seems to be cut out of the same simple material as her dog. Lady Bertram's formula is, "I am kindly, but must not be fatigued," and she functions out of it. But at the end there is a catastrophe. Her two daughters come to grief—to the worst grief known to Miss

Chapter 9
Edward Morgan Forster
爱德华·摩根·福斯特

Austen's universe, far worse than the Napoleonic wars. Julia elopes; Maria, who is unhappily married, runs off with a lover. What is Lady Bertram's reaction? The sentence describing it is significant: "Lady Bertram did not think deeply, but, guided by Sir Thomas, she thought justly on all important points, and she saw therefore in all its enormity, what had happened, and neither endeavoured herself, nor required Fanny to advise her, to think little of guilt and infamy." These are strong words, and they used to worry me because I thought Jane Austen's moral sense was getting out of hand. She may, and of course does, **deprecate** guilt and infamy herself, and she duly causes all possible distress in the minds of Edmund and Fanny, but has she any right to agitate calm, consistent Lady Bertram? Is not it like giving pug three faces and setting him to guard the gates of Hell? Ought not her ladyship to remain on the sofa saying, "This is a dreadful and sadly exhausting business about Julia and Maria, but where is Fanny gone? I have dropped another stitch"?

I used to think this, through misunderstanding Jane Austen's method—exactly as Scott misunderstood it when he congratulated her for painting on a square of ivory. She is a **miniaturist**, but never two-dimensional. All her characters are round, or capable of **rotundity**. Even Miss Bates[1] has a mind, even Elizabeth Eliot[2] a heart, and Lady Bertram's moral fervour ceases to vex us when we realize this: the disk has suddenly extended and become a little globe. When the novel is closed, Lady Bertram goes back to the flat, it is true; the dominant impression she leaves can be summed up in a formula. But that is not how Jane Austen conceived her, and the freshness of her reappearances are due to this. Why do the characters in Jane Austen give us a slightly new pleasure each time they come in, as opposed to the merely repetitive pleasure that is caused by a character in Dickens? Why do they combine so well in a conversation, and draw one another out without seeming to do so, and never perform? The answer to this question can be put in several ways: that, unlike Dickens, she was a real artist, that she never stooped to caricature, etc.

---

1   Miss Bates: a character in *Emma* by Jane Austen 奥斯汀小说《爱玛》中的人物
2   Elizabeth Eliot: a charcter in *Persuasion* by Jane Austen 奥斯汀小说《劝说》中的人物

But the best reply is that her characters though smaller than his are more highly organized. They function all round, and even if her plot made greater demands on them than it does, they would still be adequate. Suppose that Louisa Musgrove had broken her neck on the Cobb. The description of her death would have been feeble and ladylike—physical violence is quite beyond Miss Austen's powers—but the survivors would have reacted properly as soon as the corpse was carried away, they would have brought into view new sides of their character, and though Persuasion would have been spoiled as a book, we should know more than we do about Captain Wentworth and Anne. All the Jane Austen characters are ready for an extended life, for a life which the scheme of her books seldom requires them to lead, and that is why they lead their actual lives so satisfactorily. Let us return to Lady Bertram and the crucial sentence. See how subtly it modulates from her formula into an area where the formula does not work. "Lady Bertram did not think deeply." Exactly: as per formula. "But guided by Sir Thomas she thought justly on all important points." Sir Thomas' guidance, which is part of the formula, remains, but it pushes her ladyship towards an independent and undesired morality. "She saw therefore in all its enormity what had happened." This is the moral **fortissimo**—very strong but carefully introduced. And then follows a most artful **decrescendo**, by means of negatives. "She neither endeavoured herself, nor required Fanny to advise her, to think little of guilt or infamy." The formula is reappearing, because as a rule she does try to minimize trouble, and does require Fanny to advise her how to do this; indeed Fanny has done nothing else for the last ten years. The words, though they are negatived, remind us of this, her normal state is again in view, and she has in a single sentence been inflated into a round character and collapsed back into a flat one. How Jane Austen can write! In a few words she has extended Lady Bertram, and by so doing she has increased the probability of the elopements of Maria and Julia. I say probability because the elopements belong to the domain of violent physical action, and here, as already indicated, Jane Austen is feeble and ladylike. Except in her school-girl novels, she cannot stage a crash. Everything violent has to take place "off"—Louisa's accident and Marianne Dashwood's

Chapter 9
Edward Morgan Forster
爱德华·摩根·福斯特

putrid throat are the nearest exceptions—and consequently all the comments on the elopement must be sincere and convincing, otherwise we should doubt whether it occurred. Lady Bertram helps us to believe that her daughters have run away, and they have to run away, or there would be no **apotheosis** for Fanny. It is a little point, and a little sentence, yet it shows us how delicately a great novelist can modulate into the round.

All through her works we find these characters, apparently so simple and flat, never needing re-introduction and yet never out of their depth—Henry Tilney, Mr. Woodhouse, Charlotte Lucas[1]. She may label her characters "Sense," "Pride," "Sensibility," "Prejudice," but they are not tethered to those qualities.

As for the round characters proper, they have already been defined by implication and no more need be said. All I need do is to give some examples of people in books who seem to me round so that the definition can be tested afterwards:

All the principal characters in War and Peace, all the Dostoevsky[2] characters, and some of the Proust—for example, the old family servant, the Duchess of Guermantes, M. de Charlus, and Saint Loup[3]; Madame Bovary[4]—who, like Moll Flanders[5], has her book to herself, and can expand and secrete unchecked; some people in Thackeray—for instance, Becky and Beatrix; some in Fielding—Parson Adams, Tom Jones; and some in Charlotte Brontë, most particularly Lucy Snowe[6]. (And many more—this is not a catalogue.) The test

---

1 Henry Tilney, Mr. Woodhouse, Charlotte Lucas: characters in Jane Austen's *Northanger Abbey*, *Emma* and *Pride and prejudice* 这三个人物分别来自奥斯汀小说《诺桑觉寺》《爱玛》《傲慢与偏见》

2 Destoevsky: Fyodor Destoevsky (1821-1881), russian novelist 陀斯妥耶夫斯基，俄国小说家

3 the old family servant, the Duchess of Guermantes, M. de Charlus, and Saint Loup: characters in *Remembrance of Things Past* by Proust 均为普鲁斯特《追忆似水年华》中的人物

4 Madame Bovary: protagonist in a novel of the same name by the French novelist Gustave Flaubert (1821-1880) 包法利夫人，法国小说家福楼拜同名小说中的主人公

5 Moll Flanders: protagonist in a novel of the same name by the Englishnovelist Daniel Defoe (1660-1731) 摩尔·弗兰德斯，英国小说家笛福的同名小说中的主人公

6 Lucy Snowe: protagonist in *Villette* by the English novelist Charlotte Brontë 露西·斯诺，英国小说家夏洛蒂勃朗特小说《维莱特》中的人物

of a round character is whether it is capable of surprising a convincing way. If it never surprises, it is flat. If it does not convince, it is a flat pretending to be round. It has the incalculability of life about it—life within the pages of a book. And by using it sometimes alone, more often in combination with the other kind, the novelist achieves his task of **acclimatization** and harmonizes the human race with the other aspects of his work.

I Words and Phrases

subterfuge ['sʌbtəfjuːdʒ]	n.	something intended to misrepresent the true nature of an activity 遁词，借口，托辞
servitor ['sɜːvɪtə]	n.	a person who serves another 仆人
scintillation [ˌsɪntəˈleɪʃən]	n.	a rapid change in brightness; a brief spark or flash 迸出火花
by-product ['baɪˌprɒdʌkt]	n.	secondary product 副产品；附带产生的结果；意外收获
hither ['hɪðə]	adv.	to this place (especially toward the speaker) 到此处
thither ['ðɪðə]	adv.	to or toward that place; away from the speaker 向那处
furnish ['fɜːnɪʃ]	v.	provide or supply 提供
doughty ['daʊtɪ]	adj.	brave and unyielding 勇敢刚强的
go by the board		（计划、希望等）落空；放弃；被忽视；被丢弃
diffidently ['dɪfɪdəntlɪ]	adv.	lacking self-confidence 无自信地；客气地
adroit [əˈdrɔɪt]	adj.	quick or skillful or adept in action or thought 熟练的；机敏的
galvanize ['gælvənaɪz]	v.	to stimulate to action 激励；刺激
deprecate ['deprəkeɪt]	v.	express strong disapproval of 反对；抨击
miniaturist ['mɪnɪtʃərɪst]	n.	someone who paints tiny pictures in great detail 纤细画家
rotundity [rəʊˈtʌndɪtɪ]	n.	the roundness of a 3-dimensional object 人物

Chapter 9
Edward Morgan Forster
爱德华·摩根·福斯特

形象丰满

fortissimo [fɔː'tɪsɪməʊ]	n.	(music) loud 极强音
decrescendo [ˌdiːkrɪ'ʃendəʊ]	n.	(music) a gradual decrease in loudness 渐弱音
apotheosis [əˌpɒθɪ'əʊsɪs]	n.	model of excellence or perfection of a kind 典范
acclimatization [əˌklaɪmətaɪ'zeɪʃn] n.		adaptation to a new climate (environment) 环境适应性

II Reading Comprehension Questions

1. How do you understand flat characters? Do you believe that they are best when they are comic? Please use examples to illustrate your point.
2. What is Forster's evaluation of the "novelist's touch"? Do you agree with him?
3. What is Foster's evaluation of Jane Austen? Do you agree with him?
4. How do you understand round characters? Please use examples to illustrate your point.
5. Could you feel Foster's humor in his elaboration? Please find out at least two places and analyse.

Quotes of the Author

But the body is deeper than the soul and its secrets inscrutable.

Have you ever noticed that there are people who do things which are most indelicate, and yet at the same time beautiful?

I would rather be a coward than brave because people hurt you when you are brave.

If I had to choose between betraying my country and betraying my friend, I hope I should have the guts to betray my country.

Pathos, piety, courage,—they exist, but are identical, and so is filth. Everything exists, nothing has value.

Virginia Woolf
弗吉尼亚·伍尔芙
(1882—1941)

Chapter 10

本章导读

弗吉尼亚·伍尔芙，英国女作家、文学批评家和文学理论家，意识流文学代表人物，被誉为 20 世纪现代主义与女性主义的先锋。两次世界大战期间，她是伦敦文学界的核心人物，同时也是布卢姆茨伯里派（Bloomsbury Group）的成员之一。最知名的小说包括《墙上的斑点》（*The Mark on the Wall*）、《达洛维夫人》（*Mrs. Dalloway*）、《到灯塔去》（*To the Lighthouse*）和《雅各的房间》（*Jacob's Room*）等。

1882 年 1 月 25 日伍尔芙出生于英国伦敦，父亲莱斯利·斯蒂芬爵士（Leslie Stephen）是维多利亚时代一位著名的文学评论家、学者和传记家。从 1906 年起，弗吉尼亚的兄弟在剑桥结识的朋友们经常到家里聚会，逐渐形成了一个文艺和学术的中心，也就是著名的布卢姆斯伯里集团，这里面包括了当时文化界的大批精英，其核心成员有：作家伦纳德·伍尔芙（弗吉尼亚的丈夫）、文学批评家德斯蒙德·麦卡锡，经济学家约翰·梅纳德·凯恩斯，画家邓肯·格兰特，作家福斯特等。除此之外，哲学家罗素、诗人 T.S. 艾略特、乔伊斯、小说家亨利·詹姆斯和奥尔都斯·赫胥黎也与布卢姆斯伯里团体过从甚密。弗吉尼亚·伍尔芙能与这样一批知识精英切磋文学和艺术，无疑是十分幸运的。这个团体不仅给予她友谊、智慧和信心，还将自由平等的精神灌输到她的心灵深处。她的文学创作由此别开生面，更加注重对精神内涵的探索。

伍尔芙一生勤奋，著述丰富，除小说创作外，还有大量的散文、日记等。

伍尔芙认为写作要摒弃纷繁的物质表象，在对自然与生命本质的探求中定格人类"存在的""有意味的""瞬间"，通过人物的瞬间感悟揭开生活的面纱，触探生命的哲理。伍尔芙的文学创作注重人物的精神世界。她在《论现代小说》（*Modern Fiction*）一文中指出，"心灵接纳了成千上万个印象——琐屑的、奇异的、倏忽即逝的，用锋利的钢刀深深地铭刻在心头的印象",而作家的任务就是将这些印象记录下来,从而描绘出"这种变化多端、不可名状、难以界定与解说的内在精神",来揭示内心活动的本质。她在小说中尝试意识流的写作方法,试图去描绘在人们心底里的潜意识。她在文学上的成就和创造性至今仍然产生很大的影响。伍尔芙在写作中逐步确立并完善了意识流小说创作技巧,使之成为意识流小说理论的集大成者,她本人也成为当之无愧的意识流小说的代表作家之一。

在散文方面,伍尔芙以其他人无法模仿的英国式的优美洒脱与学识渊博,而被誉为"英国散文大家中的最后一人""英国传统散文的大师"以及"新散文的首创者"。伍尔芙的创作也从诗歌、音乐、绘画中得到很多启示。诗歌和音乐的意象运用充满了她的创作,印象派绘画对她的影响表现在她致力于捕捉瞬间印象,也使她的感觉更加细腻灵敏。在本章所选的《伦敦街头历险记》中,她色调鲜明地描绘了在夜幕降临时漫步伦敦街头留给她的印象与感受。

在本文中,作者的如椽之笔像一只硕大的摄像机镜头,无所不知、无孔不入地向人们展示了一幅幅行云流水般的画面:从伦敦街头一扇窗户里的一个沏茶女人到靴子店里买鞋的矮子,从顶楼的金箔匠到转过街角碰到的犹太人,从小市民家里的小地毯到阳台上高谈阔论的首相,从旧书店到月光下奔跑的猫,直至最后定格到一家小文具店遇到吵架的店主老夫妇。时间、地点、人物的变换如天马行空。主题似乎越扯越远,直到最后仅有若有若无的文思把整篇文章贯穿在一起。伍尔芙的文字就像一个跃动的精灵,踏着舞步,旋转跳跃,充满着美感,无拘无束,散漫洒脱,活泼灵动地带着你一步一步探寻她思想的领土。

About the Author

Adeline Virginia Woolf was an English author, essayist, publisher, and writer of short stories, regarded as one of the foremost modernist literary figures of the twentieth century. Virginia Woolf was born into a prominent and intellectually well-connected family. Her formal education was limited, but she grew up reading voraciously from the vast library of her father, the critic Leslie Stephen. Her youth was a traumatic one, including the early deaths of her mother and brother, a history of sexual abuse, and the beginnings of a depression that plagued her intermittently throughout her life. During the interwar period, Woolf was a significant figure in London literary society and a central

Chapter 10
Virginia Woolf
弗吉尼亚·伍尔芙

figure in the influential Bloomsbury Group of intellectuals. She committed suicide by drowning on 28 March 1941 at the age of 59.

A skilled exponent of "Steam of consciousness" technique, Woolf is one of the great English innovators of the modern novel. Her most famous novels include *The Mark on the Wall*, *Mrs. Dalloway*, *To the Lighthouse* and *Jacob's Room*.

Woolf is concerned with women's position in the modern world. *A Room of One's Own* is an extended essay by Virginia Woolf. First published on 24 October 1929, the essay was based on a series of lectures she delivered at Newnham College and Girton College, two women's colleges at Cambridge University in October 1928. The essay is generally seen as a feminist text, and is noted in its argument for both a literal and figural space for women writers within a literary tradition dominated by patriarchy.

In the essay "Street Haunting" Virginia Woolf seems to tell us that "into each of these lives one could penetrate a little way". Also note that in this essay the quest to buy a pencil serves as an occasion to contrast "street sauntering", with its sense of carefree wandering, with "street haunting", which hints at the more disturbing aspects of walking in the city.

As an essayist, Woolf is always perfectly brisk and lucid, as can be seen from the two essays selected here.

Text A

Street Haunting: A London Adventure
(Excerpt)

Virginia Woolf

No one perhaps has ever felt passionately towards a lead pencil. But there are circumstances in which it can become supremely desirable to possess one; moments when we are set upon having an object, an excuse for walking half across London between tea and dinner. As the foxhunter hunts in order to preserve the breed of foxes, and the golfer plays in order that open spaces may be preserved from the builders, so when the desire comes upon us to go street rambling the pencil does for a pretext, and getting up we say: "Really I must buy a pencil," as if under cover of this excuse we could indulge safely in the greatest pleasure of town life in winter—rambling the streets of London.

The hour should be the evening and the season winter, for in winter the champagne brightness of the air and the sociability of the streets are grateful. We are not then **taunted** as in the summer by the longing for shade and solitude and sweet airs from the hayfields. The evening hour, too, gives us the irresponsibility which darkness and lamplight bestow. We are no longer quite ourselves. As we step out of the house on a fine evening between four and six, we shed the self our friends know us by and become part of that vast republican army of anonymous trampers, whose society is so agreeable after the solitude of one's own room. For there we sit surrounded by objects which perpetually express the oddity of our own temperaments and enforce the memories of our own experience. That bowl on the **mantelpiece**, for instance, was bought at Mantua[1] on a windy day. We were leaving the shop when the sinister old woman plucked at our skirts and said she would find herself

---

1　Mantua: a city in Northern Italy 漫图亚，意大利北部一城市

Chapter 10
Virginia Woolf
弗吉尼亚·伍尔芙

starving one of these days, but, "Take it!" she cried, and thrust the blue and white china bowl into our hands as if she never wanted to be reminded of her **quixotic** generosity. So, guiltily, but suspecting nevertheless how badly we had been **fleeced**, we carried it back to the little hotel where, in the middle of the night, the innkeeper quarreled so violently with his wife that we all leant out into the courtyard to look, and saw the vines laced about among the pillars and the stars white in the sky. The moment was stabilized, stamped like a coin **indelibly** among a million that slipped by imperceptibly. There, too, was the melancholy Englishman, who rose among the coffee cups and the little iron tables and revealed the secrets of his soul—as travelers do. All this—Italy, the windy morning, the vines laced about the pillars, the Englishman and the secrets of his soul—rise up in a cloud from the china bowl on the mantelpiece. And there, as our eyes fall to the floor, is that brown stain on the carpet. Mr. Lloyd George made that. "The man's a devil!" said Mr. Cummings, putting the kettle down with which he was about to fill the teapot so that it burnt a brown ring on the carpet.

But when the door shuts on us, all that vanishes. The shell-like covering which our souls have **excreted** to house themselves, to make for themselves a shape distinct from others, is broken, and there is left of all these wrinkles and roughnesses a central oyster of perceptiveness, an enormous eye. How beautiful a street is in winter! It is at once revealed and obscured. Here vaguely one can trace symmetrical straight avenues of doors and windows; here under the lamps are floating islands of pale light through which pass quickly bright men and women, who, for all their poverty and shabbiness, wear a certain look of unreality, an air of triumph, as if they had given life the slip, so that life, deceived of her prey, blunders on without them. But, after all, we are only gliding smoothly on the surface. The eye is not a miner, not a diver, not a seeker after buried treasure. It floats us smoothly down a stream; resting, pausing, the brain sleeps perhaps as it looks.

How beautiful a London street is then, with its islands of light, and its long groves of darkness, and on one side of it perhaps some tree-sprinkled, grass-grown space where night is folding herself to sleep naturally and, as one passes the iron railing, one hears those little cracklings and stirrings of leaf and twig which seem to suppose the silence of fields all round them, an owl hooting, and far away the rattle of a train in the valley. But this is London, we are reminded; high among the bare trees are hung **oblong** frames of reddish yellow light—windows; there are points of brilliance burning steadily like low stars—lamps; this empty ground, which holds the country in it and its peace, is only a London square, set about by offices and houses where at this hour fierce lights burn over maps, over documents, over desks where clerks sit turning with wetted **forefinger** the files of endless correspondences; or more suffusedly the firelight wavers and the lamplight falls upon the privacy of some drawing-room, its easy chairs, its papers, its china, its inlaid table, and the figure of a woman, accurately measuring out the precise number of spoons of tea which— She looks at the door as if she heard a ring downstairs and somebody asking, is she in?

But here we must stop **peremptorily**. We are in danger of digging deeper than the eye approves; we are **impeding** our passage down the smooth stream by catching at some branch or root. At any moment, the sleeping army may stir itself and wake in us a thousand violins and trumpets in response; the army of human beings may rouse itself and assert all its oddities and sufferings and **sordidities**. Let us **dally** a little longer, be content still with surfaces only—the glossy brilliance of the motor omnibuses; the carnal splendor of the butchers' shops with their yellow flanks and purple steaks; the blue and red bunches of flowers burning so bravely through the plate glass of the florists' windows.

For the eye has this strange property: it rests only on beauty; like a butterfly it seeks color and basks in warmth. On a winter's night like this, when nature has been at pains to polish and preen herself, it brings back the prettiest trophies, breaks off little lumps of emerald and coral as if the whole earth were made of precious stone. The thing it cannot do (one is speaking of the average unprofessional eye) is to compose these trophies in such a way as to bring out the more obscure angles and relationships. Hence after a prolonged diet of this simple, sugary fare, of beauty pure and uncomposed, we become conscious of satiety. We halt at the door of the boot shop and make

Chapter 10

Virginia Woolf
弗吉尼亚·伍尔芙

some little excuse, which has nothing to do with the real reason, for folding up the bright **paraphernalia** of the streets and withdrawing to some duskier chamber of the being where we may ask, as we raise our left foot obediently upon the stand: "What, then, is it like to be a dwarf?"

She came in escorted by two women who, being of normal size, looked like benevolent giants beside her.

Smiling at the shop girls, they seemed to be disclaiming any lot in her deformity and assuring her of their protection. She wore the **peevish** yet **apologetic** expression usual on the faces of the deformed. She needed their kindness, yet she resented it. But when the shop girl had been summoned and the giantesses, smiling indulgently, had asked for shoes for "this lady" and the girl had pushed the little stand in front of her, the dwarf stuck her foot out with an **impetuosity** which seemed to claim all our attention. Look at that! Look at that! She seemed to demand of us all, as she thrust her foot out, for behold it was the shapely, perfectly proportioned foot of a well-grown woman. It was arched; it was aristocratic. Her whole manner changed as she looked at it resting on the stand. She looked soothed and satisfied. Her manner became full of self-confidence. She sent for shoe after shoe; she tried on pair after pair. She got up and **pirouetted** before a glass which reflected the foot only in yellow shoes, in **fawn** shoes, in shoes of lizard skin. She raised her little skirts and displayed her little legs. She was thinking that, after all, feet are the most important part of the whole person; women, she said to herself, have been loved for their feet alone. Seeing nothing but her feet, she imagined perhaps that the rest of her body was of a piece with those beautiful feet. She was shabbily dressed, but she was ready to lavish any money upon her shoes. And as this was the only occasion upon which she was not afraid of being looked at but positively craved attention, she was ready to use any device to prolong the choosing and fitting. Look at my feet, she seemed to be saying, as she took a step this way and then a step that way. The shop girl good-humouredly must have said something flattering, for suddenly her face lit up in ecstasy. But, after all, the giantesses, benevolent though they were, had their own affairs to see to; she must make up her mind; she must decide which to choose. At length, the pair was chosen and, as she walked out between her guardians, with the parcel swinging from her finger, the ecstasy faded, knowledge returned, the old peevishness, the old apology came back, and by the time she had reached the street again she had become a dwarf only.

...

That is true: to escape is the greatest of pleasures; street haunting in winter the greatest of adventures. Still as we approach our own doorstep again, it is comforting to feel the old possessions, the old prejudices, fold us round; and the self, which has been blown about at so many street corners, which has battered like a moth at the flame of so many inaccessible lanterns, sheltered and enclosed. Here again is the usual door; here the chair turned as we left it and the china bowl and the brown ring on the carpet. And here—let us examine it tenderly, let us touch it with reverence—is the only spoil we have retrieved from all the treasures of the city, a lead pencil.

I Words and Phrases

taunt [tɔːnt]	v.	harass with persistent criticism or carping 讥讽，嘲弄
mantelpiece ['mæntlpɪs]	n.	shelf that projects from wall above fireplace 壁炉台
quixotic [kwɪk'sɒtɪk]	adj.	not sensible about practical matters; unrealistic 唐吉珂德式的；狂想家的
fleece [fliːs]	v.	to deceive and take money from 欺诈
indelibly [ɪn'deləblɪ]	adv.	in an indelible manner 不能消灭地
excrete [ɪk'skriːt]	v.	eliminate from the body 排泄；分泌
oblong ['ɒblɒŋ]	adj.	deviating from a square or circle or sphere by being elongated in one direction 椭圆形的；长方形的
forefinger ['fɔːfɪŋgə]	n.	the finger next to the thumb 食指
peremptorily [pə'remptərəlɪ]	adv.	in an imperative and commanding manner 独

Chapter 10

Virginia Woolf
弗吉尼亚·伍尔芙

		断地，断然地
impede [ɪm'piːd]	v.	make the process difficult 阻碍
sordidity ['sɔːdɪdɪtɪ]	n.	being very dirty 肮脏，污秽
dally ['dælɪ]	v.	behave carelessly or indifferently 轻率地对待
paraphernalia [ˌpærəfə'neɪlɪə]	n.	equipment consisting of miscellaneous articles needed for a particular operation or sport, etc. 随身用具；全部有关的事物；设备
peevish ['piːvɪʃ]	adj.	easily irritated or annoyed 易怒的，暴躁的
apologetic [əpɒlə'dʒetɪk]	adj.	offering or expressing apology 道歉的，赔罪的
impetuosity [ɪmˌpetʃʊ'ɒsətɪ]	n.	rash impulsiveness 冲力；猛烈
pirouette [pɪru'et]	v.	do a fast turn or spin on one foot, usually as part of a dance（芭蕾舞）以脚尖旋转
fawn [fɔːn]	n.	a color or pigment varying around a light grey-brown color 浅黄褐色

II Reading Comprehension Questions

1. In the first paragraph, does the author feel supremely desirable to possess a lead pencil?
2. Why does the author like rambling on the street in winter rather than in summer time?
3. Where does the bowl on the mantelpiece come from? What are the memories associated with it?
4. Why does the author initially only want to glide on the surface? What does she mean? Did she succeed in doing so?
5. Why does the dwarf "sent for shoe after shoe; she tried on pair after pair" in the shop? What's your impression of the dwarf?

III Questions on Writing Style and Language

1. Instead of using "street sauntering", which means carefree wandering, the author uses "street haunting", which hints at the more disturbing aspects

of walking in the city. After reading the essay, please comment on this particular word choice of the author.
2. Have you noticed any stylistic features of Woolf's writing? Please share your ideas with your classmates.
3. The author's writing is deeply influenced by impressionistic painting. Where can you see the influence?
4. How does the author account her street haunting experiences? Do you see the logic between the parts?
5. Some critics think the apparent loose, spontaneous form of Virginia Woolf's essays are alluring, do you agree with them? What are some examples or evidence you can give to support the statement?

Chapter 10

Virginia Woolf
弗吉尼亚·伍尔芙

A Room of One's Own[1]
(Excerpt)

Virginia Woolf

The scene, if I may ask you to follow me, was now changed. The leaves were still falling, but in London now, not Oxbridge; and I must ask you to imagine a room, like many thousands, with a window looking across people's hats and vans and motor-cars to other windows, and on the table inside the room a blank sheet of paper on which was written in large letters Women and Fiction, but no more. The inevitable sequel to lunching and dining at Oxbridge seemed, unfortunately, to be a visit to the British Museum. One must strain off what was personal and accidental in all these impressions and so reach the pure fluid, the essential oil of truth. For that visit to Oxbridge and the luncheon and the dinner had started a swarm of questions. Why did men drink wine and women water? Why was one sex so prosperous and the other so poor? What effect has poverty on fiction? What conditions are necessary for the creation of works of art?—a thousand questions at once suggested themselves. But one needed answers, not questions; and an answer was only to be had by consulting the learned and the unprejudiced, who have removed themselves above the strife of tongue and the confusion of body and issued the result of their reasoning and research in books which are to be found in

---

1 *A Room of One's Own* is based on a series of lectures Virginia Woolf delivered at Newnham College and Girton College, two women's colleges at Cambridge University in 1928. The book has six chapters and in each section Virginia Woolf discusses the different aspects of the topic: women and fiction. In Chapter One Virginia Woolf points out that western history so far has been the history of the patriarchy, a history written by men about men and for men. The present excerpt is from the second chapter.《一间自己的房间》是基于两篇讲稿。1928年10月20日和26日,伍尔芙自伦敦两次来剑桥大学,分别在纽纳姆女子学院和戈廷女子学院,就女性与小说一题发表演讲。此后,1929年3月,她将两次演讲合为一文,以《女性与小说》为题,发表在美国杂志《论坛》上。而此时,她的小说《奥兰多》出版,她为自己造成了一座小楼,并在这里将《女性与小说》大加修改和扩充,创作了《房间》一书。该书共6章,这是第2章内容。

the British Museum. If truth is not to be found on the shelves of the British Museum, where, I asked myself, picking up a notebook and a pencil, is truth?

Thus provided, thus confident and enquiring, I set out in the pursuit of truth. The day, though not actually wet, was dismal, and the streets in the neighborhoods of the Museum were full of open coal-holes, down which sacks were showering; four-wheeled cabs were drawing up and depositing on the pavement corded boxes containing, presumably, the entire wardrobe of some Swiss or Italian family seeking fortune or refuge or some other desirable commodity which is to be found in the boarding-houses of Bloomsbury in the winter. The usual hoarse-voiced men paraded the streets with plants on **barrows**. Some shouted; others sang. London was like a workshop. London was like a machine. We were all being shot backwards and forwards on this plain foundation to make some pattern. The British Museum was another department of the factory. The swing-doors swung open; and there one stood under the vast dome, as if one were a thought in the huge bald fore head which is so splendidly encircled by a band of famous names. One went to the counter; one took a slip of paper; one opened a volume of the catalogue, and the five dots here indicate five separate minutes of **stupefaction**, wonder and bewilderment. Have you any notion of how many books are written about women in the course of one year? Have you any notion how many are written by men? Are you aware that you are, perhaps, the most discussed animal in the universe? Here had I come with a notebook and a pencil proposing to spend a morning reading, supposing that at the end of the morning I should have transferred the truth to my notebook. But I should need to be a herd of elephants, I thought, and a wilderness of spiders, desperately referring to the animals that are reputed longest lived and most multitudinously eyed, to cope with all this. I should need claws of steel and beak of brass even to penetrate the **husk**. How shall I ever find the grains of truth embedded in all this mass of paper? I asked myself, and in despair began running my eye up and down the long list of titles. Even the names of the books gave me food for thought. Sex and its nature might well attract doctors and biologists; but what was surprising and difficult of explanation was the fact that sex—woman, that is to

Chapter 10
Virginia Woolf
弗吉尼亚·伍尔芙

say—also attracts agreeable essayists, light-fingered novelists, young men who have taken the M.A. degree; men who have taken no degree; men who have no apparent qualification save that they are not women. Some of these books were, on the face of it, **frivolous** and **facetious**; but many, on the other hand, were serious and prophetic, moral and **hortatory**. Merely to read the titles suggested innumerable schoolmasters, innumerable clergymen mounting their platforms and pulpits and holding forth with **loquacity** which far exceeded the hour usually allotted to such discourse on this one subject. It was a most strange phenomenon; and apparently—here I consulted the letter M—one confined to the male sex. Women do not write books about men—a fact that I could not help welcoming with relief, for if I had first to read all that men have written about women, then all that women have written about men, the aloe that flowers once in a hundred years would flower twice before I could set pen to paper. So, making a perfectly arbitrary choice of a dozen volumes or so, I sent my slips of paper to lie in the wire tray, and waited in my stall, among the other seekers for the essential oil of truth.

What could be the reason, then, of this curious disparity, I wondered, drawing cart-wheels on the slips of paper provided by the British taxpayer for other purposes. Why are women, judging from this catalogue, so much more interesting to men than men are to women? A very curious fact it seemed, and my mind wandered to picture the lives of men who spend their time in writing books about women; whether they were old or young, married or unmarried, red-nosed or **hump**-backed—anyhow, it was flattering, vaguely, to feel oneself the object of such attention provided that it was not entirely bestowed by the crippled and the infirm—so I pondered until all such frivolous thoughts were ended by an **avalanche** of books sliding down on to the desk in front of me. Now the trouble began. The student who has been trained in research at Oxbridge has no doubt some method of shepherding his question past all distractions till it runs into his answer as a sheep runs into its pen. The student by my side, for instance, who was copying assiduously from a scientific manual, was, I felt sure, extracting pure **nuggets** of the essential ore every ten minutes or so. His little grunts of satisfaction indicated so much.

But if, unfortunately, one has had no training in a university, the question far from being shepherded to its pen flies like a frightened flock hither and thither, **helter-skelter**, pursued by a whole pack of hounds. Professors, schoolmasters, sociologists, clergymen, novelists, essayists, journalists, men who had no qualification save that they were not women, chased my simple and single question—Why are some women poor?—until it became fifty questions; until the fifty questions leapt frantically into midstream and were carried away. Every page in my notebook was scribbled over with notes. To show the state of mind I was in, I will read you a few of them, explaining that the page was headed quite simply, Women and Poverty, in block letters; but what followed was something like this:

Condition in Middle Ages of,

Habits in the Fiji Islands of,

Worshipped as goddesses by,

Weaker in moral sense than, Idealism of,

Greater **conscientiousness** of,

South Sea Islanders, age of **puberty** among,

Attractiveness of,

Offered as sacrifice to,

Small size of brain of,

Profounder sub-consciousness of,

Less hair on the body of,

Mental, moral and physical inferiority of,

Love of children of,

Greater length of life of,

Weaker muscles of,

Strength of affections of,

Vanity of,

Higher education of,

Shakespeare's opinion of,

Lord Birkenhead's opinion of,

Dean Inge's opinion of,

Chapter 10
Virginia Woolf
弗吉尼亚·伍尔芙

La Bruyere's opinion of,

Dr. Johnson's opinion of,

Mr. Oscar Browning's opinion of, ...

Here I drew breath and added, indeed, in the margin, why does Samuel Butler say, "Wise men never say what they think of women"? Wise men never say anything else apparently. But, I continued, leaning back in my chair and looking at the vast dome in which I was a single but by now somewhat **harassed** thought, what is so unfortunate is that wise men never think the same thing about women. Here is Pope:

Most women have no character at all.

And here is La Bruyère:

Les femmes sont extrêmes, elles sont meilleures ou pires que les hommes—a direct contradiction by keen observers who were contemporary. Are they capable of education or incapable? Napoleon thought them incapable. Dr. Johnson thought the opposite. Have they souls or have they not souls? Some savages say they have none. Others, on the contrary, maintain that women are half divine and worship them on that account. Some sages hold that they are shallower in the brain; others that they are deeper in the consciousness. Goethe honoured them; Mussolini despises them. Wherever one looked men thought about women and thought differently. It was impossible to make head or tail of it all, I decided, glancing with envy at the reader next door who was making the neatest abstracts, headed often with an A or a B or a C, while my own notebook rioted with the wildest scribble of contradictory **jottings**. It was distressing, it was bewildering, it was humiliating. Truth had run through my fingers. Every drop had escaped.

"Men know that women are an overmatch for them, and therefore they choose the weakest or the most ignorant. If they did not think so, they never could be afraid of women knowing as much as themselves."... In justice to the sex, I think it but candid to acknowledge that, in a subsequent conversation, he told me that he was serious in what he said."—Boswell, the Journal of a Tour to the Hebrides.

The ancient Germans believed that there was something holy in women, and accordingly consulted them as oracles.—Frazer, Golden Bough.

I could not possibly go home, I reflected, and add as a serious contribution to the study of women and fiction that women have less hair on their bodies than men, or that the age of puberty among the South Sea Islanders is nine—or is it ninety?—even the handwriting had become in its distraction **indecipherable**. It was disgraceful to have nothing more weighty or respectable to show after a whole morning's work. And if I could not grasp the truth about W. (as for brevity's sake I had come to call her) in the past, why bother about W. in the future? It seemed pure waste of time to consult all those gentlemen who specialize in woman and her effect on whatever it may be—politics, children, wages, morality—numerous and learned as they are. One might as well leave their books unopened.

But while I pondered I had unconsciously, in my listlessness, in my desperation, been drawing a picture where I should, like my neighbour, have been writing a conclusion. I had been drawing a face, a figure. It was the face and the figure of Professor von X engaged in writing his monumental work entitled *The Mental, Moral, and Physical Inferiority of the Female Sex*. He was not in my picture a man attractive to women. He was heavily built; he had a great jowl; to balance that he had very small eyes; he was very red in the face. His expression suggested that he was labouring under some emotion that made him jab his pen on the paper as if he were killing some noxious insect as he wrote, but even when he had killed it that did not satisfy him; he must go on killing it; and even so, some cause for anger and irritation remained. Could it be his wife, I asked, looking at my picture? Was she in love with a cavalry officer? Was the cavalry officer slim and elegant and dressed in **astrakhan**? Had he been laughed at, to adopt the Freudian theory, in his cradle by a pretty girl? For even in his cradle the professor, I thought, could not have been an attractive child. Whatever the reason, the professor was made to look very angry and very ugly in my sketch, as he wrote his great book upon the mental, moral and physical inferiority of women. Drawing pictures was an idle way of finishing an unprofitable morning's work. Yet it is in our idleness, in our dreams, that the submerged truth sometimes comes to the top.

Chapter 10

Virginia Woolf
弗吉尼亚·伍尔芙

A very elementary exercise in psychology, not to be dignified by the name of psychoanalysis, showed me, on looking at my notebook, that the sketch of the angry professor had been made in anger. Anger had snatched my pencil while I dreamt. But what was anger doing there? Interest, confusion, amusement, boredom—all these emotions I could trace and name as they succeeded each other throughout the morning. Had anger, the black snake, been lurking among them? Yes, said the sketch, anger had. It referred me unmistakably to the one book, to the one phrase, which had roused the demon; it was the professor's statement about the mental, moral and physical inferiority of women. My heart had leapt. My cheeks had burnt. I had flushed with anger. There was nothing specially remarkable, however foolish, in that. One does not like to be told that one is naturally the inferior of a little man—I looked at the student next me—who breathes hard, wears a ready-made tie, and has not shaved this fortnight. One has certain foolish vanities. It is only human nature, I reflected, and began drawing cartwheels and circles over the angry professor's face till he looked like a burning bush or a flaming comet—anyhow, an apparition without human semblance or significance. The professor was nothing now but a faggot burning on the top of Hampstead Heath. Soon my own anger was explained and done with; but curiosity remained. How explain the anger of the professors? Why were they angry? For when it came to analysing the impression left by these books there was always an element of heat. This heat took many forms; it showed itself in satire, in sentiment, in curiosity, in **reprobation**. But there was another element which was often present and could not immediately be identified. Anger, I called it. But it was anger that had gone underground and mixed itself with all kinds of other emotions. To judge from its odd effects, it was anger disguised and complex, not anger simple and open.

Whatever the reason, all these books, I thought, surveying the pile on the desk, are worthless for my purposes. They were worthless scientifically, that is to say, though humanly they were full of instruction, interest, boredom, and very queer facts about the habits of the Fiji Islanders. They had been written in the red light of emotion and not in the white light of truth. Therefore they must be returned to the central desk and restored each to his own cell in the enormous honeycomb. All that I had retrieved from that morning's work had been the one fact of anger. The professors—I lumped them together thus—were angry. But why, I asked myself, having returned the books, why, I repeated, standing under the colonnade among the pigeons and the prehistoric canoes, why are they angry? And, asking myself this question, I strolled off to find a place for luncheon. What is the real nature of what I call for the moment their anger? I asked. Here was a puzzle that would last all the time that it takes to be served with food in a small restaurant somewhere near the British Museum. Some previous luncher had left the lunch edition of the evening paper on a chair, and, waiting to be served, I began idly reading the headlines. A ribbon of very large letters ran across the page. Somebody had made a big score in South Africa. Lesser ribbons announced that Sir Austen Chamberlain was at Geneva. A meat axe with human hair on it had been found in a cellar. Mr justice—commented in the *Divorce Courts upon the Shamelessness of Women*. Sprinkled about the paper were other pieces of news. A film actress had been lowered from a peak in California and hung suspended in mid-air. The weather was going to be foggy. The most transient visitor to this planet, I thought, who picked up this paper could not fail to be aware, even from this scattered testimony, that England is under the rule of a patriarchy. Nobody in their senses could fail to detect the dominance of the professor. His was the power and the money and the influence. He was the proprietor of the paper and its editor and sub-editor. He was the Foreign Secretary and the judge. He was the cricketer; he owned the racehorses and the yachts. He was the director of the company that pays two hundred per cent to its shareholders. He left millions to charities and colleges that were ruled by himself. He suspended the film actress in mid-air. He will decide if the hair on the meat axe is human; he it is who will acquit or convict the murderer, and hang him, or let him go free. With the exception of the fog he seemed to control everything. Yet he was angry. I knew that he was angry by this token. When I read what he wrote about women—I thought, not of what he was saying, but of himself. When an arguer argues dispassionately he thinks only of the argument; and the reader

Chapter 10

Virginia Woolf

弗吉尼亚·伍尔芙

cannot help thinking of the argument too. If he had written dispassionately about women, had used indisputable proofs to establish his argument and had shown no trace of wishing that the result should be one thing rather than another, one would not have been angry either. One would have accepted the fact, as one accepts the fact that a pea is green or a canary yellow. So be it, I should have said. But I had been angry because he was angry. Yet it seemed absurd, I thought, turning over the evening paper, that a man with all this power should be angry. Or is anger, I wondered, somehow, the familiar, the attendant sprite on power? Rich people, for example, are often angry because they suspect that the poor want to seize their wealth. The professors, or patriarchs, as it might be more accurate to call them, might be angry for that reason partly, but partly for one that lies a little less obviously on the surface. Possibly they were not "angry" at all; often, indeed, they were admiring, devoted, exemplary in the relations of private life. Possibly when the professor insisted a little too emphatically upon the inferiority of women, he was concerned not with their inferiority, but with his own superiority. That was what he was protecting rather hot-headedly and with too much emphasis, because it was a jewel to him of the rarest price. Life for both sexes—and I looked at them, shouldering their way along the pavement—is arduous, difficult, a perpetual struggle. It calls for gigantic courage and strength. More than anything, perhaps, creatures of illusion as we are, it calls for confidence in oneself. Without self-confidence we are as babes in the cradle. And how can we generate this imponderable quality, which is yet so invaluable, most quickly? By thinking that other people are inferior to one self. By feeling that one has some innate superiority—it may be wealth, or rank, a straight nose, or the portrait of a grandfather by Romney—for there is no end to the pathetic devices of the human imagination—over other people. Hence the enormous importance to a patriarch who has to conquer, who has to rule, of feeling that great numbers of people, half the human race indeed, are by nature inferior to himself. It must indeed be one of the chief sources of his power. But let me turn the light of this observation on to real life, I thought. Does it help to explain some of those psychological puzzles that one notes in the margin of daily life?

Does it explain my astonishment of the other day when Z, most humane, most modest of men, taking up some book by Rebecca West and reading a passage in it, exclaimed, "The arrant feminist! She says that men are snobs!" The exclamation, to me so surprising—for why was Miss West an arrant feminist for making a possibly true if uncomplimentary statement about the other sex?—was not merely the cry of wounded vanity; it was a protest against some infringement of his power to believe in himself. Women have served all these centuries as looking-glasses possessing the magic and delicious power of reflecting the figure of man at twice its natural size. Without that power probably the earth would still be swamp and jungle. The glories of all our wars would be unknown. We should still be scratching the outlines of deer on the remains of mutton bones and bartering flints for sheep skins or whatever simple ornament took our unsophisticated taste. Supermen and Fingers of Destiny would never have existed. The Czar and the Kaiser would never have worn crowns or lost them. Whatever may be their use in civilized societies, mirrors are essential to all violent and heroic action. That is why Napoleon and Mussolini both insist so emphatically upon the inferiority of women, for if they were not inferior, they would cease to enlarge. That serves to explain in part the necessity that women so often are to men. And it serves to explain how restless they are under her criticism; how impossible it is for her to say to them this book is bad, this picture is feeble, or whatever it may be, without giving far more pain and rousing far more anger than a man would do who gave the same criticism. For if she begins to tell the truth, the figure in the looking-glass shrinks; his fitness for life is diminished. How is he to go on giving judgement, civilizing natives, making laws, writing books, dressing up and speechifying at banquets, unless he can see himself at breakfast and at dinner at least twice the size he really is? So I reflected, crumbling my bread and stirring my coffee and now and again looking at the people in the street. The looking-glass vision is of supreme importance because it charges the vitality; it stimulates the nervous system. Take it away and man may die, like the drug fiend deprived of his cocaine. Under the spell of that illusion, I thought, looking out of the window, half the people on the pavement are

Chapter 10
Virginia Woolf
弗吉尼亚·伍尔芙

striding to work. They put on their hats and coats in the morning under its agreeable rays. They start the day confident, braced, believing themselves desired at Miss Smith's tea party; they say to themselves as they go into the room, I am the superior of half the people here, and it is thus that they speak with that self-confidence, that self-assurance, which have had such profound consequences in public life and lead to such curious notes in the margin of the private mind.

But these contributions to the dangerous and fascinating subject of the psychology of the other sex—it is one, I hope, that you will investigate when you have five hundred a year of your own—were interrupted by the necessity of paying the bill. It came to five shillings and ninepence. I gave the waiter a ten-shilling note and he went to bring me change. There was another ten-shilling note in my purse; I noticed it, because it is a fact that still takes my breath away the power of my purse to breed ten-shilling notes automatically. I open it and there they are. Society gives me chicken and coffee, bed and lodging, in return for a certain number of pieces of paper which were left me by an aunt, for no other reason than that I share her name.

My aunt, Mary Beton, I must tell you, died by a fall from her horse when she was riding out to take the air in Bombay. The news of my legacy reached me one night about the same time that the act was passed that gave votes to women. A solicitor's letter fell into the post-box and when I opened it I found that she had left me five hundred pounds a year forever. Of the two—the vote and the money—the money, I own, seemed infinitely the more important. Before that I had made my living by cadging odd jobs from newspapers, by reporting a donkey show here or a wedding there; I had earned a few pounds by addressing envelopes, reading to old ladies, making artificial flowers, teaching the alphabet to small children in a kindergarten. Such were the chief occupations that were open to women before 1918. I need not, I am afraid, describe in any detail the hardness of the work, for you know perhaps women who have done it; nor the difficulty of living on the money when it was earned, for you may have tried. But what still remains with me as a worse infliction than either was the poison of fear and bitterness which those days bred in me. To begin with, always to be doing work that one did not wish to do, and to do it like a slave, flattering and fawning, not always necessarily perhaps, but it seemed necessary and the stakes were too great to run risks; and then the thought of that one gift which it was death to hide—a small one but dear to the possessor—perishing and with it my self, my soul—all this became like a rust eating away the bloom of the spring, destroying the tree at its heart. However, as I say, my aunt died; and whenever I change a ten-shilling note a little of that rust and corrosion is rubbed off, fear and bitterness go. Indeed, I thought, slipping the silver into my purse, it is remarkable, remembering the bitterness of those days, what a change of temper a fixed income will bring about. No force in the world can take from me my five hundred pounds. Food, house and clothing are mine forever. Therefore not merely do effort and labour cease, but also hatred and bitterness. I need not hate any man; he cannot hurt me. I need not flatter any man; he has nothing to give me. So imperceptibly I found myself adopting a new attitude towards the other half of the human race. It was absurd to blame any class or any sex, as a whole. Great bodies of people are never responsible for what they do. They are driven by instincts which are not within their control. They too, the patriarchs, the professors, had endless difficulties, terrible drawbacks to contend with. Their education had been in some ways as faulty as my own. It had bred in them defects as great. True, they had money and power, but only at the cost of harbouring in their breasts an eagle, a vulture, forever tearing the liver out and plucking at the lungs—the instinct for possession, the rage for acquisition which drives them to desire other people's fields and goods perpetually; to make frontiers and flags; battleships and poison gas; to offer up their own lives and their children's lives. Walk through the Admiralty Arch (I had reached that monument), or any other avenue given up to trophies and cannon, and reflect upon the kind of glory celebrated there. Or watch in the spring sunshine the stockbroker and the great barrister going indoors to make money and more money and more money when it is a fact that five hundred pounds a year will keep one alive in the sunshine. These are unpleasant instincts to harbour, I reflected. They are bred of the conditions of life; of the lack of civilization, I thought, looking

Chapter 10
Virginia Woolf
弗吉尼亚·伍尔芙

at the statue of the Duke of Cambridge, and in particular at the feathers in his cocked hat, with a fixity that they have scarcely ever received before. And, as I realized these drawbacks, by degrees fear and bitterness modified themselves into pity and toleration; and then in a year or two, pity and toleration went, and the greatest release of all came, which is freedom to think of things in themselves. That building, for example, do I like it or not? Is that picture beautiful or not? Is that in my opinion a good book or a bad? Indeed my aunt's legacy unveiled the sky to me, and substituted for the large and imposing figure of a gentleman, which Milton recommended for my perpetual adoration, a view of the open sky.

So thinking, so speculating I found my way back to my house by the river. Lamps were being lit and an indescribable change had come over London since the morning hour. It was as if the great machine after labouring all day had made with our help a few yards of something very exciting and beautiful—a fiery fabric flashing with red eyes, a tawny monster roaring with hot breath. Even the wind seemed flung like a flag as it lashed the houses and rattled the hoardings.

In my little street, however, domesticity prevailed. The house painter was descending his ladder; the nursemaid was wheeling the perambulator carefully in and out back to nursery tea; the coal-heaver was folding his empty sacks on top of each other; the woman who keeps the green grocer's shop was adding up the day's takings with her hands in red mittens. But so engrossed was I with the problem you have laid upon my shoulders that I could not see even these usual sights without referring them to one centre. I thought how much harder it is now than it must have been even a century ago to say which of these employments is the higher, the more necessary. Is it better to be a coal-heaver or a nursemaid; is the charwoman who has brought up eight children of less value to the world than, the barrister who has made a hundred thousand pounds? It is useless to ask such questions; for nobody can answer them. Not only do the comparative values of charwomen and lawyers rise and fall from decade to decade, but we have no rods with which to measure them even as they are at the moment. I had been foolish to ask my professor to furnish me with "indisputable proofs" of this or that in his argument about women. Even if one could state the value of any one gift at the moment, those values will change; in a century's time very possibly they will have changed completely. Moreover, in a hundred years, I thought, reaching my own doorstep, women will have ceased to be the protected sex. Logically they will take part in all the activities and exertions that were once denied them. The nursemaid will heave coal. The shopwoman will drive an engine. All assumptions founded on the facts observed when women were the protected sex will have disappeared—as, for example (here a squad of soldiers marched down the street), that women and clergymen and gardeners live longer than other people. Remove that protection, expose them to the same exertions and activities, make them soldiers and sailors and engine-drivers and dock labourers, and will not women die off so much younger, so much quicker, than men that one will say, "I saw a woman today", as one used to say, "I saw an aeroplane". Anything may happen when womanhood has ceased to be a protected occupation, I thought, opening the door. But what bearing has all this upon the subject of my paper, Women and Fiction? I asked, going indoors.

1 Words and Phrases

barrow ['bærəu]	n.	a cart 手推车
stupefaction [ˌstjuːpɪˈfækʃn]	n.	a feeling of stupefied astonishment 惊呆
husk [hʌsk]	n.	the outer covering of a grain or a seed 皮；壳
frivolous ['frɪvələs]	adj.	not useful and wastes time or money 无聊的；无用的；无价值的
facetious [fəˈsɪʃəs]	adj.	humorous; not serious 滑稽的；不正经的
hortatory ['hɔːtətrɪ]	adj.	incentive 激励的；劝告的
loquacity [ləˈkwæsətɪ]	n.	being wordy and talkative 滔滔不绝
hump [hʌmp]	n.	a large lump on a person's back 驼背
avalanche [ˈævəlɑːnʃ]	n.	a large mass of snow that falls down the side of a mountain 雪崩

Chapter 10

Virginia Woolf
弗吉尼亚·伍尔芙

nugget ['nʌgɪt]	n.	a small lump of something, especially gold 小块东西（尤指小金块）
helter-skelter	n.	something that is hurried and disorganized 杂乱无章
conscientiousness [ˌkɒnʃɪ'enʃəsnɪs]	n.	being concerned with doing something correctly 责任心
puberty ['pju:bətɪ]	n.	the period of life when a person's body starts to become physically mature 青春期
harassed [hə'ræst]	adj.	anxious and tense 疲倦的；厌倦
jotting ['dʒɒtɪŋ]	n.	brief and informal notes 简短的笔记
indecipherable [ˌɪndɪ'saɪfərəbəl]	adj.	difficult to understand the word 难懂的
astrakhan ['æstrəkən]	n.	（用于制造大衣和帽子）阿斯特拉罕羔羊皮
reprobation [ˌreprə'beɪʃən]	n.	disapproval, blame, or censure 责怪；指责

II Reading Comprehension Questions

1. What questions occur to the author while dining at Oxbridge?
2. What is the truth the author pursues in the library?
3. What does the author mean when she says, "What is so unfortunate is that wise men never think the same thing about women"?
4. What kind of comments on women are made by great figures in this essay? And what's your opinion?
5. What did the news information the author found on the evening paper at the place of luncheon suggest?

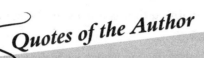

Quotes of the Author

If you do not tell the truth about yourself you cannot tell it about other people.

Women have served all these centuries as looking-glasses possessing the magic and delicious power of reflecting the figure of a man at twice its natural size.

Literature is strewn with the wreckage of men who have minded beyond reason the opinions of others.

I meant to write about death, only life came breaking in as usual.

D. H. Lawrence
D. H. 劳伦斯
(1885—1930)

本章导读

　　D. H. 劳伦斯是 20 世纪英国现实主义小说家、诗人和散文家。他的父亲是位煤矿工人，母亲是出身于中产阶级的教师。父母关系的不和对他的生活和写作都产生了很大的影响。这体现在他带有自传性质的小说《儿子与情人》中对人性中隐秘的"恋母情结"深刻且形象的挖掘。他的创作深受弗洛伊德心理分析学的影响，所以他的小说时常描述日常生活中无休止的心灵抗争，这也使他的小说弥漫着一种忧郁的情调。在短短 20 年的写作生涯中，他先后创作了 12 部长篇小说，70 多篇中短篇小说，多部诗集，大量的散文随笔和一些翻译作品。其中他的长篇小说《虹》《查泰莱夫人的情人》及《恋爱中的女人》等尤为世人所熟知。他还是英国现代文学艺术领域内罕见的文艺通才，他自幼习画，曾举办画展并出版绘画集。由于作品中对性爱的大胆描写，劳伦斯曾备受争议，但其作品中对人类灵魂的深刻剖析和对永恒的追求让他的作品经得起时间的考验。

　　劳伦斯的散文作品在欧洲文学史与思想史上也占有重要的位置，他对生命的独特阐释和深刻解读在其一系列散文创作中得到延伸和发扬。劳伦斯的散文主题主要表现在两方面，一是对西方工业文明摧残人性的揭露以及反抗；二是对大自然的热爱和人类美好生活的歌颂。在《新墨西哥风情录》中，他生动地描写自己在新墨西哥的农场的经历，并通过比较新墨西哥和澳大利亚的天空及印第安人与土著人生活等，表现了原始文明与异域文明神秘且无限的魅力，从而强调现代文明对人类心灵的压抑及他对自然天性的肯定。《鸟啼》和《沿山的耶稣像》等也都通过生动细致的刻画展现出其对自然的无限迷恋。因此劳伦斯的散文通过诗性的文风、对大自然的歌颂及其对人类心灵的洞察，传递出构建人与自然、人与人之间和谐关系的愿望，充分展现了他细腻的情感和别具一格的文字魅力。

劳伦斯的散文风格一直受到其诗歌创作的影响，因此他的散文富有诗的节奏和韵律，篇章中弥漫着诗性的思维。劳伦斯充分结合了他周游多国的经历，风景和自然之美是他散文中的创作主体，揭示了世界内在的诗性，传递出浪漫主义之美。本章所选的《鸟啼》是劳伦斯于1919年创作的一篇文辞清丽、音节优美、意义隽永的现代寓言。当时第一次世界大战刚刚结束，这场战争给参战国的普通百姓带来了肉体的苦痛和精神的摧残。战火绵延后的欧洲可谓生灵涂炭，满目疮痍，整个社会的状况正如文章开头所描绘的，呈现出一片触目惊心的死亡画面。但是，突然之间，一切都在变化。劳伦斯以诗一般的语言描写了大自然从春到冬的过渡，刻画了春天的鸟儿这一中心意象。鸟儿的鸣唱是对生命的礼赞，是对战争结束、和平来临的热烈地讴歌。因为，人类文明从来就没有真正死亡，经过短暂的停滞后它必会重新焕发春的生机。

About the Author

David Herbert Richards Lawrence (September 11, 1885–March 2, 1930) was an English novelist, poet, playwright, essayist, literary critic and painter. He is famous for his novels which deeply explored the soul of human beings and the relationship between men and women. He was recognized as a prominent novelist after the publication of *Sons and Lovers* (1913). In addition, *The Rainbow* (1915) and *Women in Love* (1920) are also masterpieces in which symbolism and complex narrative are employed more richly. Lawrence's most essential idea is opposing the influence of civilized world of mechanism over human that distorts all natural relationships between men and women. Another major characteristic of his novel is that he combines social criticism with psychological exploration. The tracing of psychological development of characters reflects the human nature. He also believes that the healthy way of individual psychological development lies in the life impulse which refers to the sexual impulse. In his eyes, love and sex are integrated with each other, which are the true life force supporting people to live in this messy world.

He started writing travelling essays during the time he and his lover Frieda eloped to Germany and Italy. Even though these essays were written for their livelihood, but still contained some artistic value. Lawrence and Frieda spent the hardest life together,

Chapter 11

D. H. Lawrence
D. H. 劳伦斯

and the essays were the fruit of their love witnessing how they kept company with each other. Afterwards, these travelling essays were published in *Twilight in Italy and Other Essays* (1916).

Later, Lawrence constantly wrote some essays. His *Sea and Sardinia* (1921) was written in grace and refinement; *Mornings in Mexico and Other Essays* (1927) became one masterpiece of exploring the Indian civilization; *Sketches of Etruscan Places and Other Italian Essays* (1932) written during his later period was created with great magnificence incorporating emotion with reason. These works reflect the essence of Lawrence's ideas in clear and elegant language. Moreover, his poetic imagination and symbolism play important roles in his essay writing, rendering his essays artistically subtle and lyrical.

Text A

Whistling of Birds

D. H. Lawrence

The frost held for many weeks, until the birds were dying rapidly. Everywhere in the fields and under the hedges lay the ragged remains of lapwings, starlings, thrushes, redwings, innumerable ragged, bloody **cloaks** of birds, whence the flesh was eaten by invisible beasts of prey.

Then, quite suddenly, one morning, the change came. The wind went to the south[1], came off the sea warm and soothing. In the afternoon there were little gleams of sunshine, and the doves began, without interval, slowly and awkwardly to coo. The doves were cooing, though with a laboured sound, as if they were still winter-stunned. Nevertheless, all the afternoon they continued their noise, in the mild air, before the frost had **thawed** off the road. At evening the wind blew gently, still gathering a bruising quality of frost from the hard earth. Then, in the yellow-gleamy sunset, wild birds began to whistle faintly in the blackthorn **thickets** of the stream-bottom.

It was startling and almost frightening, after the heavy silence of frost. How could they sing at once, when the ground was thickly **strewn** with the torn carcasses of birds? Yet out of the evening came the uncertain, silvery sounds that made ones soul start alert, almost with fear. How could the little silver bugles sound the rally so swiftly, in the soft air, when the earth was yet bound? Yet the birds continued their whistling, rather dimly and brokenly, but throwing the threads of silver, **germinating** noise into the air.

It was almost a pain to realize, so swiftly, the new world. "Le monde

---

1 The wind went to the south: 英国的春天吹的是北风，因此吹向南方

Chapter 11

D. H. Lawrence
D. H. 劳伦斯

est mort. Vive le monde!¹" But the birds omitted even the first part of the announcement, their cry was only a faint, blind, **fecund** "vive!"

There is another world. The winter is gone. There is a new world of spring. The voice of the turtle² is heard in the land. But the flesh shrinks from so sudden a transition. Surely the call is premature, while the clods are still frozen, and the ground is littered with the remains of wings! Yet we have no choice. In the bottoms of impenetrable blackthorn, each evening and morning now, out flickers a whistling of birds.

Where does it come from, the song? After so long a cruelty, how can they make it up so quickly? But it bubbles through them, they are like little well-heads, little fountain-heads whence the spring trickles and bubbles forth. It is not of their own doing. In their throats the new life distils itself into sound. It is the rising of the silvery sap of a new summer, gurgling itself forth.

All the time, whilst the earth lay choked and killed and winter-mortified, the deep undersprings were quiet. They only wait for the **ponderous encumbrance** of the old order to give way, yield in the thaw, and there theyare, a silver realm at once. Under the surge of ruin, **unmitigated** winter, liesthe silver potentiality of all blossom. One day the black tide must spend itself and fade back. Then all-suddenly appears the crocus, hovering triumphant in the year, and we know the order has changed, there is a new regime, sound of a new "Vive! Vive!"

It is no use any more to look at the torn **remnants** of birds that lie expose. It is no longer any use remembering the sullen thunder of frost and the intolerable pressure of cold upon us. For whether we will or not, they are gone. The choice is not ours. We many remain wintry and destructive for a little longer, if we wish it, but the winter is gone out of us, and **willy-nilly** our hearts sing a little at sunset.

---

1 Le monde est mort. Vive le monde!: French expression which means in English "The king is dead. Long live the (new) king". "国王驾崩，（新）国王万岁"。法国古代的传令官在通告老国王驾崩、新国王继位时常用此语。

2 turtle: turtledove, 中文名字为斑鸠。此典故出自《圣经·旧约》中的《雅歌》第二章第12节: "the flowers appear on the earth; the time of spring has come, and the voice of the turtle is heard in our land".

Even whilst we stare at the ragged horror of birds scattered broadcast, part-eaten, the soft, uneven cooing of the pigeon ripples from the outhouses, and there is a faint silver whistling in the bushes come twilight. No matter, we stand and stare at the torn and unsightly ruins of life, we watch the weary, **mutilated** columns of winter retreating under our eyes. Yet in our ears are the silver vivid bugles of a new creation advancing on us from behind, we hear the rolling of the soft and happy drums of the doves.

We may not choose the world. We have hardly any choice for ourselves. We follow with our eyes the bloody and horrid line of march of this extreme winter, as it passes away. But we cannot hold back the spring. We cannot make the birds silent, prevent the bubbling of the wood-pigeons. We cannot stay the fine world of silver-fecund creation from gathering itself and taking place upon us. Whether we will or mo, the daphne tree will soon be giving off perfume, the lambs dancing on two feet, the celandines will twinkle all over the ground, there will be new heaven and new earth[1].

For it is in us, as well as without us. Those who can may follow the columns of winter in their retreat from off the earth. Some of us, we have no choice, the spring is within us, the silver fountain begins to bubble under our breast, there is a gladness in spite of ourselves. And on the instant we accept the gladness! The first day of change, out whistles an unusual, interrupted pean, a fragment that will augment itself **imperceptibly**. And this in spite of the extreme bitter-ness of the suffering, in spite of the **myriads** of torn dead.

Such a long, long winter, and the frost only broke yesterday[2]. Yet it seems, already, we cannot remember it. It is strangely remote, like a far-off darkness. It is as unreal as a dream in the night. This is the morning of reality, when we are ourselves. This is natural and real, the glimmering of a new creation that stirs

---

1 there will be new heaven and new earth：典出《圣经·新约》中的《启示录》第21章第1节："Then I saw a new heaven and new earth; for the first heaven and the first earth had passed away, and the sea was no more."

2 the frost only broke yesterday: England underwent the severest winter starting from 1916. The frost did not break until Febuary 16th, 1917. 1916年至1917年的冬季是第一次世界大战期间英国最冷、最长的冬季，当年英国还遭受了1895年来最严重的霜冻。直至1917年2月16日霜冻结束，次日英国气温骤然升高。

Chapter 11

D. H. Lawrence
D. H. 劳伦斯

in us and about us. We know there was winter, long, fearful. We know the earth was strangled and mortified, we know the body of life was torn and scattered broadcast. But what is this **retrospective** knowledge? It is something **extraneous** to us, extraneous to this that we are now. And what we are, and what, it seems, we always have been, is this quickening lovely silver plasm of pure creativity. All the mortification and tearing, ah yes, it was upon us, encompassing us. It was like a storm or a mist or a falling from a height. It was entangled upon us, like bats in our hair, driving us mad. But it was never really our innermost self. Within, we were always apart, we were this, this **limpid** fountain of silver, then **quiescent**, rising and breaking now into the flowering.

It is strange, the utter in compatibility of death with life. Whilst there is death, life is not to be found. It is all death, one overwhelming flood. And then a new tide rises, and it is all life, a fountain of silvery blissfulness. It is one or the other.

Death takes us, and all is a torn redness, passing into darkness. Life rises, and we are faint fine jets of silver running out to blossom. All is incompatible with all. There is the silvery-speckled, **incandescent**-lovely thrush, whistling pipingly his first song in the blackthorn thicket. How is he to be connected with the bloody, feathered unsightliness of thrush-remnants just outside the bushes? There is no connection. They are not to be referred the one to the other. Where one is, the other is not. In the kingdom of death the silvery song is not. But where there is life, there is no death. No death whatever, only silvery gladness, perfect, the otherworld.

The blackbird cannot stop his song, neither can the pigeon. It takes place in him, even though all his race was yesterday destroyed. He cannot mourn, or be silent, or adhere to the dead. Of the dead he is not, since life has kept him. The dead must bury their dead[1]. Life has now taken hold on him and tossed him into the new ether of a new **firmament**, where he bursts into song as if he were **combustible**. What is the past, those others, now he is tossed clean into

---

1 The dead must bury their dead: 典出《圣经·新约》中的《马太福音》第 8 章第 22 节："Lord, first let me go and bury my father." But Jesus said to him, "Follow me, and let the dead bury their own dead."

the new, across the untranslatable difference?

In his song is heard the first brokenness and uncertainty of the transition. The transit from the grip of death into new being is a death from death, in its sheer **metempsychosis** a dizzy agony. But only for a second, the moment of **trajectory**, the passage from one state to the other, from the grip of death to the liberty of newness. In a moment he is in the kingdom of wonder, singing at the center of a new creation.

The bird did not hang back. He did not cling to his death and his dead. There is no death, and the dead have buried their dead. Tossed into the **chasm** between two worlds, he lifted his wings in dread, and found himself carried on the impulse.

We are lifted to be cast away into the new beginning. Under our hearts the fountain surges, to toss us forth. Who can thwart the impulse that comes upon us? It comes from the unknown upon us, and it **behoves** us to pass delicately and exquisitely upon the subtle new wind from heaven, conveyed like birds in unreasoning migration from death to life.

1 Words and Phrases

cloak [kləʊk]	n.	a loose sleeveless outer garment 斗篷，披风
thaw [θɔː]	v.	become less hard, less numb, less icy etc. as a result of being warmed 软化；解冻
thicket ['θɪkɪt]	n.	a dense growth of bushes 繁茂处；灌木丛
strew [struː]	v.	spread by scattering 撒满，布满
germinate ['dʒɜːmɪneɪt]	v.	produce buds or sprout 发芽，开始生长
fecund [fiːkənd]	adj.	capable of producing offspring or vegetation 多产的，丰饶的
ponderous ['pɑːndərəs]	adj.	slow and laborious because of weight 笨重的；乏味的
encumbrance [ɪn'kʌmbrəns]	n.	any obstruction that impedes or is burdensome 累赘

Chapter 11

D. H. Lawrence
D. H. 劳伦斯

unmitigated [ʌn'mɪtɪgeɪtɪd]	*adj.*	not diminished or moderated in intensity or severity; sometimes used as an intensifier 未缓和的；十足的
remnant ['remnənt]	*n.*	a small part or portion that remains after the main part no longer exists 残余，剩余物
willy-nilly [ˌwɪlɪ'nɪlɪ]	*adv.*	without having a choice 不管愿意不愿意
mutilate ['mjuːtɪleɪt]	*v.*	having a part of the body crippled 使残缺不全，破坏
imperceptibly [ˌɪmpə'septəblɪ]	*adv.*	in an imperceptible manner or to an imperceptible degree 极微小地；逐步地
myriad ['mɪrɪəd]	*n.*	a large indefinite number 极大数量
retrospective [ˌretrə'spektɪv]	*adj.*	concerned with or related to the past 回顾的；追溯的
extraneous [ɪk'streɪnɪəs]	*adj.*	not belonging to that in which it is contained; introduced from an outside source 外来的
limpid ['lɪmpɪd]	*adj.*	clear and bright 清澈的
quiescent [kwɪ'esnt]	*adj.*	being quiet or still or inactive 静止的；寂静的；不活动的
incandescent [ˌɪnkæn'desnt]	*adj.*	emitting light as a result of being heated 光亮的；炽热的
firmament ['fɜːməmənt]	*n.*	the apparent surface of the imaginary sphere on which celestial bodies appear to be projected 苍穹
combustible [kəm'bʌstəbl]	*adj.*	capable of igniting and burning 易燃的；燃烧性的
metempsychosis [ˌmetəmsaɪ'kəʊsɪs]	*n.*	after death the soul begins a new cycle of existence in another human body 轮回
trajectory [trə'dʒektərɪ]	*n.*	the path followed by an object moving through space 轨道
chasm ['kæzəm]	*n.*	a deep opening in the earth's surface 鸿沟；裂痕
behove [bɪ'həʊv]	*v.*	be appropriate or necessary 理应；应该；有必要

II Reading Comprehension Questions

1. In the first paragraph, what kind of scene is described?
2. Based on an understanding of the historical background of the essay, what do you think the severe winter symbolize?
3. Why can the birds sing over the carcasses of other birds? What does the author try to express? Just the mercilessness of those birds or is there any deeper meaning?
4. What does the whistling of birds symbolize according to your understanding?
5. Please discuss with your classmates about the theme of the essay.

III Questions on Writing Style and Language

1. What is the stylistic feature of this essay? What do you feel upon reading his sentences?
2. How does the author describe the horrific winter and the new spring? In addition to birds, what specific images does he use?
3. Synaesthesia is a figure of speech which refers to the mixing of sensations or the stimulation of one sense that produces a mental impression associated with a different sense. Can you find any examples of synaesthesia in the sixth paragraph?
4. "In their throats the new life distils itself into sound. It is the rising of the silvery sap of a new summer, gurgling itself forth." In this sentence, what rhetorical devices are used?
5. "Those who can may follow the columns of winter in their retreat from off the earth. Some of us, we have no choice." (Para. 11) What figure of speech does the author use here? Who can retreat from off the earth? Who have no choice?

Chapter 11
D. H. Lawrence
D. H. 劳伦斯

Give Her a Pattern

D. H. Lawrence

The real trouble about women is that they must always go on trying to adapt themselves to men's theories of women, as they always have done. When a woman is thoroughly herself, she is being what her type of man wants her to be. When a woman is hysterical it's because she doesn't quite know what to be, which pattern to follow, which man's picture of woman to live up to.

For, of course, just as there are many men in the world, there are many masculine theories of what women should be. But men run to type, and it is the type, not the individual, that produces the theory, or "ideal" of woman. Those very **grasping** gentry, the Romans, produced a theory or ideal of the matron, which fitted in very nicely with the Roman property lust. "Caesar's wife should be above suspicion." So Caesar's wife kindly proceeded to be above it, no matter how far below it the Caesar fell. Later gentlemen like Nero produced the "**fast**" theory of woman, and later ladies were fast enough for everybody.

Dante arrived with a chaste and untouched Beatrice, and chaste and untouched Beatrices began to march self-importantly through the centuries. The Renaissance discovered the learned woman, and learned women buzzed mildly into verse and prose. Dickens invented the child-wife, so child-wives have swarmed ever since. He also fished out his version of the chaste Beatrice, a chaste but marriageable Agnes. George Eliot imitated this pattern, and it became confirmed. The noble woman, the pure spouse, the devoted mother took the field, and was simply worked to death. Our own poor mothers were this sort. So we younger men, having been a bit frightened of our noble mothers, tended to revert to the child-wife. We weren't very inventive. Only the child-wife must be a boyish little thing—that was the new touch we added. Because young men are definitely frightened of the real female. She's too risky a quantity. She is too untidy, like David's Dora. No, let her be a boyish little thing, it's safer. So a boyish little thing she is.

There are, of course, other types. Capable men produce the capable woman ideal. Doctors produce the capable nurse. Business men produce the capable secretary. And so you get all sorts. You can produce the masculine sense of honour (whatever that highly mysterious quantity may be) in women, if you want to.

There is, also, the eternal secret ideal of men—the prostitute. Lots of women live up to this idea: just because men want them to.

And so, poor woman, destiny makes away with her. It isn't that she hasn't got a mind—she has. She's got everything that man has. The only difference is that she asks for a pattern. Give me a pattern to follow! That will always be woman's cry. Unless of course she has already chosen her pattern quite young, then she will declare she is herself absolutely, and no man's idea of women has any influence over her.

Now the real tragedy is not that women ask and must ask for a pattern of womanhood. The tragedy is not, even, that men give them such **abominable** patterns, child-wives, little-boy-baby-face girls, perfect secretaries, noble spouses, self-sacrificing mothers, pure women who bring forth children in virgin coldness, prostitutes who just make themselves low, to please the men; all the atrocious patterns of womanhood that men have supplied to woman; patterns all perverted from any real natural fullness of a human being. Man is willing to accept woman as an equal, as a man in skirts, as an angel, a devil, a baby-face, a machine, an instrument, a bosom, a womb, a pair of legs, a servant, an encyclopaedia, an ideal or an obscenity; the one thing he won't accept her as, is a human being, a real human being of the feminine sex.

And of course women love living up to strange patterns, weird patterns, the more uncanny the better. What could be more uncanny than the present pattern of the Eton-boy girl with flower-like artificial complexion? It is just weird. And for its very weirdness women like living up to it. What can be more

Chapter 11
D. H. Lawrence
D. H. 劳伦斯

gruesome than the little-boy-baby-face pattern? Yet the girls take it on with **avidity**.

But even that isn't the real root of the tragedy.

The absurdity, and often, as in the Dante-Beatrice business, the inhuman nastiness of the pattern—for Beatrice had to go on being chaste and untouched all her life, according to Dante's pattern, while Dante had a cosy wife and kids at home—even that isn't the worst of it. The worst of it is, as soon as a woman has really lived up to the man's pattern, the man dislikes her for it. There is intense secret dislike for the Eton-young-man girl, among the boys, now that she is actually produced. Of course, she's very nice to show in public, absolutely the thing. But the very young men who have brought about her production detest her in private and in their private hearts are appalled by her.

When it comes to marrying, the pattern goes all to pieces. The boy marries the Eton-boy girl, and instantly he hates the type. Instantly his mind begins to play hysterically with all the other types, noble Agneses, chaste Beatrices, clinging Doras and **lurid** filles de joie. He is in a wild **welter** of confusion.

Whatever pattern the poor woman tries to live up to, he'll want another. And that's the condition of modern marriage.

Modern woman isn't really a fool. But modern man is. That seems to me the only plain way of putting it. The modern man is a fool, and the modern young man a prize fool. He makes a greater mess of his women than men have ever made. Because he absolutely doesn't know what he wants her to be. We shall see the changes in the woman-pattern follow one another fast and furious now, because the young men hysterically don't know what they want. Two years hence women may be in **crinolines**—there was a pattern for you!—or a bead flap, like naked negresses in mid-Africa—or they may be wearing brass armour, or the uniform of the Horse Guards. They may be anything. Because the young men are off their heads, and don't know what they want.

The women aren't fools, but they must live up to some pattern or other. They know the men are the fools. They don't really respect the pattern. Yet a pattern they must have, or they can't exist.

Women are not fools. They have their own logic, even if it's not the masculine sort. Women have the logic of emotion, men have the logic of reason. The two are complementary and mostly in opposition. But the woman's logic of emotion is no less real and **inexorable** than the man's logic of reason. It only works differently.

And the woman never really loses it. She may spend years living up to a masculine pattern. But in the end, the strange and terrible logic of emotion will work out the smashing of that pattern, if it has not been emotionally satisfactory. This is the partial explanation of the astonishing changes in women. For years they go on being chaste Beatrices or child-wives. Then on a sudden—bash! The chaste Beatrice becomes something quite different, the child-wife becomes a roaring lioness! The pattern didn't suffice, emotionally.

Whereas men are fools. They are based on a logic of reason or are supposed to be. And then they go and behave, especially with regard to women, in a more-than-feminine unreasonableness. They spend years training up the little-boy-baby-face type, till they've got her perfect. Then the moment they marry her, they want something else. Oh, beware, young women, of the young men who adore you! The moment they've got you they'll want something utterly different. The moment they marry the little-boy-baby face, instantly they begin to **pine** for the noble Agnes, pure and majestic, or the infinite mother with deep bosom of consolation, or the perfect business-woman, or the lurid prostitute on black silk sheets: or, most idiotic of all, a combination of all the lot of them at once. And that is the logic of reason! When it comes to women, modern men are idiots. They don't know what they want, and so they never want, permanently, what they get. They want a cream cake that is at the same time ham and eggs and at the same time porridge. They are fools. If only women weren't bound by fate to play up to them!

For the fact of life is that women must play up to man's pattern. And she only gives her best to a man when he gives her a satisfactory pattern to play up to. But today, with a stock of ready-made, worn-out idiotic patterns to live up to, what can women give to men but the trashy side of their emotions! What could a woman possibly give to a man who wanted her to be a boy-baby

Chapter 11

D. H. Lawrence
D. H. 劳伦斯

face? What could she possibly give him but the **dribblings** of an idiot? And, because women aren't fools, and aren't fooled even for very long at a time, she gives him some nasty cruel digs with her claws, and makes him cry for mother dear!—abruptly changing his pattern.

Bah! Men are fools. If they want anything from women, let them give women a decent, satisfying idea of womanhood—not these trick patterns of **washed-out** idiots.

1 Words and Phrases

grasping ['grɑːspɪŋ]	*adj.* immoderately desirous of acquiring e.g. wealth 贪心的，贪婪的
fast [fɑːst]	*adj.* profligate, pleasure-loving, immoral 放荡的
abominable [əˈbɒmɪnəbl]	*adj.* detestable, unpleasant 讨厌的，令人憎恶的
gruesome [ˈɡruːsəm]	*adj.* shockingly repellent; inspiring horror 可怕的，阴森的
avidity [əˈvɪdətɪ]	*n.* a positive feeling of wanting to push ahead with something 渴望
lurid [ˈlʊərɪd]	*adj.* horrible in fierceness or savagery 可怕的
welter [ˈweltə]	*n.* a confused multitude of things 混乱
crinoline [ˈkrɪnəlɪn]	*n.* a full stiff petticoat made of crinoline fabric 裙衬
inexorable [ɪnˈeksərəbl]	*adj.* full of determination 坚定不移的
pine [paɪn]	*v.* have a desire for something or someone who is not present 渴望
dribble [drɪbl]	*v.* flow in drops 慢慢流下
washed-out [ˈwɒʃtˈaʊt]	*adj.* having lost freshness or brilliance of colour 褪色的

II Reading Comprehension Questions

1. According to the author, there are many masculine theories of what women should be. Can you give some examples to illustrate these theories?
2. According to the author, what is the real root of the tragedy?
3. According to the essay, what is the condition of modern marriage?
4. Why does a woman need to live in a pattern?
5. How, in your opinion, can men and women find the balance in their relationships?

Chapter 11

D. H. Lawrence
D. H. 劳伦斯

Quotes of the Author

Instead of chopping yourself down to fit the world, chop the world down to fit yourself.

One must learn to love, and go through a good deal of suffering to get to it... and the journey is always towards the other soul.

Love is the flower of life, and blossoms unexpectedly and without law, and must be plucked where it is found, and enjoyed for the brief hour of its duration.

In every living thing there is the desire for love.

One doesn't know, till one is a bit at odds with the world, how much one's friends who believe in one rather generously mean to one.

George Orwell
乔治·奥威尔
(1903—1950)

本章导读

乔治·奥威尔是 20 世纪最发人深省且文笔最为生动的散文家之一。

1903 年，乔治·奥威尔出生于英属印度彭加尔省（孟加拉邦）的一个政府下级官员的家庭，其父亲供职于印度总督府鸦片局，家境并不宽裕，奥威尔自称家庭属于"上层中产阶级偏下，即没有钱的中产家庭"。1905 年，除了父亲仍任职于印度总督府的鸦片局外，全家返回英国牛津。由于无力就读贵族学校，1911 年，奥威尔进入一个二流的私立寄宿学校——圣·塞浦里安预备学校。该寄宿学校带有许多极权主义社会的特点，如鞭子教育、等级制、恃强凌弱、规范化、反智，等等。1917 年，奥威尔依靠自己的努力考取奖学金，进入英国最著名的中学——伊顿公学，但他贫穷的家庭背景使他备受歧视。1921 年，奥威尔从伊顿公学毕业后，由于家庭经济状况无力供他升学，他只得投考公务员，成为了英国在缅甸的殖民警察，服役五年。作为英籍警官，他享有很多特权，能够近距离观察审判、笞刑、监禁和绞死囚犯的过程。这一阶段的经历让奥威尔细致地观察、体会到人性中残暴冷酷的一面，使他对西方殖民主义政策产生了反思，更进一步地认识了极权主义。在缅甸的经历使他憎恨帝国主义和殖民制度，也对他之后主张维护个人自由的思想产生了很大的影响。

1927 年，奥威尔辞去了警察职务回到欧洲，开始了长达四年的流浪生活。在这四年里，他辗转英国本岛和欧洲大陆，深入社会底层，先后做过酒店洗碗工、教师、书店店员和码头工人，但他的上层社会身份和在伊顿公学形成的贵族口音使他很难被底层社会真正接纳。但这一段时期的经历也使他更深切地感受到了社会整体对个人的压迫和普遍的社会不公现象的存在，并且最终他接受了社会主义思想。奥威尔自己曾经提到"贫困的生活和失败的感觉增强了我天生对权威的憎恨，使我第一次意识到工

Chapter 12
George Orwell
乔治·奥威尔

人阶级的存在"。

西班牙内战期间，奥威尔以记者的身份赴马德里参加反法西斯战斗，不幸负伤，之后思想右倾，转而反对自己曾经深信不疑的社会主义。第二次世界大战全面爆发后，奥威尔应征入伍，并参与英国广播公司对印度的广播。1950年1月，奥威尔因肺结核于伦敦的大学医院去世。

使乔治·奥威尔成为广为人知的作家的是他的两部著名的政治讽喻小说《一九八四》和《动物农场》，但是在奥威尔一生的文学成就中扮演极其重要角色的是他的散文。在奥威尔短暂的一生里，他以敏锐的洞察力和犀利的文笔审视和记录着他所生活的那个时代，以亲身经历为素材写成一篇篇尖锐、深刻的散文，揭露社会的阴暗和丑陋的谎言，并将此作为己任，向其广大读者展示社会最真实的一面，甚至作出了许多超越时代的预言。因此，他被称为"一代人的冷峻良知"。

奥威尔的散文风格简洁明快，他摒弃了华丽浮泛、矫揉造作的文风，以简约自然的风格描写自然现象和社会现象，表达重要、深刻的政治内容。他使用的句子简短，选择的词汇普通、常见，叙事质朴，议论直截了当。他散文写作最突出、最显著的风格就是他十分巧妙地将美妙的艺术性与尖刻的政治性有机地结合在一起，使两者融为一体。奥威尔在《我为什么要写作》中说他一生中要做的事情就是使政治写作成为一种艺术，"我所以写一本书，是因为我有一个谎言要揭露，我有一个事实要引起大家的注意。我最关心的事就是要有一个让大家来听我说话的机会。但是如果这不能同时也成为一次审美的活动，我是不会写一本书的，甚至不会写一篇杂志长文"。他的散文既洋溢着艺术的色彩、气氛，给读者一种审美、愉悦的享受，同时又带有鲜明、犀利的政治性色彩，将他的政治思想与主张传达给读者，给读者以思想的启蒙与迷惘时的豁然开朗。

About the Author

Eric Arthur Blair (25 June, 1903–21 January, 1950), who used the pen name George Orwell, was an English novelist, essayist, journalist and critic.

Orwell was born in India, while his father was in the British Civil service. After finishing his school at Eton, he served for five years in Burma with the imperial police, finally quitting in disgust at the effects of imperialism on human freedom and dignity. He returned to Europe, and for about eighteen months lived in Paris, supporting himself by washing dishes in restaurants and by various odds and ends of teaching. During World War II, Orwell became an overseas broadcaster for the British Broadcasting System and as a part-time factory worker. Orwell died in London in 1950.

Commonly ranked as one of the most influential 20th century English writers and chroniclers of English culture, Orwell wrote literary criticism, poetry, fiction, and polemical journalism. He is best known for the dystopian novel *Nineteen Eighty-Four* (1949) and the allegorical novella *Animal Farm* (1945). His nonfiction works, including *The Road to Wigan Pier* (1937), documenting his experience of working class life in the north of England, and *Homage to Catalonia* (1938), an account of his experiences in the Spanish Civil War, are widely acclaimed, as are his essays on politics, literature, language, and culture.

George Orwell was one of the best essayists in the 20th century. His work is marked by lucid prose, awareness of social injustice, opposition to totalitarianism, and commitment to democratic socialism. In 2008, *The Times* ranked him second on a list of "The 50 greatest British writers since 1945".

Chapter 12

George Orwell
乔治·奥威尔

Text A

Some Thoughts on The Common Toad

George Orwell

Before the swallow, before the daffodil, and not much later than the snowdrop, the common toad salutes the coming of spring after his own fashion, which is to emerge from a hole in the ground, where he has lain buried since the previous autumn, and crawl as rapidly as possible towards the nearest suitable patch of water. Something—some kind of **shudder** in the earth, or perhaps merely a rise of a few degrees in the temperature—has told him that it is time to wake up: though a few toads appear to sleep the clock round and miss out a year from time to time—at any rate, I have more than once dug them up, alive and apparently well, in the middle of the summer.

At this period, after his long fast, the toad has a very spiritual look[1], like a strict Anglo-Catholic towards the end of Lent[2]. His movements are **languid** but purposeful, his body is shrunken, and by contrast his eyes look abnormally large. This allows one to notice, what one might not at another time, that a toad has about the most beautiful eye of any living creature. It is like gold, or more exactly it is like the golden-coloured semi-precious stone which one sometimes sees in signet-rings, and which I think is called a **chrysoberyl.**

For a few days after getting into the water the toad concentrates on building up his strength by eating small insects. Presently he has swollen to his normal size again, and then he goes through a phase of intense sexiness. All he knows, at least if he is a male toad, is that he wants to get his arms round something, and if you offer him a stick, or even your finger, he will cling to it

---

1 spiritual look: 得道高僧的神色
2 like a strict Anglo-Catholic towards the end of Lent: Lent, 四旬斋, 是指从复活节之前的四十天, 被基督徒视为禁食和忏悔的斋戒期。这里的 Anglo-Catholic 指英国国教高派教会之教徒。

with surprising strength and take a long time to discover that it is not a female toad. Frequently one comes upon shapeless masses of ten or twenty toads rolling over and over in the water, one clinging to another without distinction of sex. By degrees, however, they sort themselves out into couples, with the male duly sitting on the female's back. You can now distinguish males from females, because the male is smaller, darker and sits on top, with his arms tightly **clasped** round the female's neck. After a day or two the **spawn** is laid in long strings which wind themselves in and out of the **reeds** and soon become invisible. A few more weeks, and the water is alive with masses of tiny **tadpoles** which rapidly grow larger, sprout hind-legs, then forelegs, then shed their tails: and finally, about the middle of the summer, the new generation of toads, smaller than one's thumb-nail but perfect in every particular, crawl out of the water to begin the game anew.

    I mention the spawning of the toads because it is one of the phenomena of spring which most deeply appeal to me, and because the toad, unlike the skylark and the primrose, has never had much of a boost from poets. But I am aware that many people do not like **reptiles** or **amphibians**, and I am not suggesting that in order to enjoy the spring you have to take an interest in toads. There are also the crocus, the missel-thrush, the cuckoo, the blackthorn, etc. The point is that the pleasures of spring are available to everybody, and cost nothing. Even in the most **sordid** street the coming of spring will register itself by some sign or other, if it is only a brighter blue between the chimney pots or the vivid green of an elder sprouting on a blitzed site. Indeed it is remarkable how Nature goes on existing unofficially, as it were, in the very heart of London. I have seen a **kestrel** flying over the Deptford **gasworks**, and I have heard a first-rate performance by a blackbird in the Euston Road.[1] There must be some hundreds of thousands, if not millions, of birds living inside the four-mile **radius**, and it is rather a pleasing thought that none of them pays a halfpenny of rent.

---

1   I have seen a kestrel flying over the Deptford gasworks, and I have heard a first-rate performance by a blackbird in the Euston Road: 这句话中的 Deptford 指德普津，是伦敦西南部泰晤士河南岸的一个城区；Euston Road 指尤斯顿路，是伦敦市中心城区的一条街道。

Chapter 12

George Orwell
乔治·奥威尔

As for spring, not even the narrow and gloomy streets round the Bank of England are quite able to exclude it. It comes **seeping** in everywhere, like one of those new poison gases which pass through all filters. The spring is commonly referred to as "a miracle", and during the past five or six years this worn-out figure of speech has taken on a new lease of life. After the sorts of winters we have had to endure recently, the spring does seem miraculous, because it has become gradually harder and harder to believe that it is actually going to happen. Every February since 1940 I have found myself thinking that this time winter is going to be permanent[1]. But Persephone[2], like the toads, always rises from the dead at about the same moment. Suddenly, towards the end of March, the miracle happens and the decaying slum in which I live is transfigured. Down in the square the **sooty privets** have turned bright green, the leaves are thickening on the chestnut trees, the daffodils are out, the wallflowers are budding, the policeman's tunic looks positively a pleasant shade of blue, the **fishmonger** greets his customers with a smile, and even the sparrows are quite a different colour, having felt the balminess of the air and nerved themselves to take a bath, their first since last September.

Is it wicked to take a pleasure in spring and other seasonal changes? To put it more precisely, is it politically **reprehensible**, while we are all groaning, or at any rate ought to be groaning, under the shackles of the capitalist system, to point out that life is frequently more worth living because of a blackbird's song, a yellow **elm** tree in October, or some other natural phenomenon which does not cost money and does not have what the editors of left-wing newspapers call a class angle? There is no doubt that many people think so. I know by experience that a favourable reference to "Nature" in one of my articles is liable to bring me abusive letters, and though the key-word

---

1 Every February since 1940 I have found myself thinking that this time winter is going to be permanent: 1939 年 9 月 "二战" 爆发，英、法对德宣战，英国国内随即处于战争状态，国内民生极为困苦，这一状态一直持续到 1945 年秋，德、日相继投降之后。本文作于 1946 年，正是战争刚刚结束，英国国内正值满目疮痍、百废待兴之际。

2 Persephone: 珀尔塞福涅，希腊神话中宙斯和德墨忒耳的女儿，被冥王哈迪斯劫娶为冥后。宙斯闻讯令冥王将女儿送回，但冥王已经给她吃冥食，宙斯无奈，只好同意让珀尔塞福涅每年在冥界待四个月，其余时间回到人间和她妈妈在一起。

in these letters is usually "sentimental", two ideas seem to be mixed up in them. One is that any pleasure in the actual process of life encourages a sort of political quietism[1]. People, so the thought runs, ought to be discontented, and it is our job to multiply our wants and not simply to increase our enjoyment of the things we have already. The other idea is that this is the age of machines and that to dislike the machine, or even to want to limit its domination, is backward-looking, reactionary and slightly ridiculous. This is often backed up by the statement that a love of Nature is a foible of urbanized people who have no notion what Nature is really like. Those who really have to deal with the soil, so it is argued, do not love the soil, and do not take the faintest interest in birds or flowers, except from a strictly utilitarian point of view. To love the country one must live in the town, merely taking an occasional week-end ramble at the warmer times of year.

This last idea is demonstrably false. Medieval literature, for instance, including the popular ballads, is full of an almost Georgian[2] enthusiasm for Nature, and the art of agricultural peoples such as the Chinese and Japanese centre always round trees, birds, flowers, rivers, mountains. The other idea seems to me to be wrong in a subtler way. Certainly we ought to be discontented, we ought not simply to find out ways of making the best of a bad job, and yet if we kill all pleasure in the actual process of life, what sort of future are we preparing for ourselves? If a man cannot enjoy the return of spring, why should he be happy in a labor-saving Utopia[3]? What will he do with the leisure that the machine will give him? I have always suspected that if our economic and political problems are ever really solved, life will become simpler instead of more complex, and that the sort of pleasure one gets from finding the first primrose will loom larger than the sort of pleasure one gets

---

1 political quietism: 寂静主义，指基督教神秘主义的一种形式，主张消极的冥思和精神的平和，指政治上的无为思想。

2 Georgian: 乔治王时代艺术风格的。乔治王时代指 1714 年到 1830 年连续四位乔治王统治英国的时期，适逢英国工业革命时期。

3 a labour-saving Utopia: 一个无须劳动的理想国

Chapter 12

George Orwell
乔治·奥威尔

from eating an ice to the tune of a Wurlitzer[1]. I think that by retaining one's childhood love of such things as trees, fishes, butterflies and—to return to my first instance—toads, one makes a peaceful and decent future a little more probable, and that by preaching the doctrine that nothing is to be admired except steel and concrete, one merely makes it a little surer that human beings will have no outlet for their surplus energy except in hatred and leader worship.

At any rate, spring is here, even in London N.1[2], and they can't stop you enjoying it. This is a satisfying reflection. How many a time have I stood watching the toads mating, or a pair of hares having a boxing match in the young corn, and thought of all the important persons who as you are not actually ill, hungry, frightened or immured in a prison or a holiday camp, spring is still spring. The atom bombs are piling up in the factories, the police are prowling through the cities, the lies are streaming from the loudspeakers, but the earth is still going round the sun, and neither the dictators nor the bureaucrats, deeply as they disapprove of the process, are able to prevent it.

1 Words and Phrases

shudder ['ʃʌdə]	n.	an involuntary vibration (as if from illness or fear) 发抖, 战栗; 震动
languid ['læŋgwɪd]	adj.	lacking spirit or liveliness 倦怠的, 呆滞的
chrysoberyl [krɪsə'berɪl]	n.	a rare hard yellow green mineral consisting of beryllium aluminate in crystal form; used as a gemstone 金绿玉
clasp [klɑːsp]	v.	hold firmly and tightly 紧抱, 扣紧
spawn [spɔːn]	n.	the mass of eggs deposited by fish or amphibians or molluscs 卵

---

1 Wurlitzer: 美国最大的乐器制造商之一
2 London N.1: 伦敦北一区

reed [ri:d]	n.	tall woody perennial grasses with hollow slender stems especially of the genera Arundo and Phragmites 芦苇
tadpole ['tædpəʊl]	n.	a larval frog or toad 蝌蚪
reptile ['reptaɪl]	n.	any cold-blooded vertebrate of the class Reptilia including tortoises, turtles, snakes, lizards, alligators, crocodiles and extinct forms 爬行动物
amphibian [æm'fɪbɪən]	n.	cold-blooded vertebrate typically living on land but breeding in water; aquatic larvae undergo metamorphosis into adult form 两栖动物
sordid ['sɔ:dɪd]	adj.	foul and run-down and repulsive 肮脏的，污秽的
kestrel ['kestr(ə)l]	n.	small North American falcon 茶隼；小鹰
gasworks ['gæswɜ:ks]	n.	a factory for making gas from coal 煤气厂
radius ['reɪdɪəs]	n.	the length of a line segment between the center and circumference of a circle or sphere 半径
seep [si:p]	v.	pass gradually or leak through or as if through small openings 漏，渗出
sooty ['sʊtɪ]	adj.	of the blackest black; similar to the color of jet or coal 乌黑的；煤烟熏黑的
privet ['prɪvɪt]	n.	any of various Old World shrubs having smooth entire leaves and terminal panicles of small white flowers followed by small black berries; many used for hedges 水蜡树；女贞
fishmonger ['fɪʃmʌŋgə]	n.	someone who sells fish 鱼贩，鱼商
reprehensible [reprɪ'hensɪbl]	adj.	bringing or deserving severe rebuke or censure 应斥责的，应该谴责的
elm [elm]	n.	any of various trees of the genus Ulmus: important timber or shade trees 榆树

Chapter 12

George Orwell
乔治·奥威尔

II Reading Comprehension Questions

1. Among all the lovely things in spring, why does the author take a special interest in the common toad?
2. How do you understand the following sentence: "Every February since 1940 I have found myself thinking that this time winter is going to be permanent"? Can we understand it literally?
3. Why do people think that any pleasure in the actual process of life encourages a sort of political quietism? Do you agree to it or not?
4. What do you think is the theme of this essay?
5. This essay and D.H. Lawrence's *Whistling of Birds* are both eulogies to nature and spring. Can you make a comparison between the two essays in terms of theme and writing style?

III Questions on Writing Style and Language

1. The first paragraph used a series of short clauses to describe the coming of Spring. What is the stylistic function of the use of these short clauses?
2. Why does the author mention the spawning of the toadsin the third paragraph? What is the function of it in terms of text organization?
3. Can you find uses of simile in the essay? What are the effects of using this rhetorical device?
4. Can you find uses of parallel structure in the essay? What are the effects of using this rhetorical device?
5. Orwell's style is characterized by a perfect combination of political argument and artistic aesthetics. Can you use this essay to analyze this feature?

Reflections on Gandhi

George Orwell

Saints should always be judged guilty until they are proved innocent, but the tests that have to be applied to them are not, of course, the same in all cases. In Gandhi's case the questions one feels inclined to ask are: to what extent was Gandhi moved by vanity—by the consciousness of himself as a humble, naked old man, sitting on a praying mat and shaking empires by sheer spiritual power—and to what extent did he compromise his own principles by entering politics, which of their nature are inseparable from **coercion** and fraud? To give a definite answer one would have to study Gandhi's acts and writings in immense detail, for his whole life was a sort of **pilgrimage** in which every act was significant. But this partial autobiography, which ends in the nineteen-twenties, is strong evidence in his favor, all the more because it covers what he would have called the unregenerate part of his life and reminds one that inside the saint, or near-saint, there was a very shrewd, able person who could, if he had chosen, have been a brilliant success as a lawyer, an administrator or perhaps even a businessman.

At about the time when the autobiography first appeared I remember reading its opening chapters in the ill-printed pages of some Indian newspaper. They made a good impression on me, which Gandhi himself at that time did not. The things that one associated with him—home-spun cloth, "soul forces" and vegetarianism—were unappealing, and his medievalist program was obviously not viable in a backward, starving, over-populated country. It was also apparent that the British were making use of him, or thought they were making use of him. Strictly speaking, as a Nationalist, he was an enemy, but since in every crisis he would exert himself to prevent violence—which, from the British point of view, meant preventing any effective action whatever—

Chapter 12
George Orwell
乔治·奥威尔

he could be regarded as "our man". In private this was sometimes cynically admitted. The attitude of the Indian millionaires was similar. Gandhi called upon them to repent, and naturally they preferred him to the Socialists and Communists who, given the chance, would actually have taken their money away. How reliable such calculations are in the long run is doubtful; as Gandhi himself says, "in the end deceivers deceive only themselves"; but at any rate the gentleness with which he was nearly always handled was due partly to the feeling that he was useful. The British Conservatives only became really angry with him when, as in 1942, he was in effect turning his non-violence against a different conqueror.

But I could see even then that the British officials who spoke of him with a mixture of amusement and disapproval also genuinely liked and admired him, after a fashion. Nobody ever suggested that he was corrupt, or ambitious in any vulgar way, or that anything he did was actuated by fear or **malice**. In judging a man like Gandhi one seems instinctively to apply high standards, so that some of his virtues have passed almost unnoticed. For instance, it is clear even from the autobiography that his natural physical courage was quite outstanding: the manner of his death was a later illustration of this, for a public man who attached any value to his own skin would have been more adequately guarded. Again, he seems to have been quite free from that **maniacal** suspiciousness which, as E. M. Forster rightly says in *A Passage to India*, is the **besetting** Indian vice, as hypocrisy is the British vice. Although no doubt he was shrewd enough in detecting dishonesty, he seems wherever possible to have believed that other people were acting in good faith and had a better nature through which they could be approached. And though he came of a poor middle-class family, started life rather unfavorably, and was probably of unimpressive physical appearance, he was not afflicted by envy or by the feeling of inferiority. Color feeling when he first met it in its worst form in South Africa, seems rather to have astonished him. Even when he was fighting what was in effect a color war, he did not think of people in terms of race or status. The governor of a province, a cotton millionaire, a half-starved Dravidian **coolie**, a British private soldier were all equally human beings, to be approached in much the same way. It is noticeable that even in the worst possible circumstances, as in South Africa when he was making himself unpopular as the champion of the Indian community, he did not lack European friends.

Written in short lengths for newspaper **serialization**, the autobiography is not a literary masterpiece, but it is the more impressive because of the commonplaceness of much of its material. It is well to be reminded that Gandhi started out with the normal ambitions of a young Indian student and only adopted his extremist opinions by degrees and, in some cases, rather unwillingly. There was a time, it is interesting to learn, when he wore a top hat, took dancing lessons, studied French and Latin, went up the Eiffel Tower and even tried to learn the violin—all this was the idea of assimilating European civilization as throughly as possible. He was not one of those saints who are marked out by their phenomenal piety from childhood onwards, nor one of the other kind who forsake the world after sensational **debaucheries**. He makes full confession of the misdeeds of his youth, but in fact there is not much to confess. As a frontispiece to the book there is a photograph of Gandhi's possessions at the time of his death. The whole outfit could be purchased for about 5 pounds, and Gandhi's sins, at least his fleshly sins, would make the same sort of appearance if placed all in one heap. A few cigarettes, a few mouthfuls of meat, a few **annas pilfered** in childhood from the maidservant, two visits to a brothel (on each occasion he got away without "doing anything"), one narrowly escaped lapse with his landlady in Plymouth, one outburst of temper—that is about the whole collection. Almost from childhood onwards he had a deep earnestness, an attitude ethical rather than religious, but, until he was about thirty, no very definite sense of direction. His first entry into anything describable as public life was made by way of vegetarianism. Underneath his less ordinary qualities one feels all the time the solid middle-class businessmen who were his ancestors. One feels that even after he had abandoned personal ambition he must have been a resourceful, energetic lawyer and a hard-headed political organizer, careful in keeping down expenses, an **adroit** handler of committees and an indefatigable chaser

Chapter 12

George Orwell

乔治·奥威尔

of subscriptions. His character was an extraordinarily mixed one, but there was almost nothing in it that you can put your finger on and call bad, and I believe that even Gandhi's worst enemies would admit that he was an interesting and unusual man who enriched the world simply by being alive. Whether he was also a lovable man, and whether his teachings can have much for those who do not accept the religious beliefs on which they are founded, I have never felt fully certain.

Of late years it has been the fashion to talk about Gandhi as though he were not only sympathetic to the Western Left-wing movement, but were integrally part of it. **Anarchists** and **pacifists**, in particular, have claimed him for their own, noticing only that he was opposed to centralism and State violence and ignoring the other-worldly, anti-humanist tendency of his doctrines. But one should, I think, realize that Gandhi's teachings cannot **be squared with** the belief that Man is the measure of all things and that our job is to make life worth living on this earth, which is the only earth we have. They make sense only on the assumption that God exists and that the world of solid objects is an illusion to be escaped from. It is worth considering the disciplines which Gandhi imposed on himself and which—though he might not insist on every one of his followers observing every detail—he considered indispensable if one wanted to serve either God or humanity. First of all, no meat-eating, and if possible no animal food in any form. (Gandhi himself, for the sake of his health, had to compromise on milk, but seems to have felt this to be a **backsliding**.) No alcohol or tobacco, and no spices or **condiments** even of a vegetable kind, since food should be taken not for its own sake but solely in order to preserve one's strength. Secondly, if possible, no sexual intercourse. If sexual intercourse must happen, then it should be for the sole purpose of begetting children and presumably at long intervals. Gandhi himself, in his middle thirties, took the vow of brahmacharya[1], which means not only complete chastity but the elimination of sexual desire. This condition, it seems, is difficult to attain without a special diet and frequent fasting. One of the

---

1 brahmacharya: literally means "going after Brahman (Supreme Reality, Self, God)". In Indian religions, Brahmacharya implies, among other things, mandatory renouncing of sex and marriage. It is considered necessary for a monk's spiritual practice.（婆罗门教的）禁欲；独身

dangers of milk-drinking is that it is apt to arouse sexual desire. And finally - this is the cardinal point—for the seeker after goodness there must be no close friendships and no exclusive loves whatever.

Close friendships, Gandhi says, are dangerous, because "friends react on one another" and through loyalty to a friend one can be led into wrong-doing. This is unquestionably true. Moreover, if one is to love God, or to love humanity as a whole, one cannot give one's preference to any individual person. This again is true, and it marks the point at which the humanistic and the religious attitude cease to be **reconcilable**. To an ordinary human being, love means nothing if it does not mean loving some people more than others. The autobiography leaves it uncertain whether Gandhi behaved in an inconsiderate way to his wife and children, but at any rate it makes clear that on three occasions he was willing to let his wife or a child die rather than administer the animal food prescribed by the doctor. It is true that the threatened death never actually occurred, and also that Gandhi—with, one gathers, a good deal of moral pressure in the opposite direction—always gave the patient the choice of staying alive at the price of committing a sin: still, if the decision had been solely his own, he would have forbidden the animal food, whatever the risks might be. There must, he says, be some limit to what we will do in order to remain alive, and the limit is well on this side of chicken broth. This attitude is perhaps a noble one, but, in the sense which—I think—most people would give to the word, it is inhuman. The essence of being human is that one does not seek perfection, that one is sometimes willing to commit sins for the sake of loyalty, that one does not push asceticism to the point where it makes friendly intercourse impossible, and that one is prepared in the end to be defeated and broken up by life, which is the inevitable price of fastening one's love upon other human individuals. No doubt alcohol, tobacco, and so forth, are things that a saint must avoid, but sainthood is also a thing that human beings must avoid. There is an obvious retort to this, but one should be wary about making it. In this yogi-ridden age, it is too readily assumed that "non-attachment" is not only better than a full acceptance of earthly life, but that the ordinary man only rejects it because it is too difficult:

Chapter 12
George Orwell
乔治·奥威尔

in other words, that the average human being is a failed saint. It is doubtful whether this is true. Many people genuinely do not wish to be saints, and it is probable that some who achieve or aspire to sainthood have never felt much temptation to be human beings. If one could follow it to its psychological roots, one would, I believe, find that the main motive for "non-attachment" is a desire to escape from the pain of living, and above all from love, which, sexual or non-sexual, is hard work. But it is not necessary here to argue whether the other-worldly or the humanistic ideal is "higher". The point is that they are incompatible. One must choose between God and Man, and all "radicals" and "progressives", from the mildest Liberal to the most extreme Anarchist, have in effect chosen Man.

However, Gandhi's pacifism can be separated to some extent from his other teachings. Its motive was religious, but he claimed also for it that it was a definitive technique, a method, capable of producing desired political results. Gandhi's attitude was not that of most Western pacifists. Satyagraha, first evolved in South Africa, was a sort of non-violent warfare, a way of defeating the enemy without hurting him and without feeling or arousing hatred. It entailed such things as civil disobedience, strikes, lying down in front of railway trains, enduring police charges without running away and without hitting back, and the like. Gandhi objected to "passive resistance" as a translation of Satyagraha: in Gujarati, it seems, the word means "firmness in the truth." In his early days Gandhi served as a stretcher-bearer on the British side in the Boer War, and he was prepared to do the same again in the war of 1914–1918. Even after he had completely **abjured** violence he was honest enough to see that in war it is usually necessary to take sides. He did not—indeed, since his whole political life centred round a struggle for national independence, he could not—take the sterile and dishonest line of pretending that in every war both sides are exactly the same and it makes no difference who wins. Nor did he, like most Western pacifists, specialize in avoiding awkward questions. In relation to the late war, one question that every pacifist had a clear obligation to answer was: "What about the Jews? Are you prepared to see them exterminated? If not, how do you propose to save them without resorting to war?" I must say that I have never heard, from any Western pacifist, an honest answer to this question, though I have heard plenty of evasions, usually of the "you're another" type. But it so happens that Gandhi was asked a somewhat similar question in 1938 and that his answer is on record in Mr. Louis Fischer's Gandhi and Stalin. According to Mr. Fischer, Gandhi's view was that the German Jews ought to commit collective suicide, which "would have aroused the world and the people of Germany to Hitler's violence." After the war he justified himself: the Jews had been killed anyway, and might as well have died significantly. One has the impression that this attitude staggered even so warm an admirer as Mr. Fischer, but Gandhi was merely being honest. If you are not prepared to take life, you must often be prepared for lives to be lost in some other way. When, in 1942, he urged non-violent resistance against a Japanese invasion, he was ready to admit that it might cost several million deaths.

At the same time there is reason to think that Gandhi, who after all was born in 1869, did not understand the nature of **totalitarianism** and saw everything in terms of his own struggle against the British government. The important point here is not so much that the British treated him forbearingly as that he was always able to command publicity. As can be seen from the phrase quoted above, he believed in "arousing the world", which is only possible if the world gets a chance to hear what you are doing. It is difficult to see how Gandhi's methods could be applied in a country where opponents of the regime disappear in the middle of the night and are never heard of again. Without a free press and the right of **assembly**, it is impossible not merely to appeal to outside opinion, but to bring a mass movement into being, or even to make your intentions known to your adversary. Is there a Gandhi in Russia at this moment? And if there is, what is he accomplishing? The Russian masses could only practise civil disobedience if the same idea happened to occur to all of them simultaneously, and even then, to judge by the history of the Ukraine famine, it would make no difference. But let it be granted that non-violent resistance can be effective against one's own government, or against an occupying power: even so, how does one put it into practise internationally? Gandhi's various conflicting statements on the late war seem to show that

Chapter 12

George Orwell
乔治·奥威尔

he felt the difficulty of this. Applied to foreign politics, pacifism either stops being pacifist or becomes appeasement. Moreover the assumption, which served Gandhi so well in dealing with individuals, that all human beings are more or less approachable and will respond to a generous gesture, needs to be seriously questioned. It is not necessarily true, for example, when you are dealing with lunatics. Then the question becomes: Who is sane? Was Hitler sane? And is it not possible for one whole culture to be insane by the standards of another? And, so far as one can gauge the feelings of whole nations, is there any apparent connection between a generous deed and a friendly response? Is gratitude a factor in international politics?

These and kindred questions need discussion, and need it urgently, in the few years left to us before somebody presses the button and the rockets begin to fly. It seems doubtful whether civilization can stand another major war, and it is at least thinkable that the way out lies through non-violence. It is Gandhi's virtue that he would have been ready to give honest consideration to the kind of question that I have raised above; and, indeed, he probably did discuss most of these questions somewhere or other in his innumerable newspaper articles. One feels of him that there was much he did not understand, but not that there was anything that he was frightened of saying or thinking. I have never been able to feel much liking for Gandhi, but I do not feel sure that as a political thinker he was wrong in the main, nor do I believe that his life was a failure. It is curious that when he was assassinated, many of his warmest admirers exclaimed sorrowfully that he had lived just long enough to see his life work in ruins, because India was engaged in a civil war which had always been foreseen as one of the byproducts of the transfer of power. But it was not in trying to smooth down Hindu-Moslem rivalry that Gandhi had spent his life. His main political objective, the peaceful ending of British rule, had after all been attained. As usual the relevant facts cut across one another. On the other hand, the British did get out of India without fighting, and event which very few observers indeed would have predicted until about a year before it happened. On the other hand, this was done by a Labour government, and it is certain that a Conservative government, especially a government headed by Churchill, would have acted differently. But if, by 1945, there had grown up in Britain a large body of opinion sympathetic to Indian independence, how far was this due to Gandhi's personal influence? And if, as may happen, India and Britain finally settle down into a decent and friendly relationship, will this be partly because Gandhi, by keeping up his struggle obstinately and without hatred, disinfected the political air? That one even thinks of asking such questions indicates his stature. One may feel, as I do, a sort of aesthetic distaste for Gandhi, one may reject the claims of sainthood made on his behalf (he never made any such claim himself, by the way), one may also reject sainthood as an ideal and therefore feel that Gandhi's basic aims were anti-human and reactionary: but regarded simply as a politician, and compared with the other leading political figures of our time, how clean a smell he has managed to leave behind!

I Words and Phrases

coercion [kəʊˈɜːʃn]	n.	the act of compelling by force of authority 高压政治；强迫，强制
pilgrimage [ˈpɪlɡrɪmɪdʒ]	n.	a journey to a sacred place 朝圣之旅
malice [ˈmælɪs]	n.	feeling a need to see others suffer 恶意；恶感；怨恨
maniacal [məˈnaɪəkl]	adj.	wildly disordered 发狂的；癫狂的
besetting [bɪˈsetɪŋ]	adj.	constantly present or attacking 不断攻击的
coolie [ˈkuːlɪ]	n.	an offensive name for an unskilled Asian labore 苦力；小工（尤指旧时印度、中国等的）当地非熟练工人
serialization [ˌsɪərɪəlaɪˈzeɪʃn]	n.	publication in serial form 连载长篇
debauchery [dɪˈbɔːtʃ(ə)rɪ]	n.	a wild gathering involving excessive drinking 放荡，淫逸
anna [ænə]	n.	a former copper coin of Pakistan 安那（巴基斯坦的旧铜币）

Chapter 12

George Orwell
乔治·奥威尔

pilfer ['pɪlfə]	v.	steal things that are usually not very valuable 偷窃（小东西）
adroit [ə'drɔɪt]	adj.	skillful (or showing skill) in adapting means to ends; quick or skillful or adept in action or thought 熟练的；机敏的；机巧；一把好手
anarchist ['ænəkɪst]	n.	a person who believes in anarchism 无政府主义者
pacifist ['pæsɪfɪst]	n.	a person who believes that violence is wrong and refuses to take part in wars 和平主义者；反战主义者
be squared with		be in accordance with 与……保持一致
backsliding ['bækslaɪdɪŋ]	n.	a failure to maintain a higher state 滑坡；倒退，退步；故态复萌
condiments ['kɒndɪmənt]	n.	a substance such as salt, pepper, or mustard that is added to food to improve the flavor 调味品，佐料
reconcilable [,rekən'saɪləbl]	adj.	capable of being reconciled 可和解的；可调和的
abjure [æb'dʒʊə]	v.	to renounce uponoath; to reject solemnly; to abstrain from 发誓放弃；宣布撤回（声明等）；避免
totalitarianism [təʊ,tælə'teərɪənɪzəm]	n.	a form of government in which the ruler is an absolute dictator (not restricted by a constitution or laws or opposition etc.) 极权主义
assembly [ə'semblɪ]	n.	a group of machine parts that fit together to form a self-contained unit; the act of constructing something (as a piece of machinery) 立法机构；议会；集会；装配

II Reading Comprehension Questions

1. Do you believe that "Saints should always be judged guilty until they are proved innocent"? How much do you know about Gandhi? Do you consider him as a saint?
2. What are the reasons for George Orwell's dislike of Gandhi at the beginning?
3. According to George Orwell, though the autobiography of Gandhi "is not a literary masterpiece, but it is the more impressive because of the commonplaceness of much of its material." Have you ever had similiar experiences reading biographic works?
4. Why is Russia cited as an example during the discussion?
5. Have you gained a better understanding of Gandhi after the reading? Can you summarize George Orwell's reflections on Gandhi in your own words?

Chapter 12

George Orwell
乔治·奥威尔

Quotes of the Author

All animals are equal but some animals are more equal than others.

The quickest way of ending a war is to lose it.

In certain kinds of writing, particularly in art criticism and literary criticism, it is normal to come across long passages which are almost completely lacking in meaning.

Every generation imagines itself to be more intelligent than the one that went before it, and wiser than the one that comes after it.

To see what is in front of one's nose needs a constant struggle.

PART II American Essays and Essayists

Benjamin Franklin
本杰明·富兰克林
(1706—1790)

本章导读

　　本杰明·富兰克林是北美启蒙运动的杰出代表，也是那个时代理性主义者最完美的体现。

　　富兰克林于 1706 年 1 月 17 日出生于北美洲波士顿。他的父亲是一个以做蜡烛和肥皂为生的工匠，生有 17 个孩子，富兰克林排行 15。由于家庭条件的不足，年轻的富兰克林没有像其他孩子一样接受正规的教育，而是零星地读了一些书。12 岁时，富兰克林就在哥哥詹姆斯经营的小印刷厂做学徒。在近十年的印刷工人生涯中，他从未中断过学习。富兰克林从伙食费中节省下钱买书，同时也通过几个书店朋友从书店偷偷借书来看。他的阅读范围很广，从自然科学技术方面的通俗读物到著名科学家的论文以及名作家的作品。

　　哥哥詹姆斯出版的《新英格兰周报》引发了富兰克林对新闻和文学的浓厚兴趣。当时只有 16 岁的他通过模仿英国文学期刊《旁观者》上的短文，形成了自己的行文风格，并用一个具有讽刺意味的笔名"寂寞的行善者"在该报发表了 14 篇文章，受到读者的欢迎。1723 年富兰克林离开了波士顿，分别到费城和英国印刷厂做工。1726 年他回到费城，凭借精湛的印刷技术开始独立经营印刷厂，印刷并发行了费城第一张报纸《宾夕法尼亚报》，并出版了《穷理查历书》，这本书当时被译成 12 种文字，行销欧美各国。《穷理查历书》中辑录的格言警句对北美人民价值观、道德观的形成起着重要作用。另外，他还发表了一些讽刺时事、促进社会进步和民族觉醒的"随感"，如《幸福论》《奸商论》《教育论》等。富兰克林于 1771 年开始到临终前创作了自传，他也是自传文体的开创者。《自传》总结了他个人奋斗的成功经验，体现了他作为一个启蒙主义者的思想观点和生活态度，《自传》被誉为"自我教育的

Chapter 13
Benjamin Franklin
本杰明·富兰克林

光辉范例""对千百万人都有教育意义",开创了美国传记文学的优秀传统。

富兰克林的语言表达简练生动,通俗易懂,却又不失内涵丰富的哲理和思想;结构精悍流畅,节奏紧凑,形式多样,多富有启发性和创造性;内容上充分体现了时代特色——启蒙思想和清教主义思想。他用启发式和探索式的行文,为读者提供了充分的思考空间。他的爱国热忱和关于自强、创业的言论和自力更生的精神,对于美国人民的人生观、价值观和道德观都产生了深远的影响。

About the Author

Benjamin Franklin was one of the founding fathers of the United States and in many ways was "the First American". A renowned polymath, Franklin was a leading author, printer, political theorist, politician, postmaster, scientist, inventor, civic activist, statesman, and diplomat. As a scientist, he was a major figure in the American Enlightenment and the history of physics for his discoveries and theories regarding electricity. As an inventor, he was known for the lightning rod, bifocals, and the Franklin stove, among other inventions. He facilitated many civic organizations, including Philadelphia's fire department and a university. Franklin was foundational in defining the American ethos as a marriage of the practical values of thrift, hard work, education, community spirit, self-governing institutions, and opposition to authoritarianism both political and religious, with the scientific and tolerant values of the Enlightenment.

In the field of Literature, Benjamin Franklin's reputation rested chiefly upon his two masterpieces, *The Autobiography* and *Poor Richard's Almanac*. *The Autobiography* reflects the author's unwavering resolution in self-study, self-cultivation, creation, research and tells of his fight for progress and public well-being.

In his *Autobiography*, Franklin describes how he used copies of *The Spectator* papers for imitation in forming his own standards of writing. Franklin's prose style is marked by clarity, concision, flexibility and order. Highly polished and graceful, his wiring is abound in wit, shrewdness, simplicity, and vigor of the plain speech of the people, as can be seen from the two essays followed.

Text A

The Way to Wealth
—Preface to *Poor Richard Improved*

Benjamin Franklin

Courteous Reader,

  I have heard that nothing gives an Author so great Pleasure, as to find his Works respectfully quoted by other learned Authors. This Pleasure I have seldom enjoyed; for tho' I have been, if I may say it without Vanity, an *eminent Author* of **Almanacks** annually now a full Quarter of a Century, my Brother Authors in the same Way, for what Reason I know not, have ever been very **sparing** in their Applauses; and no other Author has taken the least Notice of me, so that did not my Writings produce me some solid *Pudding*, the great Deficiency of *Praise* would have quite discouraged me.

  I concluded at length, that the People were the best Judges of my Merit; for they buy my Works; and besides, in my Rambles, where I am not personally known, I have frequently heard one or other of my **Adages** repeated, with, *as Poor Richard says*, at the End on't; this gave me some Satisfaction, as it showed not only that my Instructions were regarded, but discovered likewise some Respect for my Authority; and I own, that to encourage the Practice of remembering and repeating those wise Sentences, I have sometimes *quoted myself* with great Gravity.

  Judge then how much I must have been gratified by an Incident I am going to relate to you. I stopt my Horse lately where a great Number of People were collected at a **Vendue** of Merchant Goods. The Hour of Sale not being come, they were conversing on the Badness of the Times, and one of the Company call'd to a plain clean old Man, with white Locks, *Pray, Father*

Chapter 13

Benjamin Franklin
本杰明·富兰克林

Abraham, what think you of the Times? Won't these heavy Taxes quite ruin the Country? How shall we be ever able to pay them? What would you advise us to? —— Father Abraham stood up, and reply'd, If you'd have my Advice, I'll give it you in short, for *a Word to the Wise is enough,* and *many Words won't fill a Bushel,* as Poor Richard says. They join'd in desiring him to speak his Mind, and gathering round him, he proceeded as follows;

Friends, says he, and Neighbours, the Taxes are indeed very heavy, and if those laid on by the Government were the only Ones we had to pay, we might more easily discharge them; but we have many others, and much more **grievous** to some of us. We are taxed twice as much by our *Idleness,* three times as much by our *Pride,* and four times as much by our *Folly,* and from these Taxes the Commissioners cannot ease or deliver us by allowing an Abatement. However let us hearken to good Advice, and something may be done for us; *God helps them that help themselves,* as Poor Richard says, in his Almanack of 1733.

It would be thought a hard Government that should tax its People one tenth Part of their *Time,* to be employed in its Service. But *Idleness* taxes many of us much more, if we reckon all that is spent in absolute **Sloth**, or doing of nothing, with that which is spent in idle Employments or Amusements, that amount to nothing. *Sloth,* by bringing on Diseases, absolutely shortens Life. *Sloth, like Rust, consumes faster than Labour wears, while the used Key is always bright,* as Poor Richard says. But *dost thou love Life, then do not* **squander** *Time, for that's the Stuff Life is made of,* as Poor Richard says. How much more than is necessary do we spend in Sleep! forgetting that *The sleeping Fox catches no Poultry,* and that *there will be sleeping enough in the Grave,* as Poor Richard says. If Time be of all Things the most precious, *wasting Time* must be, as Poor Richard says, *the greatest* **Prodigality**, since, as he elsewhere tells us, *Lost Time is never found again;* and what we call *Time-enough, always proves little enough*: Let us then be up and be doing, and doing to the Purpose; so by Diligence shall we do more with less Perplexity. *Sloth makes all Things difficult, but Industry all easy,* as Poor Richard says; and *He that riseth late, must* **trot** *all Day, and shall scarce overtake his Business at Night.* While *Laziness travels so slowly, that Poverty soon* *overtakes him*, as we read in Poor Richard, who adds, *Drive thy Business, let not that drive thee*; and *Early to Bed, and early to rise, makes a Man healthy, wealthy and wise.*

So what signifies *wishing* and *hoping* for better Times. We may make these Times better if we **bestir** ourselves. *Industry need not wish*, as Poor Richard says, and *He that lives upon Hope will die fasting. There are no Gains, without Pains*; then *Help Hands, for I have no Lands*, or if I have, they are smartly taxed. And, as Poor Richard likewise observes, *He that hath a Trade hath an Estate*, and *He that hath a Calling hath an Office of Profit and Honour*; but then the *Trade* must be worked at, and the *Calling* well followed, or neither the *Estate*, nor the *Office*, will enable us to pay our Taxes. If we are industrious we shall never starve; for, as Poor Richard says, *At the working Man's House Hunger looks in, but dares not enter*. Nor will the **Bailiff** nor the Constable enter, for *Industry pays Debts, while Despair encreaseth them*, says Poor Richard. What though you have found no Treasure, nor has any rich Relation left you a Legacy, *Diligence is the Mother of Good luck*, as Poor Richard says, and *God gives all Things to Industry*. Then *plough deep, while* **Sluggards** *sleep, and you shall have Corn to sell and to keep*, says Poor Dick. Work while it is called To-day, for you know not how much you may be hindered To-morrow, which makes Poor Richard say, *One To-day is worth two Tomorrows*; and farther, *Have you somewhat to do To-morrow, do it To-day*. If you were a Servant, would you not be ashamed that a good Master should catch you idle? Are you then your own Master, *be ashamed to catch yourself idle*, as Poor Dick says. When there is so much to be done for yourself, your Family, your Country, and your gracious King, be up by Peep of Day; *Let not the Sun look down and say, Inglorious here he lies*. Handle your Tools without Mittens; remember that *the Cat in Gloves catches no Mice*, as Poor Richard says. 'Tis true there is much to be done, and perhaps you are weak handed, but stick to it steadily, and you will see great Effects, for *constant Dropping wears away Stones*, and by *Diligence and Patience the Mouse ate in two the Cable*; and *little Strokes fell great Oaks*, as Poor Richard says in his Almanack, the Year I cannot just now remember.

Methinks I hear some of you say, *Must a Man afford himself no Leisure?* I

Chapter 13

Benjamin Franklin
本杰明·富兰克林

will tell thee, my Friend, what Poor Richard says, *Employ thy Time well if thou meanest to gain Leisure*; and, *since thou art not sure of a Minute, throw not away an Hour*. Leisure, is Time for doing something useful; this Leisure the diligent Man will obtain, but the lazy Man never; so that, as Poor Richard says, *a Life of Leisure and a Life of Laziness are two Things*. Do you imagine that Sloth will afford you more Comfort than Labour? No, for as Poor Richard says, *Trouble springs from Idleness, and grievous Toil from needless Ease*. Many without Labour, would live by their WITS only, but they break for want of Stock. Whereas Industry gives Comfort, and Plenty, and Respect: *Fly Pleasures, and they'll follow you. The diligent Spinner has a large Shift*; and *now I have a Sheep and a Cow, every Body bids me Good morrow*; all which is well said by Poor Richard.

But with our Industry, we must likewise be *steady, settled* and *careful*, and oversee our own Affairs *with our own Eyes*, and not trust too much to others; for, as Poor Richard says,

> *I never saw an oft removed Tree,*
> *Nor yet an oft removed Family,*
> *That throve so well as those that settled be.*

And again, *Three Removes is as bad as a Fire*; and again, *Keep thy Shop, and thy Shop will keep thee*; and again, *If you would have your Business done, go; If not, send*. And again,

> *He that by the Plough would thrive,*
> *Himself must either hold or drive.*

And again, *The Eye of a Master will do more Work than both his Hands*; and again, *Want of Care does us more Damage than Want of Knowledge*; and again, *Not to oversee Workmen, is to leave them your Purse open*. Trusting too much to others Care is the Ruin of many; for, as the Almanack says, *In the Affairs of this World, Men are saved, not by Faith, but by the Want of it*; but a Man's own Care is profitable; for, saith Poor Dick, *Learning is to the Studious*, and *Riches to the Careful*, as well as *Power to the Bold*, and *Heaven to the Virtuous*. And farther, *If you would have a faithful Servant, and one that you like, serve yourself*. And again, he adviseth to **Circumspection** and Care, even in the smallest Matters, because sometimes *a little Neglect may breed great Mischief*; adding, *For want of a*

Nail the Shoe was lost; for want of a Shoe the Horse was lost; and for want of a Horse the Rider was lost, being overtaken and slain by the Enemy, all for want of Care about a Horse-shoe Nail.

So much for Industry, my Friends, and Attention to one's own Business; but to these we must add **Frugality**, if we would make our *Industry* more certainly successful. A Man may, if he knows not how to save as he gets, *keep his Nose all his Life to the Grindstone*, and die not worth a *Groat* at last. *A fat Kitchen makes a lean Will*, as Poor Richard says; and,

> *Many Estates are spent in the Getting,*
> *Since Women for Tea forsook Spinning and Knitting,*
> *And Men for Punch forsook Hewing and Splitting.*

If you would be wealthy, says he, in another Almanack, *think of Saving as well as of Getting: The Indies have not made Spain rich, because her* Outgoes *are greater than her* Incomes. Away then with your expensive Follies, and you will not have so much Cause to complain of hard Times, heavy Taxes, and chargeable Families; for, as Poor Dick says,

> *Women and Wine, Game and Deceit,*
> *Make the Wealth small, and the Wants great.*

And farther, *What maintains one Vice, would bring up two Children.* You may think perhaps, That a *little* Tea, or a *little* Punch now and then, Diet a *little* more costly, Clothes a *little* finer, and a *little* Entertainment now and then, can be no *great* Matter; but remember what Poor Richard says, *Many* a Little *makes a Mickle*; and farther, *Beware of* little *Expences; a small Leak will sink a great Ship*; and again, *Who Dainties love, shall Beggars prove*; and moreover, *Fools make Feasts, and wise Men eat them.*

Here you are all got together at this Vendue of *Fineries* and *Knicknacks*. You call them *Goods*, but if you do not take Care, they will prove *Evils* to some of you. You expect they will be sold *cheap*, and perhaps they may for less than they cost; but if you have no Occasion for them, they must be *dear* to you. Remember what Poor Richard says, *Buy what thou hast no Need of, and ere long thou shalt sell thy Necessaries.* And again, *At a great Pennyworth pause a while:* He means, that perhaps the Cheapness is *apparent* only, and not *real*;

Chapter 13

Benjamin Franklin
本杰明·富兰克林

or the Bargain, by straitning thee in thy Business, may do thee more Harm than Good. For in another Place he says, *Many have been ruined by buying good Pennyworths*. Again, Poor Richard says, *'Tis foolish to lay out Money in a Purchase of Repentance*; and yet this Folly is practised every Day at Vendues, for want of minding the Almanack. *Wise Men*, as Poor Dick says, *learn by others Harms, Fools scarcely by their own*; but, *Felix quem faciunt aliena Pericula cautum*. Many a one, for the Sake of Finery on the Back, have gone with a hungry Belly, and half starved their Families; *Silks and Sattins, Scarlet and Velvets*, as Poor Richard says, *put out the Kitchen Fire*. These are not the *Necessaries* of Life; they can scarcely be called the *Conveniencies*, and yet only because they look pretty, how many *want* to *have* them. The *artificial* Wants of Mankind thus become more numerous than the *natural*; and, as Poor Dick says, *For one* poor *Person, there are an hundred* indigent. By these, and other Extravagancies, the Genteel are reduced to Poverty, and forced to borrow of those whom they formerly despised, but who through *Industry* and *Frugality* have maintained their Standing; in which Case it appears plainly, that a *Ploughman on his Legs is higher than a Gentleman on his Knees*, as Poor Richard says. Perhaps they have had a small Estate left them, which they knew not the Getting of; they think 'tis Day, and will never be Night; that a little to be spent out of *so much*, is not worth minding; (*a Child and a Fool*, as Poor Richard says, *imagine Twenty Shillings and Twenty Years can never be spent*) but, *always taking out of the Meal-tub, and never putting in, soon comes to the Bottom*; then, as Poor Dick says, *When the Well's dry, they know the Worth of Water*. But this they might have known before, if they had taken his Advice; *If you would know the Value of Money, go and try to borrow some*; for, *he that goes a borrowing goes a sorrowing*; and indeed so does he that lends to such People, when he goes *to get it in again*. Poor Dick farther advises, and says,

        Fond Pride of Dress, *is sure a very Curse*;
        E'er Fancy *you consult, consult your Purse.*

And again, *Pride is as loud a Beggar as Want, and a great deal more saucy.* When you have bought one fine Thing you must buy ten more, that your Appearance may be all of a Piece; but Poor Dick says, *'Tis easier to* suppress *the* first Desire, than to satisfy *all that follow it*. And 'tis as truly Folly for the Poor to ape the Rich, as for the Frog to swell, in order to equal the Ox.

Great Estates may venture more,
But little Boats should keep near Shore.

'Tis however a Folly soon punished; for *Pride that dines on Vanity sups on Contempt*, as Poor Richard says. And in another Place, *Pride breakfasted with Plenty, dined with Poverty, and supped with* **Infamy**. And after all, of what Use is this *Pride of Appearance*, for which so much is risked, so much is suffered? It cannot promote Health, or ease Pain; it makes no Increase of Merit in the Person, it creates Envy, it hastens Misfortune.

What is a Butterfly? At best
He's but a Caterpillar drest.
The gaudy Fop's his Picture just,

as Poor Richard says.

But what Madness must it be to *run in Debt* for these Superfluities! We are offered, by the Terms of this Vendue, *Six Months Credit*; and that perhaps has induced some of us to attend it, because we cannot spare the ready Money, and hope now to be fine without it. But, ah, think what you do when you run in Debt; *You give to another Power over your Liberty*. If you cannot pay at the Time, you will be ashamed to see your Creditor; you will be in Fear when you speak to him; you will make poor pitiful sneaking Excuses, and by Degrees come to lose your **Veracity**, and sink into base downright lying; for, as Poor Richard says, *The second Vice is Lying, the first is running in Debt*. And again, to the same Purpose, *Lying rides upon Debt's Back*. Whereas a freeborn Englishman ought not to be ashamed or afraid to see or speak to any Man living. But Poverty often deprives a Man of all Spirit and Virtue: *'Tis hard for an empty Bag to stand upright*, as Poor Richard truly says. What would you think of that Prince, or that Government, who should issue an **Edict** forbidding you to dress like a Gentleman or a Gentlewoman, on Pain of Imprisonment or Servitude? Would you not say, that you are free, have a Right to dress as you please, and that such an Edict would be a Breach of your Privileges, and such a Government tyrannical? And yet you are about to put yourself under that Tyranny when

Chapter 13
Benjamin Franklin
本杰明·富兰克林

you run in Debt for such Dress! Your Creditor has Authority at his Pleasure to deprive you of your Liberty, by confining you in Goal for Life, or to sell you for a Servant, if you should not be able to pay him! When you have got your Bargain, you may, perhaps, think little of Payment; but *Creditors*, Poor Richard tells us, *have better Memories than Debtors*; and in another Place says, *Creditors are a superstitious Sect, great Observers of set Days and Times*. The Day comes round before you are aware, and the Demand is made before you are prepared to satisfy it. Or if you bear your Debt in Mind, the Term which at first seemed so long, will, as it lessens, appear extreamly short. *Time* will seem to have added Wings to his Heels as well as Shoulders. *Those have a short Lent*, saith Poor Richard, *who owe Money to be paid at Easter*. Then since, as he says, *The Borrower is a Slave to the Lender, and the Debtor to the Creditor*, disdain the Chain, preserve your Freedom; and maintain your Independency: Be *industrious* and *free*; be *frugal* and *free*. At present, perhaps, you may think yourself in thriving Circumstances, and that you can bear a little Extravagance without Injury; but,

For Age and Want, save while you may;
No Morning Sun lasts a whole Day,

as Poor Richard says. Gain may be temporary and uncertain, but ever while you live, Expence is constant and certain; and *'tis easier to build two Chimnies than to keep one in Fuel*, as Poor Richard says. So *rather go to Bed supperless than rise in Debt*.

Get what you can, and what you get hold;
'Tis the Stone that will turn all your Lead into Gold,

as Poor Richard says. And when you have got the Philosopher's Stone, sure you will no longer complain of bad Times, or the Difficulty of paying Taxes.

This Doctrine, my Friends, is *Reason* and *Wisdom*; but after all, do not depend too much upon your own *Industry*, and *Frugality*, and *Prudence*, though excellent Things, for they may all be **blasted** without the Blessing of Heaven; and therefore ask that Blessing humbly, and be not uncharitable to those that at present seem to want it, but comfort and help them. Remember Job suffered, and was afterwards prosperous.

And now to conclude, *Experience keeps a dear School, but Fools will learn in no other, and scarce in that*; for it is true, *we may give Advice, but we cannot give Conduct*, as Poor Richard says: However, remember this, *They that won't be counselled, can't be helped*, as Poor Richard says: And farther, That *if you will not hear Reason, she'll surely rap your Knuckles.*

Thus the old Gentleman ended his **Harangue**. The People heard it, and approved the Doctrine, and immediately practised the contrary, just as if it had been a common Sermon; for the Vendue opened, and they began to buy extravagantly, notwithstanding all his Cautions, and their own Fear of Taxes. I found the good Man had thoroughly studied my Almanacks, and digested all I had dropt on those Topicks during the Course of Five-and-twenty Years. The frequent Mention he made of me must have tired any one else, but my Vanity was wonderfully delighted with it, though I was conscious that not a tenth Part of the Wisdom was my own which he ascribed to me, but rather the *Gleanings* I had made of the Sense of all Ages and Nations. However, I resolved to be the better for the Echo of it; and though I had at first determined to buy Stuff for a new Coat, I went away resolved to wear my old One a little longer. *Reader*, if thou wilt do the same, thy Profit will be as great as mine. I am, as ever, Thine to serve thee,

Richard Saunders

July 7, 1757

I Words and Phrases

almanac ['ɔːlmənæk]	n.	a book published every year that contains information about events connected with a particular subject or activity, and facts and statistics about that activity 年鉴
sparing ['speərɪŋ]	adj.	using or giving only in very small quantities 节约的

Chapter 13
Benjamin Franklin
本杰明·富兰克林

adage ['ædɪdʒ]	n.	a condensed but memorable saying embodying some important fact of experience that is taken as true by many people 格言；谚语
vendue [ven'djuː]	n.	the public sale of something to the highest bidder 公开拍卖
grievous ['griːvəs]	adj.	causing fear or anxiety by threatening great harm 痛苦的；剧烈的
sloth [sləʊθ]	n.	a disinclination to work or exert oneself 懒惰
squander ['skwɒndə]	v.	spend extravagantly 浪费
prodigality [prɒdɪ'gælətɪ]	n.	the trait of spending extravagantly 浪费
trot [trɒt]	v.	run at a moderately swift pace 小跑；快步走
bestir [bɪ'stɜː]	v.	make become active 激励
bailiff ['beɪlɪf]	n.	an officer of the court who is employed to execute writs, processes and make arrests etc. 法警；执行官
sluggard ['slʌgəd]	n.	an idle slothful person 懒鬼，偷懒者
circumspection [səːkəm'spekʃən]	n.	the trait of being circumspect and prudent 慎重；细心
frugality [fruː'gælɪtɪ]	n.	prudence in avoiding waste 节省，节俭
infamy ['ɪnfəmɪ]	n.	evil fame or public reputation 声名狼藉；恶行
veracity [və'ræsətɪ]	n.	unwillingness to tell lies 诚实，老实
edict ['iːdɪkt]	n.	a formal or authoritative proclamation 布告
blast [blɑːst]	v.	hit hard 损害；使枯萎
harangue [hə'ræŋ]	n.	a loud bombastic declamation expressed with strong emotion 长篇大论

II Reading Comprehension Questions

1. According to the author, what is the incident he encountered at a vendee one day by which he was greatly gratified?
2. According to Poor Richard, what's Father Abraham's advice on people's complaint about heavy taxes?
3. Poor Richard says "Poverty often deprives a man of all spirit and virtue", do you agree to it?
4. Besides industry, what are some other virtues Poor Richard advocated in this essay?
5. Among all the teachings by Poor Richard, which one is most enlightening to you? Please give your reasons.

III Questions on Writing Style and Language

1. Have you noticed any stylistic features of Benjamin Franklin's writing? Are his sentences long or short? What particular effect is produced by these sentences?
2. Do you think Franklin's writing old fashioned by contemporary standards? Could you make a comparison between Franklin and some contemporary writers?
3. *Poor Richard's Almanac* is full of maxims which the author collected from various sources. Can you find some from the text and try to remember?
4. Franklin has a great gift for pungency and imagery. Can you make an analysis of his pungency and imagery on this text?
5. What do you think is the role of Father Abraham? How does the author convey his ideas through this figure?

Chapter 13

Benjamin Franklin
本杰明·富兰克林

The Art of Procuring Pleasant Dreams

As a great part of our life is spent in sleep, during which we have sometimes pleasant and sometimes painful dreams, it becomes of some consequence to obtain the one kind and avoid the other; for whether real or imaginary, pain is pain and pleasure is pleasure. If we can sleep without dreaming, it is well that painful dreams are avoided. If, while we sleep, we can have any pleasant dreams, it is, as the French say, autant de gagné, so much added to the pleasure of life.

To this end it is, in the first place, necessary to be careful in preserving health by due exercise and great **temperance**; for in sickness the imagination is disturbed, and disagreeable, sometimes terrible, ideas are apt to present themselves. Exercise should **precede** meals, not immediately follow them; the first promotes, the latter, unless moderate, **obstructs** digestion. If, after exercise, we feed **sparingly**, the digestion will be easy and good, the body lightsome, the temper cheerful, and all the animal functions performed agreeably. Sleep, when it follows, will be natural and undisturbed, while **indolence**, with full feeding, **occasions** nightmares and horrors inexpressible; we fall from **precipices**, are assaulted by wild beasts, murderers, and demons, and experience every variety of distress. Observe, however, that the quantities of food and exercise are relative things: those who move much may, and indeed ought to, eat more; those who use little exercise should eat little. In general, mankind, since the improvement of cookery, eats about twice as much as nature requires. Suppers are not bad if we have not dined; but restless nights follow hearty suppers after full dinners. Indeed, as there is a difference in constitutions, some rest well after these meals; it costs them only a frightful dream and an **apoplexy**, after which they sleep till doomsday. Nothing is more common in the newspapers than instances of people who, after eating a hearty supper, are found dead abed in the morning.

Another means of preserving health to be attended to is the having a constant supply of fresh air in your bedchamber. It has been a great mistake, the sleeping in rooms exactly closed and the beds surrounded by curtains. No outward air that may come in to you is so unwholesome as the unchanged air, often breathed, of a close chamber. As boiling water does not grow hotter by long boiling if the **particles** that receive greater heat can escape, so living bodies do not **putrefy** if the particles, so fast as they become putrid, can be thrown off. Nature expels them by the pores of the skin and lungs, and in a free, open air they are carried off; but in a close room we receive them again and again, though they become more and more corrupt. A number of persons crowded into a small room thus spoil the air in a few minutes, and even render it mortal as the Black Hole at Calcutta. A single person is said to spoil only a gallon of air per minute, and therefore requires a longer time to spoil a chamberful; but it is done, however, in proportion, and many putrid disorders hence have their origin. It is recorded of Methuselah, who, being the longest liver, may be supposed to have best preserved his health, that he slept always in the open air; for when he had lived five hundred years an angel said to him: "Arise, Methuselah, and build thee an house, for thou shalt live yet five hundred years longer." But Methuselah answered and said: "If I am to live but five hundred years longer, it is not worthwhile to build me an house; I will sleep in the air, as I have been used to do." Physicians, after having for ages **contended** that the sick should not be indulged with fresh air, have at length discovered that it may do them good. It is therefore to be hoped that they may in time discover likewise that it is not hurtful to those who are in health, and that we may then be cured of the **aerophobia** that at present distresses weak minds, and makes them choose to be **stifled** and poisoned rather than leave open the window of a bedchamber or put down the glass of a coach.

Confined air, when **saturated** with perspirable matter, will not receive more, and that matter must remain in our bodies and occasion diseases; but it gives us some previous notice of its being about to be hurtful by producing certain uneasiness, slight indeed at first, such as with regard to the lungs is

Chapter 13

Benjamin Franklin
本杰明·富兰克林

a **trifling** sensation and to the pores of the skin a kind of restlessness which is difficult to describe, and few that feel it know the cause of it. But we may **recollect** that sometimes, on waking in the night, we have, if warmly covered, found it difficult to get asleep again. We turn often, without finding repose in any position. This **fidgetiness** (to use a vulgar expression for want of a better) is occasioned wholly by uneasiness in the skin, owing to the **retention** of the perspirable matter, the bedclothes having received their quantity, and being saturated, refusing to take any more. To become sensible of this by an experiment, let a person keep his position in the bed, throw off the bedclothes, and suffer fresh air to approach the part uncovered of his body; he will then feel that part suddenly refreshed, for the air will immediately relieve the skin by receiving, licking up, and carrying off the load of perspirable matter that approaches the warm skin, in receiving its part of that vapor, receives therewith a degree of heat that rarefies and renders it lighter, by cooler and therefore heavier fresh air, which for a moment supplies its place, and then, being likewise changed and warmed, gives way to a succeeding quantity.

Here, then, is one great and general cause of unpleasing dreams. For when the body is uneasy the mind will be disturbed by it, and disagreeable ideas of various kinds will in sleep be the natural consequences. The remedies, preventive and curative, follow.

1. By eating moderately (as before advised for health's sake) less perspirable matter is produced in a given time; hence the bedclothes receive it longer before they are saturated, and we may therefore sleep longer before we are made uneasy by their refusing to receive any more.

2. By using thinner and more porous bedclothes, which will suffer the perspirable matter more easily to pass through them, we are less incommoded, such being longer tolerable.

3. When you are awakened by this uneasiness and find you cannot easily sleep again, get out of bed, beat up and turn your pillow, shake the bedclothes well, with at least twenty shakes, then throw the bed open and leave it to cool; in the meanwhile, continuing undressed, walk about your chamber till your skin has had time to discharge its load, which it will do sooner as the air may

be dryer and colder. When you begin to feel the cold air unpleasant, then return to your bed and you will soon fall asleep, and your sleep will be sweet and pleasant. All the scenes presented to your fancy will be, too, of a pleasing kind. I am often as agreeably entertained with them as by the scenery of an opera. If you happen to be too indolent to get out of bed, you may, instead of it, lift up your bedclothes with one arm and leg, so as to draw in a good deal of fresh air, and by letting them fall force it out again. This, repeated twenty times, will so clear them of the perspirable matter they have imbibed as to permit your sleeping well for some time afterward. But this latter method is not equal to the former.

Those who do not love trouble and can afford to have two beds will find great luxury in rising, when they wake in a hot bed, and going into the cool one. Such shifting of beds would also be of great service to persons ill of a fever, as it refreshes and frequently procures sleep. A very large bed that will admit a removal so distant from the first situation as to be cool and sweet may in a degree answer the same end.

One or two observations more will conclude this little piece. Care must be taken, when you lie down, to dispose your pillow so as to suit your manner of placing your head and to be perfectly easy; then place your limbs so as not to bear inconveniently hard upon one another, as, for instance, the joints of your ankles; for though a bad position may at first give but little pain and be hardly noticed, yet a continuance will render it less tolerable, and the uneasiness may come on while you are asleep and disturb your imagination. These are the rules of the art. But though they will generally prove effectual in producing the end intended, there is a case in which the most punctual observance of them will be totally fruitless. I need not mention the case to you, my dear friend; but my account of the art would be imperfect without it. The case is when the person who desires to have pleasant dreams has not taken care to preserve, what is necessary above all things,

A GOOD CONSCIENCE. (1786)

Chapter 13
Benjamin Franklin
本杰明·富兰克林

I Words and Phrases

temperance ['tempərəns]	*n.*	the trait of avoiding excesses 节制
precede [prɪ'siːd]	*v.*	be earlier in time; go back further 在……之前发生
obstruct [əb'strʌkt]	*v.*	hinder or prevent the progress or accomplishment of 妨碍
sparingly ['speərɪŋli]	*adv.*	to a meager degree or in a meager manner 节俭地
indolence ['ɪndələns]	*n.*	inactivity resulting from a dislike of work 懒惰
occasion [ə'keɪʒ(ə)n]	*v.*	bring something about 引起
precipice ['presɪpɪs]	*n.*	high cliff or crag 悬崖
apoplexy ['æpəpleksɪ]	*n.*	stroke caused by brain hemorrhage 中风
particle ['pɑːtɪk(ə)l]	*n.*	unit or element 颗粒
putrefy ['pjuːtrɪfaɪ]	*v.*	decay; spoil 腐烂
contend [kən'tend]	*v.*	to argue or claim that something is true 主张
aerophobia [ˌeərə'fəʊbɪə]	*n.*	fear or strong dislike of flying high; strong dislike of fresh air 恐高症；新鲜空气恐怖症
stifle ['staɪf(ə)l]	*v.*	kill by depriving of air 使窒息
confined [kən'faɪnd]	*adj.*	small, cramped, and completely enclosed 幽闭的
saturate ['sætʃəreɪt]	*v.*	fill completely with something 使饱和
trifling ['traɪflɪŋ]	*adj.*	small and unimportant; not worth considering 微不足道的
recollect [ˌrekə'lekt]	*v.*	recall knowledge from memory 回想起
fidgetiness ['fɪdʒɪtnɪs]	*n.*	a feeling of agitation expressed in continual motion 烦躁不安
retention [rɪ'tenʃ(ə)n]	*n.*	the act of keeping in your possession 滞留

II Reading Comprehension Questions

1. Have you had dreadful dreams or insomnia? Please describe your experiences.
2. According to the author, what's the relationship between preserving health and procuring pleasant dreams?
3. What's the advice given by the author for preserving health? Consider which recommendations may still be worth heeding in our own time.
4. What's the meaning of the last sentence in the essay?
5. As you read Frankline's suggestions, can you find any similarities between his advice and some principles and customs embeded in our culture related to having pleasant sleeps? Please talk about the commonalities and differeces.

Chapter 13
Benjamin Franklin
本杰明·富兰克林

Quotes of the Author

A countryman between two lawyers is like a fish between two cats.

A slip of the foot you may soon recover, but a slip of the tongue you may never get over.

All human situations have their inconveniences. We feel those of the present but neither see nor feel those of the future; and hence we often make troublesome changes without amendment, and frequently for the worse.

All would live long, but none would be old.

Washington Irving
华盛顿·欧文
(1783—1859)

Chapter 14

本章导读

华盛顿·欧文（1783—1859）是美国第一位获得国际声誉的作家，以随笔和短篇小说见长。他的《见闻札记》是美国第一部闻名世界的文学作品。在美国文学史上，欧文无疑占有重要的地位。美国的浪漫主义文学从一开始便具有许多特点，它所表达的是一种建立在一个全新的国家基础上的经历与精神。因此，许多美国作家开始以自己独特的文化环境作为创作源泉，在美国这个新的舞台上描绘与欧洲"旧世界"不同的新文学。欧文正是美国浪漫主义文学真正意义上的开端。《见闻札记》是欧文1819年至1820年间发表的34篇散文、随笔和短篇故事的合集，于1820年出版。其中《里普·范·温克尔》和《睡谷传说》是最为出名的作品，其他文章也很好地体现了欧文的散文创作水平。其中大部分作品是作者在英国时对英国风土人情所作的记录。《圣诞节》《平安夜》《圣诞日》《圣诞晚宴》《驿车》等文对英国圣诞节习俗进行了全面的展示；《英国的乡村生活》《乡村教堂》《乡葬巡礼》等文真实地再现了英国乡村的风情。欧文标志性的流畅而清新的文风在他描写景物、记录风俗时体现得尤为明显。不同于以往美国散文的是，欧文尽量减少了作品中的说教意味，并还原了散文的本色，将眼前一景一物结合自己天马行空的想象展现在读者面前，并抒发自己的感想，使文章富于哲理，这一点在欧文许多描写乡村的文章里得到了充分的体现。欧文的行文结构则如行云流水一般自然而畅达。在写景抒情的文章里，欧文仿佛手捧摄像机，用镜头向读者展现他所看到的每个细节，然后在其间不时露出脸来，向读者倾诉他的沉思和感受。阅读欧文的散文，读者一定会被他文字中流淌的自然、优雅气息所打动。

Chapter 14
Washington Irving
华盛顿·欧文

About the Author

Washington Irving (April 3, 1783–November 28, 1859) was the first great prose stylist of American romanticism. Familiar essayist, short story writer biographer, historian, and diplomat of the early 19th century, Irving is sometimes called the Father of American literature because he was the first American author to win international recognition.

Born into a successful New York merchant, Irving was trained as a lawyer at an early age. But he like literature better and amused himself by writing for periodicals. He made his literary debut in 1802 with a series of observational letters to the *Morning Chronicle*, written under the pseudonym Jonathan Oldstyle. After moving to England for the family business in 1815, he achieved international fame with the publication of *The Sketch Book of Geoffrey Crayon, Gent.* in 1819–1820. He continued to publish regularly—and almost always successfully—throughout his life, and completed a five-volume biography of George Washington just eight months before his death, at age 76, in Tarrytown, New York. Irving served as the U.S. ambassador to Spain from 1842 to 1846.

Irving was the first American writer of imaginative literature to gain international fame. His writings are usually classical in form though romantic in subjects. Master of a graceful and unobtrusively sophisticated prose style, Irving excels in writing gentle, refined, lucid and beautiful language. It was regarded as a model of English and American prose throughout the nineteenth century.

Text A

Old Christmas

Washington Irving

There is nothing in England that exercises a more delightful spell over my imagination than the lingerings of the holiday customs and rural games of former times. They recall the pictures my fancy used to draw in the May morning of life, when as yet I only knew the world through books, and believed it to be all that poets had painted it; and they bring with them the flavor of those honest days of **yore**, in which, perhaps with equal fallacy, I am apt to think the world was more home-bred, social, and joyous than at present. I regret to say that they are daily growing more and more faint, being gradually worn away by time, but still more obliterated by modern fashion. They resemble those picturesque **morsels** of Gothic architecture which we see crumbling in various parts of the country, partly **dilapidated** by the waste of ages, and partly lost in the additions and alterations of latter days. Poetry, however, clings with cherishing fondness about the rural game and holiday revel, from which it has derived so many of its themes,—as the ivy winds its rich foliage about the Gothic arch and mouldering tower, gratefully repaying their support by clasping together their tottering remains, and, as it were, embalming them in **verdure**.

Of all the old festivals, however, that of Christmas awakens the strongest and most heart felt associations. There is a tone of solemn and sacred feeling that blends with our **conviviality**, and lifts the spirit to a state of hallowed and elevated enjoyment. The services of the church about this season are extremely tender and inspiring. They dwell on the beautiful story of the origin of our faith, and the pastoral scenes that accompanied its announcement. They gradually increase in fervor and pathos during the season of Advent, until they break forth in full **jubilee** on the morning that

Chapter 14
Washington Irving
华盛顿·欧文

brought peace and good-will to men. I do not know a grander effect of music on the moral feelings than to hear the full choir and the pealing organ performing a Christmas anthem in a cathedral, and filling every part of the vast pile with triumphant harmony.

It is a beautiful arrangement, also derived from days of yore, that this festival, which commemorates the announcement of the religion of peace and love, has been made the season for gathering together of family connections, and drawing closer again those bands of kindred hearts which the cares and pleasures and sorrows of the world are continually operating to cast loose; of calling back the children of a family who have launched forth in life, and wandered widely **asunder**, once more to assemble about the paternal hearth, that rallying place of the affections, there to grow young and loving again among the endearing mementos of childhood.

There is something in the very season of the year that gives a charm to the festivity of Christmas. At other times we derive a great portion of our pleasures from the mere beauties of nature. Our feelings **sally forth** and dissipate themselves over the sunny landscape, and we "live abroad and everywhere". The song of the bird, the murmur of the stream, the breathing fragrance of spring, the soft **voluptuousness** of summer, the golden pomp of autumn; earth with its mantle of refreshing green, and heaven with its deep delicious blue and its cloudy magnificence, all fill us with mute but exquisite delight, and we revel in the luxury of mere sensation. But in the depth of winter, when nature lies despoiled of every charm, and wrapped in her shroud of sheeted snow, we turn for our gratifications to moral sources. The dreariness and desolation of the landscape, the short gloomy days and darksome nights, while they **circumscribe** our wanderings, shut in our feelings also from rambling abroad, and make us more keenly disposed for the pleasures of the social circle. Our thoughts are more concentrated; our friendly sympathies more aroused. We feel more sensibly the charm of each other's society, and are brought more closely together by dependence on each other for enjoyment. Heart calleth unto heart; and we draw our pleasures from the deep wells of living kindness, which lie in the quiet recesses of our bosoms: and which when resorted to, furnish forth the pure element of domestic felicity.

  The **pitchy** gloom without makes the heart dilate on entering the room filled with the glow and warmth of the evening fire. The **ruddy** blaze diffuses an artificial summer and sunshine through the room, and lights up each countenance into a kindlier welcome. Where does the honest face of hospitality expand into a broader and more cordial smile—where is the shy glance of love more sweetly eloquent—than by the winter fireside? and as the hollow blast of wintry wind rushes through the hall, claps the distant door, whistles about the casement, and rumbles down the chimney, what can be more grateful than that feeling of sober and sheltered security with which we look around upon the comfortable chamber and the scene of domestic hilarity?

  The English, from the great prevalence of rural habits throughout every class of society, have always been fond of those festivals and holidays which agreeably interrupt the stillness of country life; and they were, in former days, particularly observant of the religious and social rites of Christmas. It is inspiring to read even the dry details which some antiquarians have given of the quaint humours, the **burlesque** pageants, the complete abandonment to mirth and good-fellowship with which this festival was celebrated. It seemed to throw open every door, and unlock every heart. It brought the peasant and the peer together, and blended all ranksin one warm generous flow of joy and kindness. The old halls of castles and manor-houses resounded with the harp and the Christmas carol, and their ample boards groaned under the weight of hospitality. Even the poorest cottage welcomed the festive season with green decorations of bay and holly—the cheerful fire glanced its rays through the **lattice**, inviting the passenger to raise the latch, and join the gossip knot huddled around the hearth, **beguiling** the long evening with legendary jokes and oft-told Christmas tales.

  One of the least pleasing effects of modern refinement is the **havoc** it has made among the hearty old holiday customs. It has completely taken off the sharp touchings and spirited reliefs of these embellishments of life, and has worn down society into a more smooth and polished, but certainly a less characteristic surface. Many of the games and ceremonials of Christmas have

Chapter 14
Washington Irving
华盛顿·欧文

entirely disappeared, and like the sherris sack[1] of old Falstaff, are become matters of speculation and dispute among commentators. They flourished in times full of spirit and lustihood, when men enjoyed life roughly, but heartily and vigorously; times wild and picturesque, which have furnished poetry with its richest materials, and the drama with its most attractive variety of characters and manners. The world has become more worldly. There is more of dissipation, and less of enjoyment. Pleasure has expanded into a broader, but a shallower stream, and has forsaken many of those deep and quiet channels where it flowed sweetly through the calm bosom of domestic life. Society has acquired a more enlightened and elegant tone; but it has lost many of its strong local peculiarities, its homebred feelings, its honest fireside delights. The traditionary customs of golden-hearted antiquity, its feudal hospitalities, and lordly sailings, have passed away with the baronial castles and stately manor-houses in which they were celebrated. They **comported** with the shadowy hall, the great oaken gallery, and the tapestried parlour, but are unfitted to the light showy saloons and gay drawing-rooms of the modern villa.

Shorn, however, as it is, of its ancient and festive honours, Christmas is still a period of delightful excitement in England. It is gratifying to see that home feeling completely aroused which seems to hold so powerful a place in every English bosom. The preparations making on every side for the social board that is again to unite friends and kindred; the presents of good cheer passing and repassing, those tokens of regard, and quickeners of kind feelings; the evergreens distributed about houses and churches, **emblems** of peace and gladness; all these have the most pleasing effect in producing fond associations, and kindling benevolent sympathies. Even the sound of the waits, rude as may be their **minstrelsy**, breaks upon the mid-watches of a winter night with the effect of perfect harmony. As I have been awakened by them in that still and solemn hour, "when deep sleep falleth upon man",

---

1 sack: an antiquated wine term referring to white fortified wine imported from mainland Spain or the Canary Islands. The term "sherris sack" later gave way to "sherry" as the English term for fortified wine from Jerez Sack. 指原产于西班牙和加纳利群岛的一种加强型雪利酒。sherris sack 后来在英国被称作 sherry，用来指产自西班牙赫雷斯城的雪利酒。

I have listened with a hushed delight, and, connecting them with the sacred and joyous occasion, have almost fancied them into another celestial choir, announcing peace and good-will to mankind.

How delightfully the imagination, when wrought upon by these moral influences, turns every thing to melody and beauty: The very crowing of the cock, who is sometimes heard in the profound repose of the country, "telling the night-watches to his feathery dames," was thought by the common people to announce the approach of this sacred festival:

"Some say that ever 'gainst that season comes

Wherein our Saviour's birth is celebrated,

This bird of dawning singeth all night long:

And then, they say, no spirit dares stir abroad;

The nights are wholesome—then no planets strike,

No fairy takes, no witch hath power to charm,

Amidst the general call to happiness, the bustle of the spirits, and stir of the affections, which prevail at this period, what bosom can remain insensible? It is, indeed, the season of regenerated feeling—the season for kindling, not merely the fire of hospitality in the hall, but the genial flame of charity in the heart.

The scene of early love again rises green to memory beyond the sterile waste of years; and the idea of home, fraught with the fragrance of home-dwelling joys, reanimates the drooping spirit, —as the Arabian breeze will sometimes waft the freshness of the distant fields to the weary pilgrim of the desert.

Stranger and sojourner as I am in the land, —though for me no social hearth may blaze, no hospitable roof throw open its doors, nor the warm grasp of friendship welcome me at the threshold, —yet I feel the influence of the season beaming into my soul from the happy looks of those around me. Surely happiness is reflective, like the light of heaven; and every countenance, bright with smiles, and glowing with innocent enjoyment, is a mirror transmitting to others the rays of a supreme and ever shining benevolence. He who can turn **churlishly** away from contemplating the felicity of his fellow beings, and

Chapter 14
Washington Irving
华盛顿·欧文

sit down darkling and repining in his loneliness when all around is joyful, may have his moments of strong excitement and selfish gratification, but he wants the genial and social sympathies which constitute the charm of a merry Christmas.

I Words and Phrases

yore [jɔː]	n.	time long past 往昔，昔时
morsel ['mɔːs(ə)l]	n.	a small piece of food; a small amount 一口食物；一小块
dilapidate [dɪ'læpɪdeɪt]	v.	to bring or fall into a state of partial ruin, decay, or disrepair; to squander 使荒废；浪费
verdure ['vɜːdjʊə]	n.	the lush greenness of flourishing vegetation 青翠的树木；新鲜
conviviality [kən'vɪvɪəlɪtɪ]	adj.	being sociable 随和的，好交际的；欢庆的
jubilee ['dʒuːbɪliː]	n.	a specially celebrated anniversary, especially a 50th anniversary; a season or occasion of joyful celebration 五十年节；欢乐的节日
asunder [ə'sʌndə]	adv.	into separate parts or pieces; apart from each other either in position or in direction 分开，分离；化为碎片
sally forth		to go out in order to do something, especially something that you expect to be difficult or dangerous 毅然出发；兴冲冲地离开
voluptuousness [və'lʌptʃʊəsnɪs]	n.	being attractive in a sexual way with large breasts and hips 丰满，性感
circumscribe ['sɜːkəmskraɪb]	v.	draw a line around; encircle; limit narrowly; restrict 划定范围；限制
pitchy ['pɪtʃɪ]	adj.	extremely dark; black 沥青的；漆黑的
ruddy ['rʌdɪ]	adj.	having a healthy, reddish color 红润的，血色好的

burlesque [bɜːˈlesk]	n.	a variety show characterized by broad ribald comedy, dancing, and striptease; a literary or dramatic work that makes fun of something, often by means of outlandish exaggeration 滑稽娱乐；滑稽讽刺作品或表演
lattice [ˈlætɪs]	n.	an open framework made of strips of metal, wood or similar material overlapped or overlaid in a regular, usually crisscross pattern 格子框架
beguile [bɪˈgaɪl]	v.	trick sb into doing sth; attract or interest 吸引某人；使感兴趣
havoc [ˈhævək]	n.	widespread destruction; disorder or chaos 大破坏；大混乱，大骚动
comport [kəmˈpɔːt]	v.	behave (oneself) in a particular manner 行为表现；举止
emblem [ˈembləm]	n.	a design or picture that represents a country or organization 徽章；标记
minstrelsy [ˈmɪnstr(ə)lsɪ]	n.	the art or profession of a minstrel 吟唱；吟游诗人
churlishly [ˈtʃɜːlɪʃlɪ]	adv.	in a way that is 脾气坏的；无礼的

II Reading Comprehension Questions

1. In the beginning of the essay, the author says "There is nothing in England that exercises a more delightful spell over my imagination than the lingerings of the holiday customs and rural games of former times". Do you ever have similiar feelings towards holidays and festives? Please descibe them.

2. In the second paragraph, the author writes "Of all the old festivals, however, that of Christmas awakens the strongest and most heartfelt associations". Read the essay carefully and find all the reasons listed.

Chapter 14
Washington Irving
华盛顿·欧文

3. What is "something in the very season of the year" that gives a charm to the festivity of Christmas?
4. What is the havoc modern refinement has made among the hearty old holiday customs?
5. What festival in China does this essay remind you of? Please describe it in your own words.

III Questions on Writing Style and Language

1. Have you noticed any stylistic features of Washington Irving's writing? What particular effect is produced by these sentences?
2. The first paragraph says little about Christmas. What is the function of it then?
3. Simile is a figure of speech which makes a comparison between two unlike elements having at least one quality or characteristic in common. To make the comparison, words like *as, as...as, as if* and *like* are used to transfer the quality we associate with one to the other. Can you find uses of similes in the essay? What are the effects of using this rhetorical device?
4. Can you find uses of parallel structure in the essay? What are the effects of using this rhetorical device?
5. Irving's style is characterized by lucidity, elegance, poise and easy flow. Can you pick out a paragraph and analyze it?

Westminster Abbey

Washington Irving

On one of those sober and rather melancholy days in the latter part of autumn when the shadows of morning and evening almost mingle together, and throw a gloom over the decline of the year, I passed several hours in rambling about Westminster Abbey. There was something **congenial** to the season in the mournful magnificence of the old pile, and as I passed its threshold it seemed like stepping back into the regions of **antiquity** and losing myself among the shades of former ages.

I entered from the inner court of Westminster School, through a long, low, **vaulted** passage that had an almost subterranean look, being dimly lighted in one part by circular **perforations** in the massive walls. Through this dark avenue I had a distant view of the **cloisters**, with the figure of an old **verger** in his black gown moving along their shadowy vaults, and seeming like a **spectre** from one of the neighboring tombs. The approach to the abbey through these gloomy monastic remains prepares the mind for its solemn contemplation. The cloisters still retain something of the quiet and seclusion of former days. The gray walls are discolored by damps and crumbling with age; a coat of hoary moss has gathered over the inscriptions of the mural monuments, and obscured the death's heads and other funeral **emblems**. The sharp touches of the **chisel** are gone from the rich **tracery** of the arches; the roses which adorned the keystones have lost their leafy beauty; everything bears marks of the gradual **dilapidations** of time, which yet has something touching and pleasing in its very decay.

The sun was pouring down a yellow autumnal ray into the square of the cloisters, beaming upon a scanty plot of grass in the centre, and lighting up an angle of the vaulted passage with a kind of dusky splendor. From between the

Chapter 14
Washington Irving
华盛顿·欧文

arcades the eye glanced up to a bit of blue sky or a passing cloud, and beheld the sun-gilt pinnacles of the abbey towering into the azure heaven.

As I paced the cloisters, sometimes contemplating this mingled picture of glory and decay, and sometimes endeavoring to decipher the inscriptions on the tombstones which formed the pavement beneath my feet, my eye was attracted to three figures rudely carved in relief, but nearly worn away by the footsteps of many generations. They were the effigies of three of the early **abbots**; the epitaphs were entirely effaced; the names alone remained, having no doubt been renewed in later times (Vitalis. Abbas. 1082, and Gislebertus Crispinus. Abbas. 1114, and Laurentius. Abbas. 1176). I remained some little while, musing over these casual relics of antiquity thus left like wrecks upon this distant shore of time, telling no tale but that such beings had been and had perished, teaching no moral but the futility of that pride which hopes still to exact homage in its ashes and to live in an inscription. A little longer, and even these faint records will be obliterated and the monument will cease to be a memorial. Whilst I was yet looking down upon the gravestones I was roused by the sound of the abbey clock, **reverberating** from **buttress** to buttress and echoing among the cloisters. It is almost startling to hear this warning of departed time sounding among the tombs and telling the lapse of the hour, which, like a billow, has rolled us onward towards the grave. I pursued my walk to an arched door opening to the interior of the abbey. On entering here the magnitude of the building breaks fully upon the mind, contrasted with the vaults of the cloisters. The eyes gaze with wonder at clustered columns of gigantic dimensions, with arches springing from them to such an amazing height, and man wandering about their bases, shrunk into insignificance in comparison with his own handiwork. The spaciousness and gloom of this vast edifice produce a profound and mysterious awe. We step cautiously and softly about, as if fearful of disturbing the hallowed silence of the tomb, while every footfall whispers along the walls and chatters among the **sepulchres**, making us more sensible of the quiet we have interrupted.

It seems as if the awful nature of the place presses down upon the soul and hushes the beholder into noiseless reverence. We feel that we are surrounded by the congregated bones of the great men of past times, who have filled history with their deeds and the earth with their renown.

And yet it almost provokes a smile at the vanity of human ambition to see how they are crowded together and **jostled** in the dust; what **parsimony** is observed in doling out a scanty nook, a gloomy corner, a little portion of earth, to those whom, when alive, kingdoms could not satisfy, and how many shapes and forms and artifices are devised to catch the casual notice of the passenger, and save from forgetfulness for a few short years a name which once aspired to occupy ages of the world's thought and admiration.

I passed some time in Poet's Corner, which occupies an end of one of the transepts or cross aisles of the abbey. The monuments are generally simple, for the lives of literary men afford no striking themes for the sculptor. Shakespeare and Addison have statues erected to their memories, but the greater part have busts, medallions, and sometimes mere inscriptions. **Notwithstanding** the simplicity of these memorials, I have always observed that the visitors to the abbey remained longest about them. A kinder and fonder feeling takes place of that cold curiosity or vague admiration with which they gaze on the splendid monuments of the great and the heroic. They linger about these as about the tombs of friends and companions, for indeed there is something of companionship between the author and the reader. Other men are known to posterity only through the medium of history, which is continually growing faint and obscure; but the intercourse between the author and his fellowmen is ever new, active, and immediate. He has lived for them more than for himself; he has sacrificed surrounding enjoyments, and shut himself up from the delights of social life, that he might the more intimately commune with distant minds and distant ages. Well may the world cherish his renown, for it has been purchased not by deeds of violence and blood, but by the diligent dispensation of pleasure. Well may posterity be grateful to his memory, for he has left it an inheritance not of empty names and sounding actions, but whole treasures of wisdom, bright gems of thought, and golden veins of language.

From Poet's Corner I continued my stroll towards that part of the abbey which contains the sepulchres of the kings. I wandered among what once

Chapter 14

Washington Irving
华盛顿·欧文

were chapels, but which are now occupied by the tombs and monuments of the great. At every turn I met with some illustrious name or the cognizance of some powerful house renowned in history. As the eye darts into these dusky chambers of death it catches glimpses of quaint effigies—some kneeling in niches, as if in devotion; others stretched upon the tombs, with hands piously pressed together; warriors in armor, as if reposing after battle; prelates, with crosiers and **mitres**; and nobles in robes and coronets, lying as it were in state. In glancing over this scene, so strangely populous, yet where every form is so still and silent, it seems almost as if we were treading a mansion of that fabled city where every being had been suddenly transmuted into stone.

I paused to contemplate a tomb on which lay the **effigy** of a knight in complete armor. A large buckler was on one arm; the hands were pressed together in supplication upon the breast; the face was almost covered by the morion; the legs were crossed, in token of the warrior's having been engaged in the holy war. It was the tomb of a crusader, of one of those military enthusiasts who so strangely mingled religion and romance, and whose exploits form the connecting link between fact and fiction, between the history and the fairytale. There is something extremely picturesque in the tombs of these adventurers, decorated as they are with rude armorial bearings and Gothic sculpture. They comport with the antiquated chapels in which they are generally found; and in considering them the imagination is apt to kindle with the legendary associations, the romantic fiction, the chivalrous pomp and pageantry which poetry has spread over the wars for the sepulchre of Christ. They are the relics of times utterly gone by, of beings passed from recollection, of customs and manners with which ours have no affinity. They are like objects from some strange and distant land of which we have no certain knowledge, and about which all our conceptions are vague and visionary. There is something extremely solemn and awful in those effigies on Gothic tombs, extended as if in the sleep of death or in the supplication of the dying hour. They have an effect infinitely more impressive on my feelings than the fanciful attitudes, the over wrought conceits, the allegorical groups which abound on modern monuments. I have been struck, also, with the superiority of many of the old sepulchral inscriptions. There was a noble way in former times of saying things simply, and yet saying them proudly; and I do not know an epitaph that breathes a loftier consciousness of family worth and honorable lineage than one which affirms of a noble house that "all the brothers were brave and all the sisters virtuous."

In the opposite transept to Poet's Corner stands a monument which is among the most renowned achievements of modern art, but which to me appears horrible rather than sublime. It is the tomb of Mrs. Nightingale, by Roubillac. The bottom of the monument is represented as throwing open its marble doors, and a sheeted skeleton is starting forth. The shroud is falling from his fleshless frame as he launches his dart at his victim. She is sinking into her affrighted husband's arms, who strives with vain and frantic effort to avert the blow. The whole is executed with terrible truth and spirit; we almost fancy we hear the gibbering yell of triumph bursting from the distended jaws of the spectre. But why should we thus seek to clothe death with unnecessary terrors, and to spread horrors round the tomb of those we love? The grave should be surrounded by everything that might inspire tenderness and veneration for the dead, or that might win the living to virtue. It is the place not of disgust and dismay, but of sorrow and meditation.

While wandering about these gloomy vaults and silent aisles, studying the records of the dead, the sound of busy existence from without occasionally reaches the ear—the rumbling of the passing equipage, the murmur of the multitude, or perhaps the light laugh of pleasure. The contrast is striking with the deathlike repose around; and it has a strange effect upon the feelings thus to hear the surges of active life hurrying along and beating against the very walls of the sepulchre.

I continued in this way to move from tomb to tomb and from chapel to chapel. The day was gradually wearing away; the distant tread of loiterers about the abbey grew less and less frequent; the sweet-tongued bell was summoning to evening prayers; and I saw at a distance the choristers in their white surplices crossing the aisle and entering the choir. I stood before the entrance to Henry the Seventh's chapel. A flight of steps leads up to it through

Chapter 14

Washington Irving
华盛顿·欧文

a deep and gloomy but magnificent arch. Great gates of brass, richly and delicately wrought, turn heavily upon their hinges, as if proudly reluctant to admit the feet of common mortals into this most gorgeous of sepulchres.

On entering the eye is astonished by the pomp of architecture and the elaborate beauty of sculptured detail. The very walls are wrought into universal ornament encrusted with tracery, and scooped into niches crowded with the statues of saints and martyrs. Stone seems, by the cunning labor of the chisel, to have been robbed of its weight and density, suspended aloft as if by magic, and the fretted roof achieved with the wonderful minuteness and airy security of a cobweb.

Along the sides of the chapel are the lofty stalls of the Knights of the Bath, richly carved of oak, though with the grotesque decorations of Gothic architecture. On the pinnacles of the stalls are affixed the helmets and crests of the knights, with their scarfs and swords, and above them are suspended their banners, emblazoned with armorial bearings, and contrasting the splendor of gold and purple and crimson with the cold gray fretwork of the roof. In the midst of this grand mausoleum stands the sepulchre of its founder—his effigy, with that of his queen, extended on a sumptuous tomb—and the whole surrounded by a superbly-wrought brazen railing.

There is a sad dreariness in this magnificence, this strange mixture of tombs and trophies, these emblems of living and aspiring ambition, close beside mementos which show the dust and oblivion in which all must sooner or later terminate. Nothing impresses the mind with a deeper feeling of loneliness than to tread the silent and deserted scene of former throng and pageant. On looking round on the vacant stalls of the knights and their esquires, and on the rows of dusty but gorgeous banners that were once borne before them, my imagination conjured up the scene when this hall was bright with the valor and beauty of the land, glittering with the splendor of jewelled rank and military array, alive with the tread of many feet and the hum of an admiring multitude. All had passed away; the silence of death had settled again upon the place, interrupted only by the casual chirping of birds, which had found their way into the chapel and built their nests among its friezes and pendants—sure signs of solitariness and desertion.

When I read the names inscribed on the banners, they were those of men scattered far and wide about the world—some tossing upon distant seas: some under arms in distant lands; some mingling in the busy intrigues of courts and cabinets,—all seeking to deserve one more distinction in this mansion of shadowy honors—the melancholy reward of a monument.

Two small aisles on each side of this chapel present a touching instance of the equality of the grave, which brings down the oppressor to a level with the oppressed and mingles the dust of the bitterest enemies together. In one is the sepulchre of the haughty Elizabeth; in the other is that of her victim, the lovely and unfortunate Mary. Not an hour in the day but some ejaculation of pity is uttered over the fate of the latter, mingled with indignation at her oppressor. The walls of Elizabeth's sepulchre continually echo with the sighs of sympathy heaved at the grave of her rival.

A peculiar melancholy reigns over the aisle where Mary lies buried. The light struggles dimly through windows darkened by dust. The greater part of the place is in deep shadow, and the walls are stained and tinted by time and weather. A marble figure of Mary is stretched upon the tomb, round which is an iron railing, much corroded, bearing her national emblem—the thistle. I was weary with wandering, and sat down to rest myself by the monument, revolving in my mind the chequered and disastrous story of poor Mary.

The sound of casual footsteps had ceased from the abbey. I could only hear, now and then, the distant voice of the priest repeating the evening service and the faint responses of the choir; these paused for a time, and all was hushed. The stillness, the desertion, and obscurity that were gradually prevailing around gave a deeper and more solemn interest to the place;

For in the silent grave no conversation,
No joyful tread of friends, no voice of lovers,
No careful father's counsel—nothing's heard,
For nothing is, but all oblivion,
Dust, and an endless darkness.

Suddenly the notes of the deep-laboring organ burst upon the ear,

Chapter 14
Washington Irving
华盛顿·欧文

falling with doubled and redoubled intensity, and rolling, as it were, huge billows of sound. How well do their volume and grandeur accord with this mighty building! With what pomp do they swell through its vast vaults, and breathe their awful harmony through these caves of death, and make the silent sepulchre vocal! And now they rise in triumphant acclamation, heaving higher and higher their accordant notes and piling sound on sound. And now they pause, and the soft voices of the choir break out into sweet gushes of melody; they soar aloft and warble along the roof, and seem to play about these lofty vaults like the pure airs of heaven. Again the pealing organ heaves its thrilling thunders, compressing air into music, and rolling it forth upon the soul. What long-drawn cadences! What solemn sweeping concords! It grows more and more dense and powerful; it fills the vast pile and seems to jar the very walls—the ear is stunned—the senses are overwhelmed. And now it is winding up in full jubilee—it is rising from the earth to heaven; the very soul seems rapt away and floated upwards on this swelling tide of harmony!

I sat for some time lost in that kind of reverie which a strain of music is apt sometimes to inspire: the shadows of evening were gradually thickening round me; the monuments began to cast deeper and deeper gloom; and the distant clock again gave token of the slowly waning day.

I rose and prepared to leave the abbey. As I descended the flight of steps which lead into the body of the building, my eye was caught by the shrine of Edward the Confessor, and I ascended the small staircase that conducts to it, to take from thence a general survey of this wilderness of tombs. The shrine is elevated upon a kind of platform, and close around it are the sepulchres of various kings and queens. From this eminence the eye looks down between pillars and funeral trophies to the chapels and chambers below, crowded with tombs, where warriors, prelates, courtiers, and statesmen lie mouldering in their "beds of darkness." Close by me stood the great chair of coronation, rudely carved of oak in the barbarous taste of a remote and Gothic age. The scene seemed almost as if contrived with theatrical artifice to produce an effect upon the beholder. Here was a type of the beginning and the end of human pomp and power; here it was literally but a step from the throne to the sepulchre. Would not one think that these incongruous mementos had been gathered together as a lesson to living greatness? —to show it, even in the moment of its proudest exaltation, the neglect and dishonor to which it must soon arrive—how soon that crown which encircles its brow must pass away, and it must lie down in the dust and disgraces of the tomb, and be trampled upon by the feet of the meanest of the multitude. For, strange to tell, even the grave is here no longer a sanctuary. There is a shocking levity in some natures which leads them to sport with awful and hallowed things, and there are base minds which delight to revenge on the illustrious dead the abject homage and grovelling servility which they pay to the living. The coffin of Edward the Confessor has been broken open, and his remains despoiled of their funereal ornaments; the sceptre has been stolen from the hand of the imperious Elizabeth; and the effigy of Henry the Fifth lies headless. Not a royal monument but bears some proof how false and fugitive is the homage of mankind. Some are plundered, some mutilated, some covered with ribaldry and insult, —all more or less outraged and dishonored.

The last beams of day were now faintly streaming through the painted windows in the high vaults above me; the lower parts of the abbey were already wrapped in the obscurity of twilight. The chapels and aisles grew darker and darker. The effigies of the kings faded into shadows; the marble figures of the monuments assumed strange shapes in the uncertain light; the evening breeze crept through the aisles like the cold breath of the grave; and even the distant footfall of a **verger**, traversing the Poet's Corner, had something strange and dreary in its sound. I slowly retraced my morning's walk, and as I passed out at the portal of the cloisters, the door, closing with a jarring noise behind me, filled the whole building with echoes.

I endeavored to form some arrangement in my mind of the objects I had been contemplating, but found they were already falling into indistinctness and confusion. Names, inscriptions, trophies, had all become confounded in my recollection, though I had scarcely taken my foot from off the threshold. What, thought I, is this vast assemblage of sepulchres but a treasury of humiliation—a huge pile of reiterated homilies on the emptiness of renown

Chapter 14

Washington Irving
华盛顿·欧文

and the certainty of oblivion? It is, indeed, the empire of death; his great shadowy palace where he sits in state mocking at the relics of human glory and spreading dust and forgetfulness on the monuments of princes. How idle a boast, after all, is the immortality of a name! Time is ever silently turning over his pages; we are too much engrossed by the story of the present to think of the characters and anecdotes that gave interest to the past; and each age is a volume thrown aside to be speedily forgotten. The idol of to-day pushes the hero of yesterday out of our recollection, and will in turn be supplanted by his successor of tomorrow. "Our fathers," says Sir Thomas Browne, "find their graves in our short memories, and sadly tell us how we may be buried in our survivors." History fades into fable; fact becomes clouded with doubt and controversy; the inscription moulders from the tablet; the statue falls from the pedestal. Columns, arches, pyramids, what are they but heaps of sand, and their epitaphs but characters written in the dust? What is the security of a tomb or the perpetuity of an embalmment? The remains of Alexander the Great have been scattered to the wind, and his empty sarcophagus is now the mere curiosity of a museum. "The Egyptian mummies, which Cambyses or time hath spared, avarice now consumeth; Mizraim cures wounds, and Pharaoh is sold for balsams."

What then is to ensure this pile which now towers above me from sharing the fate of mightier mausoleums? The time must come when its gilded vaults which now spring so loftily, shall lie in rubbish beneath the feet; when instead of the sound of melody and praise the wind shall whistle through the broken arches and the owl hoot from the shattered tower; when the garish sunbeam shall break into these gloomy mansions of death, and the ivy twine round the fallen column; and the fox-glove hang its blossoms about the nameless urn, as if in mockery of the dead. Thus man passes away; his name passes from record and recollection; his history is as a tale that is told, and his very monument becomes a ruin.

1 Words and Phrases

congenial [kən'dʒiːnɪəl]	*adj.*	suitable to one's needs or similar to one's nature 意气相投的；适意的；一致的
antiquity [æn'tɪkwɪtɪ]	*n.*	extreme oldness, ancientness; an artifact surviving from the past 高龄；古物；古代的遗物
vaulted ['vɔːltɪd]	*adj.*	having a hemispherical vault or dome 拱形的；圆顶的；有拱顶的，盖有拱顶的
perforation [pəːfə'reɪʃən]	*n.*	a line of small holes for tearing at a particular place 穿孔；孔眼；身体某部位的裂口
cloister ['klɒɪstə]	*n.*	residence that is a place of religious seclusion 回廊；修道院；修道院生活；隐居地
verger ['vɜːdʒə]	*n.*	a church officer who takes care of the interior of the building 教堂司事；执权标者；教堂管理人
spectre ['spektə]	*n.*	a ghostly appearing figure 幽灵；妖怪
emblem ['embləm]	*n.*	special design or visual object representing a quality, type, group, etc. 象征；徽章；符号
chisel ['tʃɪz(ə)l]	*n.*	an edge tool with a flat steel blade with a cutting edge 雕刻；欺骗；凿子
tracery ['treɪs(ə)rɪ]	*n.*	decoration consisting of an open pattern of interlacing ribs 窗饰；花饰窗格
dilapidation [ˌdɪlæpɪ'deɪʃ(ə)n]	*n.*	a state of deterioration due to old age or long use; the process of becoming dilapidated 破损；崩塌；荒废
abbot ['æbət]	*n.*	the superior of an abbey of monks 男修道院院长；大寺院男住持
reverberate [rɪ'vɜːbəreɪt]	*v.*	ring or echo with sound 使回响；使反射；使弹回
buttress ['bʌtrɪs]	*n.*	a support usually of stone or brick; supports the wall of a building 扶壁；拱壁；支撑物

Chapter 14
Washington Irving
华盛顿·欧文

sepulchre ['sep(ə)lkə]	n.	a chamber that is used as a grave 坟墓；圣体安置所
jostle ['dʒɒsl]	v.	force your way by pushing 竞争；争夺；推挤
parsimony ['pɑːsɪmənɪ]	n.	extreme care in spending money 吝啬，过度节俭
notwithstanding [ˌnɒtwɪθ'stændɪŋ] prep.		despite anything to the contrary 尽管；仍然
mitre ['maɪtə]	n.	a liturgical headdress worn by bishops on formal occasions. 斜接；主教法冠；僧帽
effigy ['efɪdʒɪ]	n.	a representation of a person (especially in the form of sculpture) 雕像；肖像

II Reading Comprehension Questions

1. Please find on line a sketch of the Westminster Abbey and try to mark the places Irving Visited in a chronological order.
2. As the author paced the cloisters, what did he see and what was he thinking about?
3. Why do the visitors to the abbey remain longest about the Poet's Corner?
4. What was the author thinking about when he saw the sepulchres of Elizabeth and Mary?
5. What kind of mood was Irving in when he came out of the Abbey?

Quotes of the Author

There is sacredness in tears. They are not the mark of weakness, but of power.

A tart temper never mellows with age; and a sharp tongue is the only edged tool that grows keener with constant use.

There is a healthful hardiness about real dignity that never dreads contact and communion with others, however humble.

A father may turn his back on his child, but a mother's love endures through all.

A kind heart is a fountain of gladness, making everything in its vicinity freshens into smiles.

Ralph Waldo Emerson
拉尔夫·瓦尔多·爱默生
(1803—1882)

本章导读

拉尔夫·瓦尔多·爱默生是 19 世纪中期美国文学巨匠，他不仅是一位卓越的散文家，还是出色的演说家，更以其超验主义文学实践为美国留下了宝贵的文化财富。

爱默生于 1803 年 5 月 25 日出生于波士顿的一个牧师家庭。其父在他 7 岁时去世，他的母亲不得不独自抚养 5 个儿子，并依靠招收寄宿学生的费用过活。在亲戚们的帮助下，爱默生接受了良好的教育，9 岁时进入波士顿拉丁学校，14 岁进入哈佛大学。毕业后，爱默生执教于波士顿女子学院，后又返回哈佛大学神学院学习。1829 年，爱默生被任命为波士顿第二教堂牧师。1832 年，因自己的思想与传统教义不合，爱默生辞去了教职。之后的一年中，爱默生游历了欧洲各国，在此期间他结识了威廉·华兹华斯和塞缪尔·泰勒·柯勒律治等著名文人，开始了他的演说生涯，传播超验主义思想。

1836 年，爱默生定居康科德，与梭罗等人不定期聚会，交流思想，组成了非正式的"超验主义俱乐部"。1840 年到 1844 年，俱乐部出版了评论刊《日晷》（*The Dial*），针砭时弊，宣传超验思想。

爱默生的文学创作开始于 1836 年出版的《论自然》（*Nature*）。这部作品的问世，震撼了美国文化思想界，把美国浪漫主义推向一个新阶段——新英格兰超验主义阶段。1837 年，爱默生在哈佛大学优等生联谊会上发表了著名演讲《论美国学者》（*The American Scholar*），为美国文学的未来大声疾呼，轰动一时。之后，爱默生将自己的文学作品和演讲稿编辑成册，并于 1841 年出版了《散文选：第一辑》（*Essays: First Series*），其中包括《论自助》（*Self-Reliance*）、《论超灵》（*The Over-Soul*）、《论补偿》（*Compensation*）等 12 篇文章。1844 年，他又将《诗人》（*The Poet*）和《经验》（*Experience*）等文收入了《散文选：第二辑》（*Essays: Second Series*）。除此之外，爱默生的作品集还包括《代表人物》（*Representative Men*）和《英国人的特性》（*English Traits*）等。

张爱玲曾经指出："爱默森的作品即使在今日看来，也仍旧没有失去时效，这一点最使我们感到惊异。他有许多见解都适用于当前的政局，或是对于我们个人有切身之感。"爱默生的散文作品中的许多思想在今天依然适用，足见其作品的超前性及其经典、隽永。尽管在结构上略显跳跃，爱默生的散文却总能给人文采斐然，目不暇接之感。他的散文语言高雅大方，充满诗意。为了使文章更加生动，爱默生经常性穿插比喻，使文章更加形象化。

About the Author

Ralph Waldo Emerson (May 25, 1803—April 27, 1882) was an American essayist, lecturer, and poet who led the Transcendentalist movement of the mid-19th century. He was seen as a champion of individualism and a prescient critic of the countervailing pressures of society, and he disseminated his thoughts through dozens of published essays and more than 1,500 public lectures across the United States.

Emerson gradually moved away from the religious and social beliefs of his contemporaries, formulating and expressing the philosophy of Transcendentalism in his 1836 essay, "Nature". Following this ground-breaking work, he gave a speech entitled "The American Scholar" in 1837, which was considered as America's "Intellectual Declaration of Independence".

Emerson wrote on a number of subjects, never espousing fixed philosophical tenets, but developing certain ideas such as individuality, freedom, the ability for humankind to realize almost anything, and the relationship between the soul and the surrounding world. Emerson wrote most of his important essays as lectures first, then revised them for print. His first two collections of essays "Essays: First Series" and "Essays: Second Series", published respectively in 1841 and 1844—represent the core of his thinking, and include such well-known essays as "Self-Reliance", "The Over-Soul", "Circles", "The Poet and Experience". Together with "Nature", these essays made the decade from the mid-1830s to

Chapter 15

Ralph Waldo Emerson
拉尔夫·瓦尔多·爱默生

the mid-1840s Emerson's most fertile period.

Emerson remains among the linchpins of the American romantic movement, and his work has greatly influenced the thinkers, writers and poets that have followed him. He is also well known as a mentor and friend of fellow Transcendentalist Henry David Thoreau.

Text A

Nature

To go into solitude, a man needs to retire as much from his chamber as from society. I am not solitary whilst I read and write, though nobody is with me. But if a man would be alone, let him look at the stars. The rays that come from those heavenly worlds, will separate between him and what he touches. One might think the atmosphere was made transparent with this design, to give man, in the heavenly bodies, the **perpetual** presence of the sublime. Seen in the streets of cities, how great they are! If the stars should appear one night in a thousand years, how would men believe and adore; and preserve for many generations the remembrance of the city of God which had been shown! But every night come out these **envoys** of beauty, and light the universe with their **admonishing** smile.

The stars awaken a certain reverence, because though always present, they are inaccessible; but all natural objects make a kindred impression, when the mind is open to their influence. Nature never wears a mean appearance. Neither does the wisest man **extort** her secret, and lose his curiosity by finding out all her perfection. Nature never became a toy to a wise spirit. The flowers, the animals, the mountains, reflected the wisdom of his best hour, as much as they had delighted the simplicity of his childhood.

When we speak of nature in this manner, we have a distinct but most poetical sense in the mind. We mean the integrity of impression made by manifold natural objects. It is this which distinguishes the stick of timber of the wood-cutter, from the tree of the poet. The charming landscape which I saw this morning, is **indubitably** made up of some twenty or thirty farms. Miller owns this field, Locke that, and Manning the woodland beyond. But none of them owns the landscape. There is a property in the horizon which no man has but he whose eye can integrate all the parts, that is, the poet. This is the

Chapter 15

Ralph Waldo Emerson
拉尔夫·瓦尔多·爱默生

best part of these men's farms, yet to this their **warranty-deeds** give no title.

To speak truly, few adult persons can see nature. Most persons do not see the sun. At least they have a very superficial seeing. The sun illuminates only the eye of the man, but shines into the eye and the heart of the child. The lover of nature is he whose inward and outward senses are still truly adjusted to each other; who has retained the spirit of infancy even into the era of manhood. His intercourse with heaven and earth, becomes part of his daily food. In the presence of nature, a wild delight runs through the man, in spite of real sorrows. Nature says, —he is my creature, and **maugre** all his impertinent griefs, he shall be glad with me. Not the sun or the summer alone, but every hour and season yields its tribute of delight; for every hour and change corresponds to and authorizes a different state of the mind, from breathless noon to **grimmest** midnight. Nature is a setting that fits equally well a comic or a mourning piece. In good health, the air is a **cordial** of incredible virtue. Crossing a bare common, in snow puddles, at twilight, under a clouded sky, without having in my thoughts any occurrence of special good fortune, I have enjoyed a perfect **exhilaration**. I am glad to the brink of fear. In the woods too, a man casts off his years, as the snake his **slough**, and at what period **soever** of life, is always a child. In the woods, is perpetual youth. Within these plantations of God, a **decorum** and **sanctity** reign, a perennial festival is dressed, and the guest sees not how he should tire of them in a thousand years. In the woods, we return to reason and faith. There I feel that nothing can befall me in life,—no disgrace, no calamity, (leaving me my eyes,) which nature cannot repair. Standing on the bare ground,—my head bathed by the **blithe** air, and uplifted into infinite space,—all mean egotism vanishes. I become a transparent eye-ball; I am nothing; I see all; the currents of the Universal Being circulate through me; I am part or particle of God. The name of the nearest friend sounds then foreign and accidental: to be brothers, to be acquaintances, —master or servant, is then a trifle and a disturbance. I am the lover of uncontained and immortal beauty. In the wilderness, I find something more dear and **connate** than in streets or villages. In the tranquil landscape, and especially in the distant line of the horizon, man beholds somewhat as beautiful as his own nature.

  The greatest delight which the fields and woods minister, is the suggestion of an **occult** relation between man and the vegetable. I am not alone and unacknowledged. They nod to me, and I to them. The waving of the **boughs** in the storm, is new to me and old. It takes me by surprise, and yet is not unknown. Its effect is like that of a higher thought or a better emotion coming over me, when I deemed I was thinking justly or doing right.

  Yet it is certain that the power to produce this delight, does not reside in nature, but in man, or in a harmony of both. It is necessary to use these pleasures with great temperance. For, nature is not always tricked in holiday **attire**, but the same scene which yesterday breathed perfume and glittered as for the **frolic** of the nymphs, is overspread with melancholy today. Nature always wears the colors of the spirit. To a man laboring under calamity, the heat of his own fire hath sadness in it. Then, there is a kind of contempt of the landscape felt by him who has just lost by death a dear friend. The sky is less grand as it shuts down over less worth in the population.

Ⅰ Words and Phrases

perpetual [pə'petʃuəl]   *adj.* continuing forever or indefinitely; occurring so frequently as to seem ceaseless or uninterrupted 永久的；不断的；四季开花的；无期限的

envoy ['envɒɪ]   *n.* someone sent on a mission to represent the interests of someone else 使者

admonish [əd'mɒnɪʃ]   *v.* express reproof or reproach especially as a corrective 训诫；劝告

extort [ɪk'stɔːt]   *v.* obtain through intimidation; get or cause to become in a difficult or laborious manner 敲诈；侵占；强求；牵强地引出

indubitably [ɪn'dʊbɪtəblɪ]   *adv.* in a manner or to a degree that could not be doubted 无疑地，不容置疑地

Chapter 15

Ralph Waldo Emerson
拉尔夫·瓦尔多·爱默生

warranty-deed ['wɒrəntɪ diːd]	a type of deed where the grantor (seller) guarantees that he or she holds clear title to a piece of real estate and has a right to sell it (房地产) 担保契约
maugre ['mɔːgə]	*prep.* in despite of 不管
grim [grɪm]	*adj.* shockingly repellent; characterized by hopelessness; filled with gloom 冷酷的；糟糕的；残忍的
cordial ['kɔːdɪəl]	*adj.* strong highly flavored sweet liquor usually drunk after a meal 甘露酒
exhilaration [ɪɡˌzɪləˈreɪʃ(ə)n]	*n.* the feeling of lively and cheerful joy 愉快，令人高兴
slough [slaʊ]	*v.* cast off hair, skin, horn, or feathers 蜕下的皮(或壳)
soever [səʊˈevə]	*adv.* to any possible or known extent; of any or every kind that may be specified 任何，不论何种；无论
decorum [dɪˈkɔːrəm]	*n.* propriety in manners and conduct 礼仪；礼貌；端正
sanctity ['sæŋ(k)tɪtɪ]	*n.* the quality of being holy 圣洁；尊严；神圣不可侵犯性
blithe [blaɪð]	*adj.* carefree and happy and lighthearted 愉快的；快乐无忧的
connate ['kɒneɪt]	*adj.* related in nature, congenital, innate 先天的；天赋的
occult [ɒˈkʌlt]	*adj.* having an impact not apparent to the senses nor obvious to the intelligence; beyond ordinary understanding mysterious, supernatural 神秘的；超自然的；难以理解的
bough [baʊ]	*n.* any of the larger branches of a tree 大树枝
attire [əˈtaɪə]	*n.* clothing of a distinctive style or for a particular occasion 服装；盛装

frolic ['frɒlɪk]　　　　　　　　　*n.*　gay or light-hearted recreational activity for diversion or amusement 嬉闹，嬉戏

II Reading Comprehension Questions

1. Do you think it true that a person "is not solitary whilst he reads and writes"? Please share your own experience with your classmates.
2. In the author's opinion, who can own the landscape?
3. How do you understand "the sun illuminates only the eye of the man, but shines into the eye and the heart of the child"?
4. Do you think it true that "nature is a setting that fits equally well a comic or a mourning piece"? Please explain by using your own examples.
5. Why did the author say that "the power to produce this delight, does not reside in nature, but in man, or in a harmony of both"?

III Questions on Writing Style and Language

1. Have you noticed any stylistic features of Emerson's writing? What particular effect is produced by these sentences?
2. Can you find out some imaginative metaphors in the essay? In what way are they different from the commonly used metaphors?
3. When the author says "when we speak of nature in this manner, we have a distinct but most poetical sense in the mind", he uses an example to illustrate his point. Do you find the example vivid and convincing?
4. How does the author organize his ideas in this essay? Do you find any feaure of discontinuity?
5. Try to recall and describe some sacred moments you have experienced in nature.

Chapter 15

Ralph Waldo Emerson
拉尔夫·瓦尔多·爱默生

Beauty

A nobler want of man is served by nature, namely, the love of Beauty.[1]

The ancient Greeks called the world {kosmos}, beauty. Such is the **constitution** of all things, or such the plastic power of the human eye, that the primary forms, as the sky, the mountain, the tree, the animal, give us a delight in and for themselves; a pleasure arising from outline, color, motion, and grouping. This seems partly owing to the eye itself. The eye is the best of artists. By the mutual action of its structure and of the laws of light, perspective is produced, which integrates every mass of objects, of what character soever, into a well colored and shaded globe, so that where the particular objects are mean and unaffecting, the landscape which they compose, is round and symmetrical.[2] And as the eye is the best composer, so light is the first of painters. There is no object so foul that intense light will not make beautiful. And the stimulus it affords to the sense, and a sort of **infinitude** which it hath, like space and time, make all matter gay. Even the corpse has its own beauty. But besides this general grace diffused over nature, almost all the individual forms are agreeable to the eye, as is proved by our endless imitations of some of them, as the **acorn**, the grape, the pine-cone, the wheat-ear, the egg, the wings and forms of most birds, the lion's claw, the serpent, the butterfly, sea-shells, flames, clouds, buds, leaves, and the forms of many trees, as the palm.

For better consideration, we may distribute the aspects of Beauty in a

---

1 A nobler want of man is served by nature, namely, the love of Beauty: 大自然除了提供人类意识所需之外，还满足了一种更高尚的追求——那就是满足了人们的爱美之心。

2 By the mutual action of its structure and of the laws of light, perspective is produced, which integrates every mass of objects, of what character soever, into a well colored and shaded globe, so that where the particular objects are mean and unaffecting, the landscape which they compose, is round and symmetrical: 眼睛的结构与光学的法则互动，产生出所谓的"透视"，因此任何一组物体，不管它是何种东西，在我们看来都觉得色彩清晰，明暗层次鲜明，井然有序，整体就似乎是一个球；个别的物体或许形态拙劣，了无生趣，但一经组合，就变得对称而完满了。

threefold manner.

1. First, the simple perception of natural forms is a delight. The influence of the forms and actions in nature, is so needful to man, that, in its lowest functions, it seems to lie on the confines of commodity and beauty[1]. To the body and mind which have been **cramped** by **noxious** work or company, nature is medicinal and restores their tone. The tradesman, the attorney comes out of the din and craft of the street, and sees the sky and the woods, and is a man again. In their eternal calm, he finds himself. The health of the eye seems to demand a horizon. We are never tired, so long as we can see far enough.

But in other hours, Nature satisfies by its loveliness, and without any mixture of corporeal benefit. I see the spectacle of morning from the hill-top over against my house, from day-break to sun-rise, with emotions which an angel might share. The long slender bars of cloud float like fishes in the sea of crimson light. From the earth, as a shore, I look out into that silent sea. I seem to partake its rapid transformations: the active enchantment reaches my dust, and I **dilate** and conspire with the morning wind. How does Nature deify us with a few and cheap elements! Give me health and a day, and I will make the **pomp** of emperors ridiculous. The dawn is my Assyria; the sun-set and moon-rise my Paphos, and unimaginable realms of **faerie**; broad noon shall be my England of the senses and the understanding; the night shall be my Germany of mystic philosophy and dreams[2].

Not less excellent, except for our less **susceptibility** in the afternoon, was the charm, last evening, of a January sunset. The western clouds divided and subdivided themselves into pink flakes **modulated** with tints of unspeakable softness; and the air had so much life and sweetness, that it was a pain to come within doors. What was it that nature would say? Was there no meaning in the live repose of the valley behind the mill, and which Homer or

---

1 lie on the confines of commodity and beauty: 局限于实用和审美两者之间

2 The dawn is my Assyria; the sun-set and moon-rise my Paphos, and unimaginable realms of faerie; broad noon shall be my England of the senses and the understanding; the night shall be my Germany of mystic philosophy and dreams: 绚烂清晨，是我的亚述帝国；夕阳西落，皓月东升，是我的帕福斯和无法想象的超凡景致；泛泛午日，将是我感觉和思维的英格兰；深深黑夜成为我玄妙哲理和梦想的德意志。

Chapter 15

Ralph Waldo Emerson
拉尔夫·瓦尔多·爱默生

Shakspeare could not reform for me in words? The leafless trees become **spires** of flame in the sunset, with the blue east for their back-ground, and the stars of the dead **calices** of flowers, and every withered stem and **stubble** rimed with frost, contribute something to the mute music.

The inhabitants of cities suppose that the country landscape is pleasant only half the year. I please myself with the graces of the winter scenery, and believe that we are as much touched by it as by the genial influences of summer. To the attentive eye, each moment of the year has its own beauty, and in the same field, it beholds, every hour, a picture which was never seen before, and which shall never be seen again. The heavens change every moment, and reflect their glory or gloom on the plains beneath.[1] The state of the crop in the surrounding farms alters the expression of the earth from week to week. The succession of native plants in the pastures and roadsides, which makes the silent clock by which time tells the summer hours, will make even the divisions of the day sensible to a keen observer. The tribes of birds and insects, like the plants punctual to their time, follow each other, and the year has room for all. By water-courses, the variety is greater. In July, the blue **pontederia** or **pickerel-weed** blooms in large beds in the shallow parts of our pleasant river, and swarms with yellow butterflies in continual motion. Art cannot rival this pomp of purple and gold. Indeed the river is a perpetual gala, and boasts each month a new ornament.

But this beauty of Nature which is seen and felt as beauty, is the least part. The shows of day, the dewy morning, the rainbow, mountains, orchards in blossom, stars, moonlight, shadows in still water, and the like, if too eagerly hunted, become shows merely, and mock us with their unreality. Go out of the house to see the moon, and 't is mere tinsel; it will not please as when its light shines upon your necessary journey. The beauty that **shimmers** in the yellow afternoons of October, who ever could clutch it? Go forth to find it, and it is gone: 't is only a mirage as you look from the windows of diligence.

2. The presence of a higher, namely, of the spiritual element is essential

---

1 The heavens change every moment, and reflect their glory or gloom on the plains beneath: 天空变幻无穷，映衬着下界的盛衰枯荣。

to its perfection. The high and divine beauty which can be loved without effeminacy, is that which is found in combination with the human will. Beauty is the mark God sets upon virtue. Every natural action is graceful. Every heroic act is also decent, and causes the place and the bystanders to shine. We are taught by great actions that the universe is the property of every individual in it. Every rational creature has all nature for his dowry and estate. It is his, if he will. He may **divest** himself of it; he may creep into a corner, and **abdicate** his kingdom, as most men do, but he is entitled to the world by his constitution. In proportion to the energy of his thought and will, he takes up the world into himself. "All those things for which men plough, build, or sail, obey virtue;" said Sallust. "The winds and waves," said Gibbon, "are always on the side of the ablest navigators." So are the sun and moon and all the stars of heaven. When a noble act is done, perchance in a scene of great natural beauty; when Leonidas[1] and his three hundred martyrs consume one day in dying, and the sun and moon come each and look at them once in the steep defile of Thermopylae[2]; when Arnold Winkelried[3], in the high Alps, under the shadow of the **avalanche**, gathers in his side a **sheaf** of Austrian spears to break the line for his comrades; are not these heroes entitled to add the beauty of the scene to the beauty of the deed? When the bark of Columbus nears the shore of America; before it, the beach lined with savages, fleeing out of all their huts of cane; the sea behind; and the purple mountains of the Indian Archipelago[4] around, can we separate the man from the living picture? Does not the New World clothe his form with her palm-groves and savannahs as fit drapery? Ever does natural beauty steal in like air, and envelope great actions. When Sir Harry Vane[5] was dragged up the Tower-hill, sitting on a sled, to suffer death, as the champion of the English laws, one of the multitude cried out to him, "You never sate on so glorious a

---

1 Leonidas: 斯巴达国王莱奥尼达斯率领斯巴达 300 名勇士在色摩比利山与波斯的军队进行最后的决战，壮烈殉难（死于公元前 480 年）。
2 Thermopylae: 色摩比利山，即莱奥尼达斯和他的斯巴达 300 名勇士殉难的地方。
3 Arnold Winkelried: 阿诺得·温克尔里德，瑞士的民族英雄，为了突破澳军的防线，身临冰川崩溃之地，身中无数澳军的矛枪，英勇就义。
4 Indian Archipelago: 印第安列岛
5 Sir Harry Vane: 哈里·韦恩爵士（1613-1662），为捍卫英国法律的声誉，被查理二世判处死刑。

Chapter 15

Ralph Waldo Emerson
拉尔夫·瓦尔多·爱默生

seat." Charles II., to intimidate the citizens of London, caused the patriot Lord Russel to be drawn in an open coach, through the principal streets of the city, on his way to the scaffold. "But," his biographer says, "the multitude imagined they saw liberty and virtue sitting by his side." In private places, among sordid objects, an act of truth or heroism seems at once to draw to itself the sky as its temple, the sun as its candle. Nature stretcheth out her arms to embrace man, only let his thoughts be of equal greatness. Willingly does she follow his steps with the rose and the violet, and bend her lines of grandeur and grace to the decoration of her darling child. Only let his thoughts be of equal scope, and the frame will suit the picture. A virtuous man is in unison with her works, and makes the central figure of the visible sphere. Homer, Pindar, Socrates, Phocion, associate themselves fitly in our memory with the geography and climate of Greece. The visible heavens and earth sympathize with Jesus. And in common life, whosoever has seen a person of powerful character and happy genius, will have remarked how easily he took all things along with him, the persons, the opinions, and the day, and nature became ancillary to a man.

3. There is still another aspect under which the beauty of the world may be viewed, namely, as it become s an object of the intellect. Beside the relation of things to virtue, they have a relation to thought. The intellect searches out the absolute order of things as they stand in the mind of God, and without the colors of affection. The intellectual and the active powers seem to succeed each other, and the exclusive activity of the one, generates the exclusive activity of the other. There is something unfriendly in each to the other, but they are like the alternate periods of feeding and working in animals; each prepares and will be followed by the other. Therefore does beauty, which, in relation to actions, as we have seen, comes unsought, and comes because it is unsought, remain for the apprehension and pursuit of the intellect; and then again, in its turn, of the active power. Nothing divine dies. All good is eternally reproductive. The beauty of nature reforms itself in the mind, and not for barren contemplation, but for new creation.

All men are in some degree impressed by the face of the world; some men even to delight. This love of beauty is Taste. Others have the same love in such excess, that, not content with admiring, they seek to embody it in new forms. The creation of beauty is Art.

The production of a work of art throws a light upon the mystery of humanity. A work of art is an abstract or epitome of the world. It is the result or expression of nature, in miniature. For, although the works of nature are innumerable and all different, the result or the expression of them all is similar and single. Nature is a sea of forms radically alike and even unique. A leaf, a sun-beam, a landscape, the ocean, make an analogous impression on the mind. What is common to them all, that perfectness and harmony, is beauty. The standard of beauty is the entire circuit of natural forms, the totality of nature; which the Italians expressed by defining beauty "il piu nell' uno." Nothing is quite beautiful alone: nothing but is beautiful in the whole. A single object is only so far beautiful as it suggests this universal grace. The poet, the painter, the sculptor, the musician, the architect, seek each to concentrate this radiance of the world on one point, and each in his several work to satisfy the love of beauty which stimulates him to produce. Thus is Art, a nature passed through the alembic of man. Thus in art, does nature work through the will of a man filled with the beauty of her first works.

The world thus exists to the soul to satisfy the desire of beauty. This element I call an ultimate end. No reason can be asked or given why the soul seeks beauty. Beauty, in its largest and profoundest sense, is one expression for the universe. God is the all-fair. Truth, and goodness, and beauty, are but different faces of the same All. But beauty in nature is not ultimate. It is the herald of inward and eternal beauty, and is not alone a solid and satisfactory good. It must stand as a part, and not as yet the last or highest expression of the final cause of Nature.

Words and Phrases

constitution [kɒnstɪ'tjuːʃn]　　n.　the physical makeup of the individual especially zwith respect to the health, strength, and appearance of the body 体格；组成

Chapter 15

Ralph Waldo Emerson
拉尔夫·瓦尔多·爱默生

infinitude [ɪnˈfɪnɪtjuːd]	n.	the quality or state of being infinite, infinitness 无限，无穷
acorn [ˈeɪkɔːn]	n.	the nut of the oak tree 橡子
cramp [kræmp]	v.	prevent the progress or free movement of 束缚；限制；使……抽筋；以铁箍扣紧
noxious [ˈnɒkʃəs]	adj.	injurious to physical or mental health 讨厌的
dilate [daɪˈleɪt]	v.	become bigger, wider; add details to, clarify the meaning in a learned way 扩大；膨胀；详述
pomp [pɒmp]	n.	ceremonial elegance and splendor 盛况；浮华
faerie [ˈfeərɪ]	n.	fairyland 仙境，仙地
susceptibility [səˌseptɪˈbɪlɪtɪ]	n.	the state of being susceptible; easily affected 敏感性；感情
modulate [ˈmɒdjʊleɪt]	v.	fix or adjust the time, amount, degree, or rate of 调节
spire [spaɪə]	n.	a tall tower that forms the superstructure of a building (usually a church or temple) and that tapers to a point at the top 尖顶；尖塔；螺旋
calices [ˈkælɪsiːz]	n.	cups 盏（calix 的复数）；杯状窝；凹洼
stubble [ˈstʌb(ə)l]	n.	material consisting of seed coverings and small pieces of stem or leaves that have been separated from the seeds 残株；发茬；须茬
pontederia [pɒnˈtedərɪə]	n.	梭鱼草
pickerel-weed [ˈpɪkərəlˌwiːd]	n.	A freshwater plant of eastern North America, having heart-shaped leaves with long petioles and spikes of violet-blue flowers 梭鱼草，一种多年生植物（产于北美沼泽）
shimmer [ˈʃɪmə]	v.	shine with a weak or fitful light 闪烁
divest [daɪˈvest]	v.	take away possessions from someone deprive of status or authority 剥夺；使脱去；迫使放弃
abdicate [ˈæbdɪkeɪt]	v.	give up, such as power, as of monarchs and emperors, or duties and obligations 退位；放弃
avalanche [ˈævəlɑːnʃ]	n.	a large amount of snow and ice that slides

| | | suddenly down the side of a mountain 雪崩 |
| sheaf [ʃi:f] | n. | a package of several things tied together for carrying or storing 捆; 束; 扎 |

II Reading Comprehension Questions

1. According to the author, what are the three aspects of Beauty? Do you agree with him in this division? Do you have more categories to add?
2. How do you understand "The tradesman, the attorney comes out of the din and craft of the street, and sees the sky and the woods, and is a man again"?
3. Do you think Creation an important part of Beauty? Please give examples to illustrate your point.
4. How can we find the beauty of nature, since it is gone if we eagerly hunt it?
5. Do you think there is a difference among people as for the love of beauty?

Chapter 15
Ralph Waldo Emerson
拉尔夫·瓦尔多·爱默生

Quotes of the Author

A foolish consistency is the hobgoblin of little minds, adored by little statesmen and philosophers and divines.

Beware when the great God lets loose a thinker on this planet.

Children are all foreigners.

Every hero becomes a bore at last.

I hate quotations. Tell me what you know.

Chapter 16

Henry David Thoreau
亨利·大卫·梭罗
(1817—1862)

本章导读

亨利·大卫·梭罗是美国浪漫主义时期一位特立独行的作家，他的文学地位在他去世后才被世人认可。他新颖而超前的作品在美国文学史上留下了浓墨重彩的一笔。

梭罗与拉尔夫·瓦尔多·爱默生处于同一时代。这一时期，美国的经济处于上升阶段，轰轰烈烈的工业化进程将美国带入了内战前的"黄金时间"。传统的农业社会开始向工业社会转轨，对大自然资源不加节制的开发、利用出现苗头。机器的广泛应用、铁路的铺架，都大大提升了人们的生活环境。随着物质生活的改善，人们的精神生活开始出现空洞；金钱、享乐几乎占据了人的思想。意识到现实问题的梭罗于1845年离开喧嚣的城市，来到康科德城郊的瓦尔登湖畔，亲手搭建了一个简陋的小木屋，在四周开荒种地，自力更生，尽情享受大自然的馈赠，过了两年多的独居生活。在回到城市后，他将自己的经历与感悟用几年的时间进行整理，写成了他的代表作《瓦尔登湖，或林中生活》（*Walden; or, Life in the Woods*）。在这之后，他为自然的魅力所吸引，不知疲倦地观察家乡的地理风貌，还从事了一段时间的土地调查员，并四处旅行，写下自己的心得和感悟。同时，还对美国政府对外战争和奴隶制度进行了声讨。他的作品充分体现了时代特征。

梭罗一生的著述多达数百万字，后人为他出版札记全集达47卷。最能代表梭罗思想的作品当属《瓦尔登湖》。在当时物欲横流的社会中，梭罗超凡脱俗的自然观的确打破了当时世俗阶层狭隘实用的自然观，就像炎热的夏日吹来一股凉爽的清风，顿时让人神清气爽。可以说，他的作品主题超越了时代。时人虽不识其意义，但梭罗的作品却在一个世纪后焕发了生机。

Chapter 16
Henry David Thoreau
亨利·大卫·梭罗

梭罗的散文风格平易而明晰、自然而畅达，笔调生动灵活，时而记录生活细节而平铺直叙，时而描绘自然景致而诗意盎然，时而针砭时弊而不留情面，时而澄思寂虑而哲思飞扬。以《瓦尔登湖》为例，梭罗时常以流水账一般的语言记录他的生活实践经历，但没有流于表面，而是在其中不时插入轶事、寓言并引入自己的哲学思考，这就给整个文章增添了深度与魅力。当然，梭罗跳跃的叙述方式使读者不容易把握他的思维，但梭罗在讲述深奥的话题时，往往会先用一段实际生活经验引入，便于读者理解。与爱默生的超验主义文章比起来，梭罗的散文少了许多理论性，却多了几分可读性。

About the Author

Henry David Thoreau, American transcendentalist and essayist, was one of the most important 19th-century literary figures in American. He was born on July 12, 1817 in Concord, Massachusetts. When Thoreau was 16, he entered Harvard College, where he was known as a serious though unconventional scholar. While there, Henry read a small book by his Concord neighbor, Ralph Waldo Emerson, *Nature*, and in a sense he never finished exploring its ideas—although always definitely on his own terms. After graduation, he came bake to Concord, and refused all the careers his education prepared him for. Instead, he worked for several years as a surveyor and making pencils with his father, but at the age of 28 in 1845, wanting to write his first book, he went to Walden pond and built his cabin on land owned by Emerson.

Today, Thoreau is best known for his time spent at Walden Pond and the work that came out of that experience—*Walden; or, Life in the Woods*. A description of his twenty-six month retreat on the edges of a small pond—Walden, the book has become an American classic.

Thoreau's books, articles, essays, journals, and poetry total over 20 volumes. Among his lasting contributions are his writings on natural history and philosophy, where he anticipated the methods and findings of ecology and environmental history, two sources of modern-day environmentalism. His literary style interweaves close natural observation, personal experience, pointed rhetoric, symbolic meanings, and historical lore, while displaying a poetic sensibility, philosophical austerity. He was also deeply interested in the idea of survival in the face of hostile elements, historical change, and natural decay; at the same time he advocated abandoning waste and illusion in order to discover life's true essential needs.

The two essays in this chapter are both taken from *Walden*: one from the section of "Economy", and one from the section of "Solitude".

Chapter 16

Henry David Thoreau
亨利·大卫·梭罗

Text A

Economy[1]
(Excerpt)

Henry David Thoreau

Most men, even in this comparatively free country, through mere ignorance and mistake, are so occupied with the **factitious** cares and superfluously coarse labors of life that its finer fruits cannot be plucked by them. Their fingers, from excessive toil, are too clumsy and tremble too much for that. Actually, the laboring man has not leisure for a true integrity day by day; he cannot afford to sustain the manliest relations to men; his labor would be depreciated in the market. He has no time to be anything but a machine. How can he remember well his ignorance—which his growth requires—who has so often to use his knowledge? We should feed and clothe him **gratuitously** sometimes, and recruit him with our cordials, before we judge of him. The finest qualities of our nature, like the bloom on fruits, can be preserved only by the most delicate handling. Yet we do not treat ourselves nor one another thus tenderly.

Some of you, we all know, are poor, find it hard to live, are sometimes, as it were, gasping for breath. I have no doubt that some of you who read this book are unable to pay for all the dinners which you have actually eaten, or for the coats and shoes which are fast wearing or are already worn out, and have come to this page to spend borrowed or stolen time, robbing your creditors of an hour. It is very evident what mean and sneaking lives many of

---

1 Economy: the introductory part of the book, *Walden*. In this chapter, Thoreau defines what he sees as the major problem of his time: how work and the acquisition of material goods can consume your life. Thoreau did not want to live out his life like this—"when I came to die, discover that I had not lived." 经济篇是《瓦尔登湖》的第一章。在这一章里，梭罗分析了他所处时代的主要问题：工作和财富的累积正在透支人的生活。"当我将死之时，才发现我根本没有活过。" 梭罗显然不想过这样的生活。

you live, for my sight has been **whetted** by experience; always on the limits, trying to get into business and trying to get out of debt, a very ancient **slough**[1], called by the Latins æs alienum, another's brass, for some of their coins were made of brass; still living, and dying, and buried by this other's brass; always promising to pay, promising to pay, tomorrow, and dying today, insolvent; seeking to curry favor, to get custom, by how many modes, only not state-prison offenses; lying, flattering, voting, contracting yourselves into a nutshell of civility or dilating into an atmosphere of thin and vaporous generosity, that you may persuade your neighbor to let you make his shoes, or his hat, or his coat, or his carriage, or import his groceries for him; making yourselves sick, that you may lay up something against a sick day, something to be tucked away in an old chest, or in a stocking behind the plastering, or, more safely, in the brick bank; no matter where, no matter how much or how little.

I sometimes wonder that we can be so frivolous, I may almost say, as to attend to the gross but somewhat foreign form of servitude called Negro Slavery, there are so many keen and subtle masters that enslave both North and South. It is hard to have a Southern overseer; it is worse to have a Northern one; but worst of all when you are the slave-driver of yourself. Talk of a divinity in man! Look at the teamster on the highway, wending to market by day or night; does any divinity stir within him? His highest duty to **fodder** and water his horses! What is his destiny to him compared with the shipping interests? Does not he drive for Squire Make-a-stir? How godlike, how immortal, is he? See how he **cowers** and sneaks, how vaguely all the day he fears, not being immortal nor divine, but the slave and prisoner of his own opinion of himself, a fame won by his own deeds. Public opinion is a weak tyrant compared with our own private opinion. What a man thinks of himself, that it is which determines, or rather indicates, his fate. Self-emancipation even in the West Indian provinces of the fancy and imagination—what

---

1 a very ancient slough: the "Slough of Despond" in *The Pilgrim's Progress*, part 1, 1675, by John Bunyan（1628–1688）此处的深渊指的是班扬的《天路历程》中描绘的"绝望的深渊"。

Chapter 16

Henry David Thoreau
亨利・大卫・梭罗

Wilberforce[1] is there to bring that about? Think, also, of the ladies of the land weaving toilet cushions against the last day, not to betray too green an interest in their fates! As if you could kill time without injuring eternity.

The mass of men lead lives of quiet desperation. What is called resignation is confirmed desperation. From the desperate city you go into the desperate country, and have to **console** yourself with the bravery of **minks** and muskrats. A stereotyped but unconscious despair is concealed even under what are called the games and amusements of mankind. There is no play in them, for this comes after work. But it is a characteristic of wisdom not to do desperate things.

When we consider what, to use the words of the catechism[2], is the chief end of man, and what are the true necessaries and means of life, it appears as if men had deliberately chosen the common mode of living because they preferred it to any other. Yet they honestly think there is no choice left. But alert and healthy natures remember that the sun rose clear. It is never too late to give up our prejudices. No way of thinking or doing, however ancient, can be trusted without proof. What everybody echoes or in silence passes by as true today may turn out to be falsehood tomorrow, mere smoke of opinion, which some had trusted for a cloud that would sprinkle fertilizing rain on their fields. What old people say you cannot do, you try and find that you can. Old deeds for old people, and new deeds for new. Old people did not know enough once, **perchance**, to fetch fresh fuel to keep the fire a-going; new people put a little dry wood under a pot, and are whirled round the globe with the speed of birds[3], in a way to kill old people, as the phrase is. Age is no better, hardly so well, qualified for an instructor as youth, for it has not profited so much as

---

1 Wilberforce: William Wilberforce (1759–1833), English anti-slavery leader 威廉・威尔伯福斯，慈善家、废奴主义领袖

2 catechism: Westminster Catechism: "Man's chief end is to glorify God, and to enjoy Him forever." 《威斯敏斯德小教要问答》是在 1647 年英国威斯敏斯德会议产生的。它用字审慎、字义明晰，集中讨论的是基督教的教义，而不是事实，所以它的结构不是按《圣经》记载中历史的顺序，而是按教义内在的逻辑顺序。教要问答的首问：人生的首要目的是什么？答：人生的首要目的就是荣耀上帝并以他为乐，直到永远。

3 new people put a little dry wood under a pot, and are whirled round the globe with the speed of birds: the technology of a steam engine 此处所描述的是蒸汽机的技术。

it has lost. One may almost doubt if the wisest man has learned anything of absolute value by living. Practically, the old have no very important advice to give the young, their own experience has been so partial, and their lives have been such miserable failures, for private reasons, as they must believe; and it may be that they have some faith left which belies that experience, and they are only less young than they were. I have lived some thirty years on this planet, and I have yet to hear the first syllable of valuable or even earnest advice from my seniors. They have told me nothing, and probably cannot tell me anything to the purpose. Here is life, an experiment to a great extent untried by me; but it does not avail me that they have tried it. If I have any experience which I think valuable, I am sure to reflect that this my Mentors said nothing about.

One farmer says to me, "You cannot live on vegetable food solely, for it furnishes nothing to make bones with"; and so he religiously devotes a part of his day to supplying his system with the raw material of bones; walking all the while he talks behind his oxen, which, with vegetable-made bones, jerk him and his lumbering plow along in spite of every obstacle. Some things are really necessaries of life in some circles, the most helpless and diseased, which in others are luxuries merely, and in others still are entirely unknown.

The whole ground of human life seems to some to have been gone over by their predecessors, both the heights and the valleys, and all things to have been cared for. According to Evelyn[1],"the wise Solomon prescribed **ordinances** for the very distances of trees; and the Roman prætors have decided how often you may go into your neighbor's land to gather the acorns which fall on it without trespass, and what share belongs to that neighbor." Hippocrates[2] has even left directions how we should cut our nails; that is, even with the ends of the fingers, neither shorter nor longer. Undoubtedly the very tedium and ennui which presume to have exhausted the variety and the joys of life are as old as

---

1 Evelyn: John Evelyn (1620–1706), a famous English horticulturist and author. The following quote is from *Sylva, or A Discourse of Forest Trees* (1664). 约翰·伊夫林，英国著名园艺学家和作家。该处的引言来自伊夫林1664年出版的《森林志，又名林木论》。

2 Hippocrates: Greek physician (460?–377? B.C.), Father of Medicine 希波克拉底，希腊名医

Chapter 16

Henry David Thoreau
亨利·大卫·梭罗

Adam. But man's capacities have never been measured; nor are we to judge of what he can do by any precedents, so little has been tried. Whatever have been thy failures hitherto, "be not afflicted, my child, for who shall assign to thee what thou hast left undone?"

We might try our lives by a thousand simple tests; as, for instance, that the same sun which ripens my beans illumines at once a system of earths like ours. If I had remembered this it would have prevented some mistakes. This was not the light in which I hoed them. The stars are the apexes of what wonderful triangles! What distant and different beings in the various mansions of the universe are contemplating the same one at the same moment! Nature and human life are as various as our several constitutions. Who shall say what prospect life offers to another? Could a greater miracle take place than for us to look through each other's eyes for an instant? We should live in all the ages of the world in an hour; ay, in all the worlds of the ages. History, Poetry, Mythology!—I know of no reading of another's experience so startling and informing as this would be.

The greater part of what my neighbors call good I believe in my soul to be bad, and if I repent of anything, it is very likely to be my good behavior. What demon possessed me that I behaved so well? You may say the wisest thing you can, old man—you who have lived seventy years, not without honor of a kind—I hear an irresistible voice which invites me away from all that. One generation abandons the enterprises of another like stranded vessels.

I think that we may safely trust a good deal more than we do. We may waive just so much care of ourselves as we honestly bestow elsewhere. Nature is as well adapted to our weakness as to our strength. The incessant anxiety and strain of some is a well-nigh incurable form of disease. We are made to exaggerate the importance of what work we do; and yet how much is not done by us! or, what if we had been taken sick? How vigilant we are! determined not to live by faith if we can avoid it; all the day long on the alert, at night we unwillingly say our prayers and commit ourselves to uncertainties. So thoroughly and sincerely are we compelled to live, reverencing our life, and denying the possibility of change. This is the only way, we say; but there are as many ways as there can be drawn radii from one centre. All change is a miracle to contemplate; but it is a miracle which is taking place every instant. Confucius said, "To know that we know what we know, and that we do not know what we do not know, that is true knowledge." When one man has reduced a fact of the imagination to be a fact to his understanding, I foresee that all men at length establish their lives on that basis.

I Words and Phrases

factitious [fæk'tɪʃəs]	*adj.* not produced by natural forces 不自然的；虚假的
gratuitously [græ'tjuːɪtəslɪ]	*adv.* in an uncalled-for manner 平白无故地
whet [wet]	*v.* make keen or more acute 磨快；促进
slough [slaʊ]	*n.* a stagnant swamp (especially as part of a bayou) 泥沼；绝境
fodder ['fɒdə]	*n.* coarse food (especially for cattle and horses) composed of entire plants or the leaves and stalks of a cereal crop 饲料
cower ['kaʊə]	*v.* crouch or curl up 退缩；蜷缩
console [kən'səʊl]	*v.* give moral or emotional strength to 安慰，慰藉
mink [mɪŋk]	*n.* a small animal that has a thin body and soft, dark brown fur 貂
perchance [pə'tʃɑːns]	*adv.* maybe but not definitely 偶然；可能
ordinance ['ɔːdɪnəns]	*n.* a statute enacted by a city government 条例；法令

II Reading Comprehension Questions

1. "The finest qualities of our nature, like the bloom on fruits, can be preserved only by the most delicate handling." What do you think are our

Chapter 16

Henry David Thoreau
亨利·大卫·梭罗

finest qualities? What is meant by "the most delicate handling"?

2. What does the author want to suggest by the reference to Negro Slavery in the third paragraph?
3. How do you understand "The mass of men lead lives of quiet desperation?" What do you think of people's state of living nowadays?
4. What's the relation between "Economy" and what the author tries to express in the essay?
5. Can you figure out the original sentence said by Confucius in the last paragraph? Do you think the author understand the sentence properly?

III Questions on Writing Style and Language

1. Have you noticed any stylistic features of Thoreau's writing? Are his sentences long or short? What particular effect is produced by these sentences?
2. The topic the author talks about is not a simple one. How does the author begin his discussion?
3. Please analyse the figure of speech used in the following sentence and try to understand what the author trys to convey.
   "Could a greater miracle take place than for us to look through each other's eyes for an instant?"
4. What are some of the other retorical devices the author used in this text? Please pick them out and analyze.
5. Thoreau was not considered a successful man by society during his own lifetime. His published writings had few readers and little impact of whatever kind. But even if he had published nothing, his journals revealed the richness of his deep down personal success in life, which made his writings bloom with a positive spirit toward life. Where can you see his positive spirit in this text?

Text B

Solitude[1]

Henry David Thoreau

This is a delicious evening, when the whole body is one sense, and **imbibes** delight through every pore. I go and come with a strange liberty in Nature, a part of herself. As I walk along the stony shore of the pond in my shirt-sleeves, though it is cool as well as cloudy and windy, and I see nothing special to attract me, all the elements are unusually congenial to me. The bullfrogs trump to usher in the night, and the note of the **whip-poor-will** is borne on the rippling wind from over the water. Sympathy with the fluttering **alder** and poplar leaves almost takes away my breath; yet, like the lake, my serenity is rippled but not ruffled. These small waves raised by the evening wind are as remote from storm as the smooth reflecting surface. Though it is now dark, the wind still blows and roars in the wood, the waves still dash, and some creatures **lull** the rest with their notes. The repose is never complete. The wildest animals do not repose, but seek their prey now; the fox, and skunk, and rabbit, now roam the fields and woods without fear. They are Nature's watchmen—links which connect the days of animated life.

When I return to my house I find that visitors have been there and left their cards, either a bunch of flowers, or a wreath of evergreen, or a name in pencil on a yellow walnut leaf or a chip. They who come rarely to the woods take some little piece of the forest into their hands to play with by the way, which they leave, either intentionally or accidentally. One has peeled a willow

---

1 This selection is taken from the chapter of "Solitude" from *Walden*. The chapter mainly describes Thoreau's own experiment in living a simple life. Though living alone, Thoreau "is no more lonely than the loon in the pond that laughs so loud, or than Walden Pond itself." 本部分节选自《瓦尔登湖》的《孤独篇》。本章主要描写了梭罗一人住在瓦尔登湖、寂静却不寂寞的生活，探讨了独处的意义。尽管身居陋室，以物为伴，独享闲情，但梭罗"并不比那嬉水湖中的鸭子或瓦尔登湖本身更孤独"。

Chapter 16

Henry David Thoreau
亨利·大卫·梭罗

wand, woven it into a ring, and dropped it on my table. I could always tell if visitors had called in my absence, either by the bended twigs or grass, or the print of their shoes, and generally of what sex or age or quality they were by some slight trace left, as a flower dropped, or a bunch of grass plucked and thrown away, even as far off as the railroad, half a mile distant, or by the lingering odor of a cigar or pipe. Nay, I was frequently notified of the passage of a traveller along the highway sixty **rods** off by the scent of his pipe.

There is commonly sufficient space about us. Our horizon is never quite at our elbows. The thick wood is not just at our door, nor the pond, but somewhat is always clearing, familiar and worn by us, appropriated and fenced in some way, and reclaimed from Nature. For what reason have I this vast range and circuit, some square miles of unfrequented forest, for my privacy, abandoned to me by men? My nearest neighbor is a mile distant, and no house is visible from any place but the hill-tops within half a mile of my own. I have my horizon bounded by woods all to myself; a distant view of the railroad where it touches the pond on the one hand, and of the fence which skirts the woodland road on the other. But for the most part it is as solitary where I live as on the prairies. It is as much Asia or Africa as New England. I have, as it were, my own sun and moon and stars, and a little world all to myself. At night there was never a traveller passed my house, or knocked at my door, more than if I were the first or last man; unless it were in the spring, when at long intervals some came from the village to fish for **pouts**—they plainly fished much more in the Walden Pond of their own natures, and baited their hooks with darkness—but they soon retreated, usually with light baskets, and left "the world to darkness and to me," and the black kernel of the night was never **profaned** by any human neighborhood. I believe that men are generally still a little afraid of the dark, though the witches are all hung, and Christianity and candles have been introduced.

Yet I experienced sometimes that the most sweet and tender, the most innocent and encouraging society may be found in any natural object, even for the poor misanthrope and most melancholy man. There can be no very black melancholy to him who lives in the midst of Nature and has his senses still. There was never yet such a storm but it was Aeolian music[1] to a healthy and innocent ear. Nothing can rightly compel a simple and brave man to a vulgar sadness. While I enjoy the friendship of the seasons I trust that nothing can make life a burden to me. The gentle rain which waters my beans and keeps me in the house today is not drear and melancholy, but good for me too. Though it prevents my **hoeing** them, it is of far more worth than my hoeing. If it should continue so long as to cause the seeds to rot in the ground and destroy the potatoes in the low lands, it would still be good for the grass on the uplands, and, being good for the grass, it would be good for me. Sometimes, when I compare myself with other men, it seems as if I were more favored by the gods than they, beyond any **deserts** that I am conscious of; as if I had a warrant and surety at their hands which my fellows have not, and were especially guided and guarded. I do not flatter myself, but if it be possible they flatter me. I have never felt lonesome, or in the least oppressed by a sense of solitude, but once, and that was a few weeks after I came to the woods, when, for an hour, I doubted if the near neighborhood of man was not essential to a serene and healthy life. To be alone was something unpleasant. But I was at the same time conscious of a slight insanity in my mood, and seemed to foresee my recovery. In the midst of a gentle rain while these thoughts prevailed, I was suddenly sensible of such sweet and beneficent society in Nature, in the very pattering of the drops, and in every sound and sight around my house, an infinite and unaccountable friendliness all at once like an atmosphere sustaining me, as made the fancied advantages of human neighborhood insignificant, and I have never thought of them since. Every little pine needle expanded and swelled with sympathy and befriended me. I was so distinctly made aware of the presence of something kindred to me, even in scenes which we are accustomed to call wild and dreary, and also that the nearest of blood to me and humanest was not a person nor a villager, that I thought no place could ever be strange to me again.

1　Aeolian music: in Greek mythology, the Aeolian harp was the instrument of Aeolus, god of wind. The ancient Greeks made Aeolian harps that were played by moving air. 希腊神话中埃俄利亚风弦琴是风之神埃俄罗斯的乐器。传说古希腊人善于制作靠风演奏的风弦琴。

Chapter 16

Henry David Thoreau
亨利·大卫·梭罗

"Mourning untimely consumes the sad;
Few are their days in the land of the living,
Beautiful daughter of Toscar."[1]

Some of my pleasantest hours were during the long rain-storms in the spring or fall, which confined me to the house for the afternoon as well as the forenoon, soothed by their ceaseless roar and **pelting**; when an early twilight ushered in a long evening in which many thoughts had time to take root and unfold themselves. In those driving northeast rains which tried the village houses so, when the maids stood ready with mop and pail in front entries to keep the **deluge** out, I sat behind my door in my little house, which was all entry, and thoroughly enjoyed its protection. In one heavy thunder-shower the lightning struck a large **pitch pine** across the pond, making a very conspicuous and perfectly regular spiral groove from top to bottom, an inch or more deep, and four or five inches wide, as you would **groove** a walking-stick. I passed it again the other day, and was struck with awe on looking up and beholding that mark, now more distinct than ever, where a terrific and resistless **bolt** came down out of the harmless sky eight years ago[2]. Men frequently say to me, "I should think you would feel lonesome down there, and want to be nearer to folks, rainy and snowy days and nights especially." I am tempted to reply to such—This whole earth which we inhabit is but a point in space. How far apart, think you, dwell the two most distant inhabitants of yonder star, the breadth of whose disk cannot be appreciated by our instruments? Why should I feel lonely? is not our planet in the Milky Way? This which you put seems to me not to be the most important question. What sort of space is that which separates a man from his fellows and makes him solitary? I have found that no exertion of the legs can bring two minds much nearer to one another. What do we want most to dwell near to? Not to many men surely, the depot, the post-office, the bar-room, the meeting-house, the

---

1 The quotation is from *Croma* by James Macpherson (1736–1796), a Scottish writer, poet and politician. 诗句引自苏格兰诗人詹姆斯·麦克佛森的诗歌。

2 eight years ago: Thoreau lived at Walden from 1845 to 1847. *Walden* was not published until 1854. 梭罗1845年到1847年住在瓦尔登湖畔，其著作《瓦尔登湖》直到1854年才出版。

school-house, the grocery, Beacon Hill[1], or the Five Points[2], where men most congregate, but to the perennial source of our life, whence in all our experience we have found that to issue, as the willow stands near the water and sends out its roots in that direction. This will vary with different natures, but this is the place where a wise man will dig his cellar.... I one evening overtook one of my townsmen, who has accumulated what is called "a handsome property"—though I never got a *fair* view of it—on the Walden road, driving a pair of cattle to market, who inquired of me how I could bring my mind to give up so many of the comforts of life. I answered that I was very sure I liked it **passably** well; I was not joking. And so I went home to my bed, and left him to pick his way through the darkness and the mud to Brighton—or Bright-town—which place he would reach some time in the morning.

Any prospect of awakening or coming to life to a dead man makes indifferent all times and places. The place where that may occur is always the same, and indescribably pleasant to all our senses. For the most part we allow only outlying and transient circumstances to make our occasions. They are, in fact, the cause of our distraction. Nearest to all things is that power which **fashions** their being. *Next* to us the grandest laws are continually being executed. *Next* to us is not the workman whom we have hired, with whom we love so well to talk, but the workman whose work we are.

"How vast and profound is the influence of the subtile powers of Heaven and of Earth!"[3]

"We seek to perceive them, and we do not see them; we seek to hear them, and we do not hear them; identified with the substance of things, they cannot be separated from them."[4]

---

1 Beacon Hill: fashionable section of Boston 灯塔山，波士顿的一个繁华时尚之处

2 Five Points: a disreputable section of New York City throughout the 1800s, between the current NY City Hall and Chinatown 19 世纪纽约市内一个臭名昭著的地方，在今日的市政厅和中国城之间

3 "How vast and profound is the influence of the subtile powers of Heaven and of Earth!": 鬼神之为德，其盛矣乎。这一句及以下两句都选自《中庸》。

4 "We seek to perceive them, and we do not see them; we seek to hear them, and we do not hear them; identified with the substance of things, they cannot be separated from them.": 视之而弗见；听之而弗闻；体物而不可遗。

Chapter 16

Henry David Thoreau
亨利·大卫·梭罗

"They cause that in all the universe men purify and sanctify their hearts, and clothe themselves in their holiday garments to offer sacrifices and **oblations** to their ancestors. It is an ocean of subtle intelligences. They are everywhere, above us, on our left, on our right; they environ us on all sides."[1]

We are the subjects of an experiment which is not a little interesting to me. Can we not do without the society of our gossips a little while under these circumstances—have our own thoughts to cheer us? Confucius says truly, "Virtue does not remain as an abandoned orphan; it must of necessity have neighbors."[2]

With thinking we may be beside ourselves in a sane sense. By a conscious effort of the mind we can stand aloof from actions and their consequences; and all things, good and bad, go by us like a **torrent**. We are not wholly involved in Nature. I may be either the driftwood in the stream, or Indra[3] in the sky looking down on it. I *may* be affected by a theatrical exhibition; on the other hand, I *may not* be affected by an actual event which appears to concern me much more. I only know myself as a human entity; the scene, so to speak, of thoughts and affections; and am sensible of a certain doubleness by which I can stand as remote from myself as from another. However intense my experience, I am conscious of the presence and criticism of a part of me, which, as it were, is not a part of me, but spectator, sharing no experience, but taking note of it, and that is no more I than it is you. When the play, it may be the tragedy, of life is over, the spectator goes his way. It was a kind of fiction, a work of the imagination only, so far as he was concerned. This doubleness may easily make us poor neighbors and friends sometimes.

I find it wholesome to be alone the greater part of the time. To be in company, even with the best, is soon wearisome and dissipating. I love to be

---

1 "They cause that in all the universe men purify and sanctify their hearts, and clothe themselves in their holiday garments to offer sacrifices and oblations to their ancestors. It is an ocean of subtle intelligences. They are everywhere, above us, on our left, on our right; they environ us on all sides.": 使天下之人，齐明盛服，以承祭祀。洋洋乎，如在其上，如在其左右。

2 "Virtue does not remain as an abandoned orphan; it must of necessity have neighbors.": 德不孤，必有邻。这句话出自《论语·里仁》。

3 Indra: in Hinduism, chief of the Vedic gods, god of thunder and rain 印度教中主管雷雨的神

alone. I never found the companion that was so companionable as solitude. We are for the most part more lonely when we go abroad among men than when we stay in our chambers. A man thinking or working is always alone, let him be where he will. Solitude is not measured by the miles of space that intervene between a man and his fellows. The really diligent student in one of the crowded **hives** of Cambridge College is as solitary as a **dervish** in the desert. The farmer can work alone in the field or the woods all day, hoeing or chopping, and not feel lonesome, because he is employed; but when he comes home at night he cannot sit down in a room alone, at the mercy of his thoughts, but must be where he can "see the folks," and recreate, and as he thinks remunerate himself for his day's solitude; and hence he wonders how the student can sit alone in the house all night and most of the day without ennui and "the blues"; but he does not realize that the student, though in the house, is still at work in *his* field, and chopping in *his* woods, as the farmer in his, and in turn seeks the same recreation and society that the latter does, though it may be a more condensed form of it.

Society is commonly too cheap. We meet at very short intervals, not having had time to acquire any new value for each other. We meet at meals three times a day, and give each other a new taste of that old musty cheese that we are. We have had to agree on a certain set of rules, called etiquette and politeness, to make this frequent meeting tolerable and that we need not come to open war. We meet at the post-office, and at the sociable, and about the fireside every night; we live thick and are in each other's way, and stumble over one another, and I think that we thus lose some respect for one another. Certainly less frequency would suffice for all important and hearty communications. Consider the girls in a factory—never alone, hardly in their dreams. It would be better if there were but one inhabitant to a square mile, as where I live. The value of a man is not in his skin, that we should touch him.

I have heard of a man lost in the woods and dying of famine and exhaustion at the foot of a tree, whose loneliness was relieved by the grotesque visions with which, owing to bodily weakness, his diseased imagination surrounded him, and which he believed to be real. So also, owing to bodily

Chapter 16

Henry David Thoreau
亨利·大卫·梭罗

and mental health and strength, we may be continually cheered by a like but more normal and natural society, and come to know that we are never alone.

I have a great deal of company in my house; especially in the morning, when nobody calls. Let me suggest a few comparisons, that some one may convey an idea of my situation. I am no more lonely than the loon in the pond that laughs so loud, or than Walden Pond itself. What company has that lonely lake, I pray? And yet it has not the blue devils[1], but the blue angels in it, in the azure tint of its waters. The sun is alone, except in thick weather, when there sometimes appear to be two, but one is a mock sun. God is alone—but the devil, he is far from being alone; he sees a great deal of company; he is legion. I am no more lonely than a single mullein or dandelion in a pasture, or a bean leaf, or sorrel, or a horse-fly, or a bumblebee. I am no more lonely than the Mill Brook, or a weathercock, or the north star, or the south wind, or an April shower, or a January thaw, or the first spider in a new house.

I have occasional visits in the long winter evenings, when the snow falls fast and the wind howls in the wood, from an old settler and original proprietor, who is reported to have dug Walden Pond, and stoned it, and fringed it with pine woods; who tells me stories of old time and of new eternity; and between us we manage to pass a cheerful evening with social mirth and pleasant views of things, even without apples or cider—a most wise and humorous friend, whom I love much, who keeps himself more secret than ever did Goffe or Whalley[2]; and though he is thought to be dead, none can show where he is buried. An elderly dame, too, dwells in my neighborhood, invisible to most persons, in whose odorous herb garden I love to stroll sometimes, gathering simples and listening to her fables; for she has a genius of unequalled fertility, and her memory runs back farther than mythology, and she can tell me the original of every fable, and on what fact every one is founded, for the incidents occurred when she was young. A ruddy and lusty old dame, who delights in all weathers and seasons,

---

1 blue devils: hypochondriac melancholy 忧郁症
2 Goffe or Whalley: William Goffe, Edward Whalley, indicted for killing Charles I of England, lived in hiding in America. 威廉·戈夫和爱德华·华里,两人被指控杀死了英国的查理一世,秘密逃亡到美国并终生隐居在那里。

and is likely to outlive all her children yet.

What is the pill which will keep us well, serene, contented? Not my or thy great-grandfather's, but our great-grandmother Nature's universal, vegetable, botanic medicines, by which she has kept herself young always, outlived so many old Parrs[1] in her day, and fed her health with their decaying fatness. For my panacea, instead of one of those quack vials of a mixture dipped from Acheron[2] and the Dead Sea, which come out of those long shallow black-schooner looking wagons which we sometimes see made to carry bottles, let me have a draught of undiluted morning air. Morning air! If men will not drink of this at the fountainhead of the day, why, then, we must even bottle up some and sell it in the shops, for the benefit of those who have lost their subscription ticket to morning time in this world. But remember, it will not keep quite till noonday even in the coolest cellar, but drive out the stopples long ere that and follow westward the steps of Aurora[3]. I am no worshipper of Hygeia[4], who was the daughter of that old herb-doctor Aesculapius[5], and who is represented on monuments holding a serpent in one hand, and in the other a cup out of which the serpent sometimes drinks; but rather of Hebe[6],

The indescribable innocence and beneficence of Nature—of sun and wind and rain, of summer and winter—such health, such cheer, they afford forever! and such sympathy have they ever with our race, that all Nature would be affected, and the sun's brightness fade, and the winds would sigh humanely, and the clouds rain tears, and the woods shed their leaves and put on mourning in midsummer, if any man should ever for a just cause grieve. Shall I not have intelligence with the earth? Am I not partly leaves and vegetable mould myself?

---

1 Parr: Thomas Parr, an Englishman said to have lived 152 years 托马斯·帕尔，英国人，据说活了152岁
2 Acheron: in Greek mythology, a river in Hades 希腊神话中冥府的一条河流
3 Aurora: in Roman mythology, goddess of the dawn 罗马神话中的晨曦女神
4 Hygeia: in Greek mythology, goddess of health 希腊神话中的掌管健康的女神
5 Aesculapius: in Greek mythology, god of medicine 希腊神话中的掌管医药的神
6 Hebe: in Greek mythology, goddess of youth 希腊神话中的掌管青春的女神

Chapter 16
Henry David Thoreau
亨利·大卫·梭罗

cup-bearer to Jupiter[1], who was the daughter of Juno and wild lettuce[2], and who had the power of restoring gods and men to the vigor of youth. She was probably the only thoroughly sound-conditioned, healthy, and robust young lady that ever walked the globe, and wherever she came it was spring.

1 Words and Phrases

imbibe [ɪm'baɪb]	v.	(formal) to absorb something, especially information 吸收；接受
whip-poor-will ['wɪpəwɪl]	n.	a brown North American bird with a cry that sounds like its name 三声夜鹰
alder ['ɔːldə]	n.	a tree like a birch that grows in northern countries, usually in wet ground 赤杨
lull [lʌl]	v.	make calm or still 使平静；使安静
rod [rɒd]	n.	a linear measure of 16.5 feet <英国英语>竿(长度单位)
pout [paʊt]	n.	any of several large-headed fishes 大头鱼类(如鲟，条鳕，鲶鱼等)
profane [prə'feɪn]	v.	(formal) treat something holy with a lack of respect 亵渎；玷污
hoe [həʊ]	v.	break up soil, remove plants, etc. with a hoe 锄，用锄头
desert [dɪ'zɜːt]	n.	what somebody deserves, especially when it is something bad 应得的报应
pelt [pelt]	v.	(of rain) to fall very heavily（雨）猛烈地下
deluge ['deljuːdʒ]	n.	a heavy rain 暴雨
pitch pine	n.	large three-needled pine of the eastern United

---

1 Jupiter: in Roman mythology, chief of the gods 罗马神话中的众神之神
2 daughter of Juno and wild lettuce: In Roman mythology, Juno (also known as Hera), queen of heaven, conceived Hebe after eating lettuce. 罗马神话中，天后赫拉在吃了野生莱后怀孕生下了女儿。

		States and southeastern Canada 北美脂松
groove [gruːv]	n.	a long narrow cut in the surface of something hard 凹槽
bolt [bəʊlt]	n.	a sudden flash of lightning in the sky, appearing as a line 闪电
passably ['pæsəblɪ]	adv.	in a way that is acceptable or good enough 尚可地；也还过得去地
fashion ['fæʃn]	v.	to make or shape something, especially with hands 做成……的形状；把……塑成
oblation [ɒb'leɪʃən]	n.	the act of offering of the Eucharistic delments to God 祭品
torrent ['tɔːrənt]	n.	a violently fast stream of water (or other liquid) 奔流，激流
hive [haɪv]	n.	a place full of people who are busy 忙碌的地方
dervish ['dɜːvɪʃ]	n.	a member of a Muslim religious group which has a very active and lively dance as part of its worship (伊斯兰教的) 托钵僧

II Reading Comprehension Questions

1. Why did the author say that there can be no very black melancholy to him who lives in the midst of Nature and has his senses still?
2. The author found that no exertion of the legs can bring two minds much nearer to one another. Do you agree with him?
3. What are the functions of the quotations from Confucius the author used? Do you understand them all?
4. Why can the student sit alone in the house all night and most of the day without ennui and "the blues"? Do you have the same feelings as a student?
5. Do you see any significance in reading this excerpt from *Walden* nowadays?

Chapter 16
Henry David Thoreau
亨利·大卫·梭罗

Quotes of the Author

Any fool can make a rule, and any fool will mind it.

Beware of all enterprises that require new clothes.

Every generation laughs at the old fashions, but follows religiously the new.

How vain it is to sit down to write when you have not stood up to live.

I know of no more encouraging fact than the unquestioned ability of a man to elevate his life by conscious endeavour.

Henry Louis Menken
亨利·路易斯·门肯
(1880—1956)

Chapter 17

本章导读

亨利·路易斯·门肯（1880—1956），美国著名报人、评论家与语言学家，美国当代最有名的散文家之一。他出生并长期居住于马里兰州巴尔的摩市。16岁毕业于本地工艺学校。毕业后投身报界，在巴尔的摩市的《太阳报》与《时髦者》等报刊编辑部工作。1924年与剧评家拿旦着手创立《美国水星》杂志，并任主编长达十年之久。这个杂志在当时的美国颇有影响力，对美国社会与思想文化有颇多创见。正是在这些方面，门肯作为一名最勇敢的"偶像破坏者"显示了他卓越的才能。

门肯一生涉猎广泛、笔耕不辍，共撰写了25部专著以及数千篇论文、散文、小说、社论和书评。20世纪20年代前后是门肯创作的巅峰时期，他不仅完成了最具代表性的作品——6卷本文集《偏见》（*Prejudices*），还于1919年出版了《美国语言》（*The American Language*）一书。这部长达2500页的旷世佳作不仅汇集了有关美国英语极其丰富的资料，而且将英语在美国的发展、英国英语与美国英语的不同表达方式和习惯用语、美国习惯用语的起源都做出了详细解释，并且追溯了移民语言对美国英语的影响。该书至今仍然是研究美国英语的权威著作之一。

他是最令人憎恶却也最令人敬佩的美国学者之一。作为一名记者兼社会批评家，门肯以讥讽刻薄的写作方式嘲弄那些沾沾自喜的中产阶级商人、思想狭隘的美国文化生活以及严厉肃穆的美国清教徒，尤其是政客和政党的愚蠢和矫揉造作。他针对这些主题冷嘲热讽，大肆抨击。

门肯的作品被美国人广泛阅读并非因为他的抨击责难，而是他的著作富有活力及鲜明艺术风格。他的文风愉快喧闹，而且由于他的语言基础非常稳固，以至于他的挖苦嘲讽甚至都令人感到愉快。他直言不讳且一针见血，所说的每句话都充满智慧。

Chapter 17

Henry Louis Menken
亨利·路易斯·门肯

About the Author

Henry Louis Mencken was the most prominent newspaperman, book reviewer, essayist, and political commentator of his day in America.

Mencken was born and spent most of his life in the city of Baltimore, Maryland. He was the son of German immigrant parents. He completed high school but did not attend university, only graduated from Baltimore Polytechnic Institute at 16. He became a reporter on the *Baltimore Morning Herald*. A few years later, he joined the staff of its rival newspaper, the *Baltimore Sun* or *Evening Sun*, first as a reporter, then as its drama critic and editor, a position which he held until 1941. In 1924 he founded *The American Mercury* together with G. J. Nathan and was its editor until 1933.

Mencken was an important figure who influenced his age with his skeptical, cynical and irreverent attitude towards conventions, dogmas and institutions, whether literary, religious or political. He was a "libertarian" before the word came into usage. He launched the most cutting attacks of any writer against American middle class culture. He invented the word "booboisie", combining the two words "bourgeoisie" and "booby" (an awkward, foolish person). In caustic, witty essays, he derided the institution which supported the middle class. He enjoyed controversy and tried to arouse his antagonists with his direct and devastating attacks.

Mencken was renowned for his playfully combative prose style and his politically incorrect points of view. His prose is as clear as an azure sky, and his rhetoric as deadly as a rifle shot. His writing is endearing because of its wit, its crisp style, and the obvious delight he takes in it.

Text A

The Penalty of Death

H. L. Mencken

Of the arguments against capital punishment that issue from uplifters, two are commonly heard most often, to wit:

1. That hanging a man (or frying him or gassing him) is a dreadful business, degrading to those who have to do it and revolting to those who have to witness it.

2. That it is useless, for it does not deter others from the same crime.

The first of these arguments, it seems to me, is plainly too weak to need serious refutation. All it says, in brief, is that the work of the hangman is unpleasant. Granted. But suppose it is? It may be quite necessary to society for all that. There are, indeed, many other jobs that are unpleasant, and yet no one thinks of abolishing them—that of the plumber, that of the soldier, that of the garbage-man, that of the priest hearing confessions, that of the **sandhog**, and so on. Moreover, what evidence is there that any actual hangman complains of his work? I have heard none. On the contrary, I have known many who delighted in their ancient art, and practiced it proudly.

In the second argument of the abolitionists there is rather more force, but even here, I believe, the ground under them is shaky. Their fundamental error consists in assuming that the whole aim of punishing criminals is to deter other (potential) criminals—that we hang or **electrocute** A simply in order to so alarm B that he will not kill C. This, I believe, is an assumption which confuses a part with the whole. Deterrence, obviously, is one of the aims of punishment, but it is surely not the only one. On the contrary, there are at least half a dozen, and some are probably quite as important. At least one of them, practically considered, is more important. Commonly, it is described as revenge, but revenge is really not the word for it. I borrow a better term from the late Aristotle: **katharsis**. Katharsis,

Chapter 17
Henry Louis Menken
亨利·路易斯·门肯

so used, means a **salubrious** discharge of emotions, a healthy letting off of steam. A school-boy, disliking his teacher, deposits a **tack** upon the **pedagogical** chair; the teacher jumps and the boy laughs. This is katharsis. What I contend is that one of the prime objects of all judicial punishments is to afford the same grateful relief (a) to the immediate victims of the criminal punished, and (b) to the general body of moral and **timorous** men.

These persons, and particularly the first group, are concerned only indirectly with deterring other criminals. The thing they crave primarily is the satisfaction of seeing the criminal actually before them suffer as he made them suffer. What they want is the peace of mind that goes with the feeling that accounts are squared. Until they get that satisfaction they are in a state of emotional tension, and hence unhappy. The instant they get it they are comfortable. I do not argue that this yearning is noble; I simply argue that it is almost universal among human beings. In the face of injuries that are unimportant and can be borne without damage it may yield to higher impulses; that is to say, it may yield to what is called Christian charity. But when the injury is serious Christianity is **adjourned**, and even saints reach for their sidearms. It is plainly asking too much of human nature to expect it to conquer so natural an impulse. A keeps a store and has a bookkeeper, B. B steals $700, employs it in playing at dice or bingo, and is cleaned out. What is A to do? Let B go? If he does so he will be unable to sleep at night. The sense of injury, of injustice, of frustration will haunt him like **pruritus**. So he turns B over to the police, and they hustle B to prison. Thereafter A can sleep. More, he has pleasant dreams. He pictures B chained to the wall of a **dungeon** a hundred feet underground, devoured by rats and **scorpions**. It is so agreeable that it makes him forget his $700. He has got his katharsis.

The same thing precisely takes place on a larger scale when there is a crime which destroys a whole community's sense of security. Every law-abiding citizen feels menaced and frustrated until the criminals have been struck down—until the communal capacity to get even with them, and more than even, has been dramatically demonstrated. Here, manifestly, the business of deterring others is no more than an afterthought. The main thing is to destroy the concrete **scoundrels** whose act has alarmed everyone, and thus made everyone unhappy. Until they are brought to book that unhappiness continues; when the law has been executed upon them there is a sigh of relief. In other words, there is katharsis.

I know of no public demand for the death penalty for ordinary crimes, even for ordinary homicides. Its infliction would shock all men of normal decency of feeling. But for crimes involving the deliberate and inexcusable taking of human life, by men openly defiant of all civilized order—for such crimes it seems, to nine men out of ten, a just and proper punishment. Any lesser penalty leaves them feeling that the criminal has got the better of society—that he is free to add insult to injury by laughing. That feeling can be dissipated only by a recourse to katharsis, the invention of the aforesaid Aristotle. It is more effectively and economically achieved, as human nature now is, by **wafting** the criminal to realms of bliss.

The real objection to capital punishment doesn't lie against the actual extermination of the condemned, but against our brutal American habit of putting it off so long. After all, every one of us must die soon or late, and a murderer, it must be assumed, is one who makes that sad fact the cornerstone of his metaphysic. But it is one thing to die, and quite another thing to lie for long months and even years under the shadow of death. No sane man would choose such a finish. All of us, despite the Prayer Book, long for a swift and unexpected end. Unhappily, a murderer, under the irrational American system, is tortured for what, to him, must seem a whole series of eternities. For months on end he sits in prison while his lawyers carry on their idiotic **buffoonery** with **writs, injunctions, mandamuses,** and appeals. In order to get his money (or that of his friends) they have to feed him with hope. Now and then, by the **imbecility** of a judge or some trick of juridic science, they actually justify it. But let us say that, his money all gone, they finally throw up their hands. Their client is now ready for the rope or the chair. But he must still wait for months before it fetches him.

That wait, I believe, is horribly cruel. I have seen more than one man sitting in the death-house, and I don't want to see any more. Worse, it is wholly

Chapter 17

Henry Louis Menken
亨利·路易斯·门肯

useless. Why should he wait at all? Why not hang him the day after the last court **dissipates** his last hope? Why torture him as not even **cannibals** would torture their victims? The common answer is that he must have time to make his peace with God. But how long does that take? It may be accomplished, I believe, in two hours quite as comfortably as in two years. There are, indeed, no temporal limitations upon God. He could forgive a whole herd of murderers in a millionth of a second. More, it has been done.

I Words and Phrases

sandhog ['sændhɒg]	n.	a laborer who works in a caisson in driving underwater tunnels 隧道挖掘工人
electrocute [ɪ'lektrəkjuːt]	v.	kill by electrocution, as in the electric chair 以电椅处死
katharsis [kə'θɑːsɪs]	n.	purging of emotional tensions 导泻法
salubrious [sə'luːbrɪəs]	adj.	favorable to health of mind or body 清爽的；气候有益健康的
tack [tæk]	n.	a short nail with a sharp point and a large head 大头钉
pedagogical [,pedə'gɒdʒɪkl]	adj.	of or relating to pedagogy 教育学的；教育法的
timorous ['tɪm(ə)rəs]	adj.	timid by nature or revealing timidity 胆怯的，胆小的
adjourn [ə'dʒɜːn]	v.	break from a meeting or gathering, postpone 使中止；使延期
pruritus [prʊ'raɪtəs]	n.	an intense itching sensation that can have various causes (as by allergies or infection, etc.) 瘙痒症
dungeon ['dʌn(d)ʒ(ə)n]	n.	a dark cell (usually underground) where prisoners can be confined 地牢
scorpion ['skɔːpɪən]	n.	a small animal related to spiders that has a long segmented tail ending in a venomous

		sting 蝎子
scoundrel ['skaʊndr(ə)l]	n.	a wicked or evil person; someone who does evil deliberately 恶棍，流氓
waft [wɑːft]	v.	blow gently 飘荡，吹送
buffoonery [bʌ'fuːnərɪ]	n.	acting like a clown or buffoon 滑稽，打诨
writ [rɪt]	n.	(law) a legal document issued by a court or judicial officer 令状；文书
injunction [ɪn'dʒʌŋkʃən]	n.	(law) a judicial remedy issued in order to prohibit a party from doing or continuing to do a certain activity 禁令；命令
mandamus [mæn'deməs]	n.	an extraordinary writ by a superior court commanding the performance of specified official act or duty 命令书
imbecility [ˌɪmbɪ'sɪlətɪ]	n.	retardation more severe than a moron but not as severe as an idiot 愚蠢，低能
dissipate ['dɪsɪpeɪt]	v.	cause to separate and go in different directions 驱散，使消散
cannibal ['kænɪb(ə)l]	n.	a person who eats human flesh 食人者

II Reading Comprehension Questions

1. What are the two arguments against capital punishment?
2. How does the author refute these two arguments?
3. What is "katharsis" in your own words?
4. According to the author, what's the real objection to capital punishment?
5. What's your opinion towards capital punishment? Please discuss with your classmates and make a presentation.

Chapter 17

Henry Louis Menken
亨利·路易斯·门肯

III Questions on Writing Style and Language

1. What do you think is Mencken's purpose in writing this essay?
2. Straightforwardness is a remarkable feature of Menken's writing. Can you give examples to demonstrate this?
3. Have you noticed any stylistic features of Menken's writing? Are his sentences long or short? What particular effect is produced by these sentences?
4. Mencken is well-known for his bombastic style and acid sentences. Please identify examples in this essay to illustrate this point of view.
5. Mencken was an influential satirist. As you read his arguments in favor of the death penalty, consider how and why Mencken injects humor into his discussion of a grim subject.

Text B

The Libido for the Ugly

H. L. Mencken

On a winter day some years ago, coming out of Pittsburgh on one of the expresses of the Pennsylvania Railroad, I rolled eastward for an hour through the coal and steel towns of Westmoreland county.

It was familiar ground; boy and man, I had been through it often before. But somehow I had never quite sensed its appalling desolation. Here was the very heart of industrial America, the center of its most **lucrative** and characteristic activity, the boast and pride of the richest and grandest nation ever seen on earth—and here was a scene so dreadfully hideous, so intolerably bleak and **forlorn** that it reduced the whole aspiration of man to a **macabre** and depressing joke. Here was wealth beyond **computation**, almost beyond imagination—and here were human habitations so **abominable** that they would have disgraced a race of **alley** cats.

I am not speaking of mere filth. One expects steel towns to be dirty. What I **allude** to is the unbroken and agonizing ugliness, the sheer revolting monstrousness, of every house in sight. From East Liberty to Greensburg, a distance of twenty-five miles, there was not one in sight from the train that did not insult and **lacerate** the eye. Some were so bad, and they were among the most pretentious—churches, stores, warehouses, and the like—that they were **downright** startling; one blinked before them as one blinks before a man with his face shot away.

A few linger in memory, horrible even there: a crazy little church just west of Jeannette, set like a **dormer**-window on the side of a bare, **leprous** hill; the headquarters of the Veterans of Foreign Wars at another forlorn town, a steel stadium like a huge rat-trap somewhere further down the line. But most of all I recall the general effect—of hideousness without a break. There was

Chapter 17
Henry Louis Menken
亨利·路易斯·门肯

not a single decent house within eye-range from the Pittsburgh suburbs to the Greensburg yards. There was not one that was not **misshapen**, and there was not one that was not shabby.

The country itself is not **uncomely**, despite the **grime** of the endless mills. It is, in form, a narrow river valley, with deep **gullies** running up into the hills. It is thickly settled, but not noticeably overcrowded. There is still plenty of room for building, even in the larger towns, and there are very few solid blocks. Nearly every house, big and little, has space on all four sides. Obviously, if there were architects of any professional sense or dignity in the region, they would have perfected a **chalet** to hug the hillsides—a chalet with a high-pitched roof, to throw off the heavy Winter storms, but still essentially a low and clinging building, wider than it was tall. But what have they done? They have taken as their model a brick set on end. This they have converted into a thing of dingy clapboards, with a narrow, low-pitched roof. And the whole they have set upon thin, **preposterous** brick piers. By the hundreds and thousands these abominable houses cover the bare hillsides, like gravestones in some gigantic and decaying cemetery on their deep sides they are three, four and even five stories high; on their low sides they bury themselves swinishly in the mud. Not a fifth of them are perpendicular. They lean this way and that, hanging on to their bases **precariously**. And one and all they are streaked in grime, with dead and eczematous patches of paint peeping through the streaks.

Now and then there is a house of brick. But what brick! When it is new it is the color of a fried egg. When it has taken on the patina of the mills it is the color of an egg long past all hope or caring. Was it necessary to adopt that shocking color? No more than it was necessary to set all of the houses on end. Red brick, even in a steel town, ages with some dignity. Let it become downright black, and it is still sightly, especially if its trimmings are of white stone, with soot in the depths and the high spots washed by the rain. But in Westmoreland they prefer that **uremic** yellow, and so they have the most loathsome towns and villages ever seen by mortal eye.

I award this championship only after laborious research and incessant prayer. I have seen, I believe, all of the most unlovely towns of the world; they are all to be found in the United States. I have seen the mill towns of decomposing New England and the desert towns of Utah, Arizona and Texas. I am familiar with the back streets of Newark, Brooklyn and Chicago, and have made scientific explorations to Camden, N.J. and Newport News, Va. Safe in a Pullman, I have whirled through the gloomy, God-forsaken villages of Iowa and Kansas, and the malarious tide-water hamlets of Georgia. I have been to Bridgeport, Conn., and to Los Angeles. But nowhere on this earth, at home or abroad, have I seen anything to compare to the villages that huddle along the line of the Pennsylvania from the Pittsburgh yards to Greensburg. They are incomparable in color, and they are incomparable in design. It is as if some **titanic** and **aberrant** genius, uncompromisingly inimical to man, had devoted all the ingenuity of Hell to the making of them. They show grotesqueries of ugliness that, in retrospect, become almost diabolical. One cannot imagine mere human beings **concocting** such dreadful things, and one can scarcely imagine human beings bearing life in them.

Are they so frightful because the valley is full of foreigners—dull, insensate brutes, with no love of beauty in them? Then why didn't these foreigners set up similar abominations in the countries that they came from? You will, in fact, find nothing of the sort in Europe save perhaps in the more putrid parts of England. There is scarcely an ugly village on the whole Continent. The peasants, however poor, somehow manage to make themselves graceful and charming habitations, even in Spain. But in the American village and small town the pull is always toward ugliness, and in that Westmoreland valley it has been yielded to with an eagerness bordering upon passion. It is incredible that mere ignorance should have achieved such masterpieces of horror.

On certain levels of the American race, indeed, there seems to be a positive **libido** for the ugly, as on other and less Christian levels there is a libido for the beautiful. It is impossible to put down the wallpaper that **defaces** the average American home of the lower middle class to mere **inadvertence**, or to the obscene humor of the manufacturers. Such ghastly designs, it must be

Chapter 17

Henry Louis Menken
亨利·路易斯·门肯

obvious, give a genuine delight to a certain type of mind. They meet, in some unfathomable way, its obscure and unintelligible demands. They caress it as "The Palms" caresses it, or the art of Landseer, or the ecclesiastical architecture of the United States. The taste for them is as enigmatical and yet as common as the taste for vaudeville, dogmatic theology, sentimental movies, and the poetry of Edgar A. Guest. Or for the metaphysical speculations of Arthur Brisbane. Thus I suspect (though confessedly without knowing) that the vast majority of the honest folk of Westmoreland county, and especially the 100% Americans among them, actually admire the houses they live in, and are proud of them. For the same money they could get vastly better ones, but they prefer what they have got. Certainly there was no pressure upon the Veterans of Foreign Wars to choose the dreadful edifice that bears their banner, for there are plenty of vacant buildings along the trackside, and some of them are appreciably better. They might, indeed, have built a better one of their own. But they chose that clapboarded horror with their eyes open, and having chosen it, they let it mellow into its present shocking depravity. They like it as it is: beside it, the Parthenon would no doubt offend them. In precisely the same way the authors of the rat-trap stadium that I have mentioned made a deliberate choice. After painfully designing and erecting it, they made it perfect in their own sight by putting a completely impossible pent-house, painted a staring yellow, on top of it. The effect is that of a fat woman with a black eye. It is that of a Presbyterian grinning. But they like it.

Here is something that the psychologists have so far neglected: the love of ugliness for its own sake, the lust to make the world intolerable. Its habitat is the United States. Out of the melting pot emerges a race which hates beauty as it hates truth. The etiology of this madness deserves a great deal more study than it has got. There must be causes behind it; it arises and flourishes in obedience to biological laws, and not as a mere act of God. What, precisely, are the terms of those laws? And why do they run stronger in America than elsewhere? Let some honest Privat Dozent in pathological sociology apply himself to the problem.

I. Words and Phrases

lucrative ['luːkrətɪv]	*adj.* producing wealth or profit; profitable; remunerative 有利可图的；赚钱的
forlorn [fə'lɔːn]	*adj.* in pitiful condition; wretched; miserable 可怜的；悲惨的；不幸的
macabre [mə'kɑːbrə]	*adj.* gruesome; grim and horrible; ghastly 可怕的，令人毛骨悚然的，恐怖的
computation [kɒmpjʊ'teɪʃ(ə)n]	*n.* the act of computing; calculation 计算
abominable [ə'bɒm(ə)nəb(ə)l]	*adj.* nasty and disgusting; vile; loathsome 讨厌的，可恶的
alley ['ælɪ]	*n.* a narrow street or walk; specifically, between two rows of buildings that face on adjacent streets 胡同；小巷；小街
allude [ə'l(j)uːd]	*v.* refer in a casual or indirect way（随便或间接）提到，涉及；暗指
lacerate ['læsəreɪt]	*v.* tear jaggedly; mangle (something soft, as flesh); wound or hurt (one's feelings, etc.) deeply; distress 撕裂；割碎（肉等软组织）；伤害（感情等）；使……伤心
downright ['daʊnraɪt]	*adv.* thoroughly; utterly; really 彻底地，完全地；真正地
dormer ['dɔːmə]	*n.* a window set upright in a sloping roof 屋顶窗
leprous ['leprəs]	*adj.* of or like leprosy; having leprosy 麻风的；似麻风的；患麻风病的
misshapen [mɪs'ʃeɪp(ə)n]	*adj.* badly shaped; deformed 奇形怪状的；畸形的
uncomely [ʌn'kʌmlɪ]	*adj.* having unpleasant appearance 不美观的，不好看的
grime [graɪm]	*n.* dirt, esp. sooty dirt, rubbed into or covering a surface, as of the skin（尤指经摩擦而深入或覆盖皮肤等表面的）积垢；污秽

Chapter 17
Henry Louis Menken
亨利·路易斯·门肯

gully ['gʌlɪ]	n.	a channel or hollow worn by running water; small, narrow ravine 沟壑；狭沟；冲沟
chalet ['ʃæleɪ]	n.	a type of Swiss house, built of wood with balconies and overhanging eaves（瑞士的木造）农舍；山上小舍
preposterous [prɪ'pɒst(ə)rəs]	adj.	so contrary to nature, reason, or common sense as to be laughable; absurd; ridiculous 反常的，乖戾的；十分荒谬的；愚蠢的
precariously [prɪ'keərɪəslɪ]	adv.	uncertainly; insecurely; riskily 不稳定地；不安全地；危险地
uremic [jʊ'riːmɪk]	adj.	尿毒症的
titanic [taɪ'tænɪk]	adj.	of great size, strength, or power 巨大的；力大无比的；有极大权力的
aberrant [ə'ber(ə)nt]	adj.	turning away from what is right, true, etc.; deviating from what is normal or typical 与真实情况相悖的；偏离常规的，反常的
concoct [kən'kɒkt]	v.	devise, invent, or plan 计划，策划；虚构，编造
libido [lɪ'biːdəʊ]	n.	a basic form of psychic energy, comprising the primitive biglogical urges; sexual drive 欲望
deface [dɪ'feɪs]	v.	spoil the appearance of; disfigure; mar 损坏……的外表；丑化
inadvertence [ɪnəd'vɜːtəns]	n.	the quality of being inadvertent; oversight; mistake 掉以轻心，粗心大意；疏漏；错误

ⅠⅠ Reading Comprehension Questions

1. The title of this essay is very arresting. Why does the author used "libido" instead of "love", and "for the ugly" instead of "for the beautiful"?
2. What impression do you get from the houses described by the author?
3. A lot of rhetorical devices are used in the essay. Please try to find at least three and analyse the effect they produce.
4. What do you think are the reasons for such kind of "libido for the ugly"?
5. By saying "Out of the melting pot emerges a race which hates beauty as it hates truth", what does the author try to tell us?

Chapter 17
Henry Louis Menken
亨利·路易斯·门肯

Quotes of the Author

I believe that it is better to tell the truth than a lie. I believe it is better to be free than to be a slave. And I believe it is better to know than to be ignorant.

Every man sees in his relatives, and especially in his cousins, a series of grotesque caricatures of himself.

Love is like war: easy to begin but very hard to stop.

Marriage is a wonderful institution, but who would want to live in an institution?

For every complex problem there is an answer that is clear, simple, and wrong.

Chapter 18
Elwyn Brooks White
埃尔文·布鲁克斯·怀特
(1899—1985)

本章导读

埃尔文·布鲁克斯·怀特是20世纪美国著名散文家、幽默作家、文体学家，尤以散文闻名于世，其文风冷峻清丽，辛辣幽默，自成一格。

怀特的作品包括散文、随笔、速写、诗集、书信和童话。代表作品有《我的罗盘的方位》（*The Points of My Compass*，1962）、《这是纽约》（*Here is New York*，1949）、《性是否必要》（*Is Sex Necessary*，1929）、《夏洛的网》（*Charlotte's Web*，1952）和《小老鼠斯图尔特》（*Little Stuart*，1945）等。

怀特于1899年生于纽约州的佛农山庄。在康奈尔大学就读的时候，他就担任了校刊总编辑，后来又任合众社的记者和《西雅图时报》的记者。1927年怀特加入了《纽约客》杂志，撰写了大量的散文和诗歌。作为主要的撰稿人，他一手奠定了影响深远的"《纽约客》文风"。他和詹姆斯·瑟伯是初期《纽约客》的台柱。怀特的妻子凯瑟琳·安琪尔也是《纽约客》的作者。他们于1938年移居缅因州的老农舍。那儿安静的生活给了怀特很多灵感，由于他自幼喜爱自然和动物，所以在农舍居住期间创作了不少童话人物。

在怀特的创作生涯中，有一本小册子对他甚至对美国文学都有深远影响——《风格的要素》。早在怀特就读于康奈尔大学期间，他就改编了英文教授威廉·史德伦克所著的《风格的要素》。这本小册子不过薄薄的几十页，经过怀特改编后连年再版，是畅销的写作指导书。"……风格不是这么独立的个体；它不能与文章分开，不能从文章中过滤……达到风格的必经之路是简单、朴实、清楚、诚实。"这些原则无不反映了怀特写作时坚持的风格。

怀特发表了很多散文和随感，他的文风朴实、幽默、清澈、敏感而富有魅力。

Chapter 18

Elwyn Brooks White
埃尔文·布鲁克斯·怀特

　　怀特在写作中常用简单句，毫无矫情的修饰，不用复杂句式和生涩词汇，反而经常会用到一些俚语和口语以引起读者的共鸣。他曾经说自己是用耳朵来写作，也就是说他所写的，读出来，听得懂。而且他有时会用一些俚语，更能引起读者共鸣。《纽约客》主编威廉·肖恩曾盛赞道："E. B. 怀特是一位伟大的散文家、至上的文体家。他的文风是我们文字中最纯粹的。它是独特的、清晰的、易懂的、不勉强的、彻底美国化的、十全十美的。由于他的静静的影响，本国好几代作家都写得更好了。……他是永恒的。他的著作是没有时间限制的。"

　　E. B. 怀特是公认的当代美国散文大家。他一生所得到的荣誉恐怕比任何当代美国作家所得到的都多。虽然他没有获得诺贝尔文学奖，但是他所获的其他奖章甚多，包括全国文学勋章，总统颁发的自由勋章，美国文艺学院颁发的散文金质章。他所获的普立策文艺奖是颁给他的"整体著作"的。在 1985 年怀特逝世时，《纽约时报》的讣闻把他形容为"美国最宝贵的文学资源之一"。虽然没有一部"巨作"，但 E. B. 怀特凭借他精美的文字，依然称得上是美国散文史上的巨擘。

　　本章 Text A 精选了怀特最令人称赞的文章《再到湖上》（*Once More to the Lake*），写他于 1941 年带 11 岁的儿子回到缅因州的一个湖边去玩。他自己的父亲于 1904 年开始每年带他去那湖边游玩，他对那段生活怀有深厚的感情。在此文中，怀特回忆起了他童年所熟悉的湖，现在他又通过儿子的眼睛去看同样的风景，发现他儿子在湖边玩乐，与他自己在三十多年前的感受完全一样。在一种复杂的情感中，他一边通过自己儿子的视角重温自己与父亲的生活，一边却又预见到了自己的死亡。可以说《再到湖上》所谈的是时光荏苒，物是人非，是人类生命个体的代代绵延呈递。Text B 是曾入选美国中学课本的《再会，我可爱的！》（*Farewell My Lovely!*），该文中作者以细腻的笔触追忆了他所珍爱的福特旧式老爷车的种种细节与趣闻，在深情的记叙中缅怀了一个时代的逝去。

About the Author

　　Elwyn Brooks White was a leading American essayist, author, humorist, poet and literary stylist. Graduated from Cornell University with a Bachelor of Arts degree in 1921, E. B. White wrote for *The Seattle Times* and *Seattle Post-Intelligencer*, and worked for an advertising agency before returning to New York City in 1924. He published his first article in *The New Yorker* magazine in 1925, then joined the staff in 1927 and continued to contribute for six decades. Best recognized for his essays and unsigned "Notes and Comment" pieces, he gradually became one of the most important contributors to *The New Yorker* at a time when it was arguably the most important American literary magazine. He also served as a columnist for *Harper's Magazine* from 1938 to 1943.

In the late 1930s, White turned his hand to children's fiction on behalf of a niece, Janice Hart White, which resulted in a series of children's classics including *Stuart Little*, *Charlotte's Web*, and *The Trumpet of the Swan*. In 1959 he revised *The Elements of Style*, which is a grammar and language handbook by the late William Strunk, Jr., one of White's professors at Cornell. White's rework of the book was extremely well received, and it has remained a standard style manual for writers.

E. B. White's writings are among some of the finest examples of contemporary, genuinely American prose. "His voice rumbles with authority through sentences of surpassing grace. In his more than fifty years at *The New Yorker*, White set a standard of writerly craft for that supremely well-wrought magazine. In genial, perfectly poised essay after essay, he has wielded the English language with as much clarity and control as any American of his time." According to Baymond Sokolov, a critic for *Newsweek*.

In 1978, White won an honorary Pulitzer Prize for his work as a whole. Other awards he received included a Presidential Medal of Freedom in 1963, the National Medal for Literature in 1971, and memberships in a variety of literary societies throughout the United States.

Often considered a national resource to the Americans, E. B. White's work is a great pleasure to read.

Chapter 18

Elwyn Brooks White
埃尔文·布鲁克斯·怀特

Text A

Once More to the Lake

E. B. White

One summer, along about 1904, my father rented a camp on a lake in Maine and took us all there for the month of August. We all got **ringworm** from some kittens and had to rub Pond's Extract on our arms and legs night and morning, and my father rolled over in a canoe with all his clothes on; but outside of that the vacation was a success and from then on none of us ever thought there was any place in the world like that lake in Maine. We returned summer after summer—always on August 1st for one month. I have since become a salt-water man, but sometimes in summer there are days when the restlessness of the tides and the fearful cold of the sea water and the incessant wind which blows across the afternoon and into the evening make me wish for the placidity of a lake in the woods. A few weeks ago this feeling got so strong I bought myself a couple of bass hooks and a spinner and returned to the lake where we used to go, for a week's fishing and to revisit old haunts.

I took along my son, who had never had any fresh water up his nose and who had seen lily pads only from train windows. On the journey over to the lake I began to wonder what it would be like. I wondered how time would have **marred** this unique, this holy spot—the **coves** and streams, the hills that the sun set behind, the camps and the paths behind the camps. I was sure that the tarred road would have found it out and I wondered in what other ways it would be **desolated**. It is strange how much you can remember about places like that once you allow your mind to return into the **grooves** which lead back. You remember one thing, and that suddenly reminds you of another thing. I guess I remembered clearest of all the early mornings, when the lake was cool and motionless, remembered how the bedroom smelled of the lumber it was made of and of the wet woods whose scent entered through the screen. The partitions in the camp were thin and did not extend clear to the top of the rooms, and as I was always the first up I would dress softly so as not to wake the others, and sneak out into the sweet outdoors and start out in the canoe, keeping close along the shore in the long shadows of the pines. I remembered being very careful never to rub my paddle against the **gunwale** for fear of disturbing the stillness of the cathedral.

The lake had never been what you would call a wild lake. There were cottages sprinkled around the shores, and it was in farming although the shores of the lake were quite heavily wooded. Some of the cottages were owned by nearby farmers, and you would live at the shore and eat your meals at the farmhouse. That's what our family did. But although it wasn't wild, it was a fairly large and undisturbed lake and there were places in it which, to a child at least, seemed infinitely remote and primeval.

I was right about the tar: it led to within half a mile of the shore. But when I got back there, with my boy, and we settled into a camp near a farmhouse and into the kind of summertime I had known, I could tell that it was going to be pretty much the same as it had been before—I knew it, lying in bed the first morning, smelling the bedroom, and hearing the boy sneak quietly out and go off along the shore in a boat. I began to sustain the illusion that he was I, and therefore, by simple transposition, that I was my father. This sensation persisted, kept **cropping up** all the time we were there. It was not an entirely new feeling, but in this setting it grew much stronger. I seemed to be living a dual existence. I would be in the middle of some simple act, I would be picking up a bait box or laying down a table fork, or I would be saying something, and suddenly it would be not I but my father who was saying the words or making the gesture. It gave me a creepy sensation.

We went fishing the first morning. I felt the same damp moss covering the worms in the bait can, and saw the dragonfly alight on the tip of my rod as it hovered a few inches from the surface of the water. It was the arrival of this fly that convinced me beyond any doubt that everything was as it always had been, that the years were a mirage and there had been no years. The small waves were the same, **chucking** the rowboat under the chin as we fished at anchor, and the boat was the same boat, the same color green

Chapter 18

Elwyn Brooks White
埃尔文·布鲁克斯·怀特

and the ribs broken in the same places, and under the floor-boards the same freshwater leavings and debris—the dead helgramite, the wisps of moss, the rusty discarded fishhook, the dried blood from yesterday's catch. We stared silently at the tips of our rods, at the dragonflies that came and wells. I lowered the tip of mine into the water, tentatively, pensively **dislodging** the fly, which darted two feet away, poised, darted two feet back, and came to rest again a little farther up the rod. There had been no years between the **ducking** of this dragonfly and the other one—the one that was part of memory. I looked at the boy, who was silently watching his fly, and it was my hands that held his rod, my eyes watching. I felt dizzy and didn't know which rod I was at the end of.

We caught two bass, hauling them in **briskly** as though they were mackerel, pulling them over the side of the boat in a businesslike manner without any landing net, and stunning them with a blow on the back of the head. When we got back for a swim before lunch, the lake was exactly where we had left it, the same number of inches from the dock, and there was only the merest suggestion of a breeze. This seemed an utterly enchanted sea, this lake you could leave to its own devices for a few hours and come back to, and find that it had not stirred, this constant and trustworthy body of water. In the shallows, the dark, water-soaked sticks and twigs, smooth and old, were **undulating** in clusters on the bottom against the clean ribbed sand, and the track of the mussel was plain. A school of minnows swam by, each minnow with its small, individual shadow, doubling the attendance, so clear and sharp in the sunlight. Some of the other campers were in swimming, along the shore, one of them with a cake of soap, and the water felt thin and clear and insubstantial. Over the years there had been this person with the cake of soap, this **cultist**, and here he was. There had been no years.

Up to the farmhouse to dinner through the teeming, dusty field, the road under our sneakers was only a two-track road. The middle track was missing, the one with the marks of the hooves and the splotches of dried, **flaky** manure. There had always been three tracks to choose from in choosing which track to walk in; now the choice was narrowed down to two. For a moment I missed terribly the middle alternative. But the way led past the tennis court, and something about the way it lay there in the sun reassured me; the tape had loosened along the backline, the alleys were green with plantains and other weeds, and the net (installed in June and removed in September) **sagged** in the dry noon, and the whole place steamed with midday heat and hunger and emptiness. There was a choice of pie for dessert, and one was blueberry and one was apple, and the waitresses were the same country girls, there having been no passage of time, only the illusion of it as in a dropped curtain—the waitresses were still fifteen; their hair had been washed, that was the only difference—they had been to the movies and seen the pretty girls with the clean hair. Summertime, oh summertime, pattern of life **indelible**, the fade proof lake, the woods unshatterable, the pasture with the sweet fern and the **juniper** forever and ever, summer without end; this was the background, and the life along the shore was the design, the cottages with their innocent and tranquil design, their tiny docks with the flagpole and the American flag floating against the white clouds in the blue sky, the little paths over the roots of the trees leading from camp to camp and the paths leading back to the **outhouses** and the can of lime for sprinkling, and at the souvenir counters at the store the miniature birch-bark canoes and the post cards that showed things looking a little better than they looked. This was the American family at play, escaping the city heat, wondering whether the newcomers at the camp at the head of the cove were "common" or "nice", wondering whether it was true that the people who drove up for Sunday dinner at the farmhouse were turned away because there wasn't enough chicken.

It seemed to me, as I kept remembering all this, that those times and those summers had been infinitely precious and worth saving. There had been jollity and peace and goodness. The arriving (at the beginning of August) had been so big a business in itself, at the railway station the farm wagon drawn up, the first smell of the pine-laden air, the first glimpse of the smiling farmer, and the great importance of the trunks and your father's enormous authority in such matters, and the feel of the wagon under you for the long ten-mile haul, and at the top of the last long hill catching the first view of the lake after eleven months of not seeing this cherished body of water. The shouts and cries

Chapter 18
Elwyn Brooks White
埃尔文·布鲁克斯·怀特

of the other campers when they saw you, and the trunks to be unpacked, to give up their rich burden. (Arriving was less exciting nowadays, when you sneaked up in your car and parked it under a tree near the camp and took out the bags and in five minutes it was all over, no fuss, no loud wonderful fuss about trunks.)

Peace and goodness and jollity. The only thing that was wrong now, really, was the sound of the place, an unfamiliar nervous sound of the outboard motors. This was the note that jarred, the one thing that would sometimes break the illusion and set the years moving. In those other summertimes, all motors were inboard; and when they were at a little distance, the noise they made was a **sedative**, an ingredient of summer sleep. They were one-cylinder and two-cylinder engines, and some were make-and-break and some were jump-spark, but they all made a sleepy sound across the lake. The one-lungers throbbed and fluttered, and the twin-cylinder ones **purred** and purred, and that was a quiet sound too. But now the campers all had outboards. In the daytime, in the hot mornings, these motors made a **petulant**, irritable sound; at night, in the still evening when the **afterglow** lit the water, they **whined** about one's ears like mosquitoes. My boy loved our rented outboard, and his great desire was to achieve single-handed mastery over it, and authority, and he soon learned the trick of choking it a little (but not too much), and the adjustment of the needle valve. Watching him I would remember the things you could do with the old one-cylinder engine with the heavy flywheel, how you could have it eating out of your hand if you got really close to it spiritually. Motor boats in those days didn't have clutches, and you would make a landing by shutting off the motor at the proper time and coasting in with a dead rudder. But there was a way of reversing them, if you learned the trick, by cutting the switch and putting it on again exactly on the final dying revolution of the flywheel, so that it would kick back against compression and begin reversing. Approaching a dock in a strong following breeze, it was difficult to slow up sufficiently by the ordinary coasting method, and if a boy felt he had complete mastery over his motor, he was tempted to keep it running beyond its time and then reverse it a few feet from the dock.

It took a cool nerve, because if you threw the switch a twentieth of a second too soon you would catch the flywheel when it still had speed enough to go up past center, and the boat would leap ahead, charging bull-fashion at the dock.

  We had a good week at the camp. The bass were biting well and the sun shone endlessly, day after day. We would be tired at night and lie down in the accumulated heat of the little bedrooms after the long hot day and the breeze would stir almost imperceptibly outside and the smell of the swamp drift in through the rusty screens. Sleep would come easily and in the morning the red squirrel would be on the roof, tapping out his gay routine. I kept remembering everything, lying in bed in the mornings—the small steamboat that had a long rounded stern like the lip of a Ubangi, and how quietly she ran on the moonlight sails, when the older boys played their mandolins and the girls sang and we ate doughnuts dipped in sugar, and how sweet the music was on the water in the shining night, and what it had felt like to think about girls then. After breakfast we would go up to the store and the things were in the same place—the minnows in a bottle, the **plugs** and spinners disarranged and pawed over by the youngsters from the boys' camp, the fig newtons and the Beeman's gum. Outside, the road was tarred and cars stood in front of the store. Inside, all was just as it had always been, except there was more Coca Cola and not so much Moxie and root beer and birch beer and sarsaparilla. We would walk out with a bottle of pop apiece and sometimes the pop would backfire up our noses and hurt. We explored the streams, quietly, where the turtles slid off the sunny logs and dug their way into the soft bottom; and we lay on the town wharf and fed worms to the tame bass. Everywhere we went I had trouble making out which was I, the one walking at my side, the one walking in my pants.

  One afternoon while we were there at that lake a thunderstorm came up. It was like the revival of an old melodrama that I had seen long ago with childish awe. The second-act climax of the drama of the electrical disturbance over a lake in America had not changed in any important respect. This was the big scene, still the big scene. The whole thing was so familiar, the first feeling of oppression and heat and a general air around camp of not wanting

Chapter 18

Elwyn Brooks White
埃尔文·布鲁克斯·怀特

to go very far away. In mid-afternoon (it was all the same) a curious darkening of the sky, and a lull in everything that had made life tick; and then the way the boats suddenly swung the other way at their **moorings** with the coming of a breeze out of the new quarter, and the **premonitory rumble**. Then the kettle drum, then the snare, then the bass drum and cymbals, then crackling light against the dark, and the gods grinning and licking their chops in the hills. Afterward the calm, the rain steadily rustling in the calm lake, the return of light and hope and spirits, and the campers running out in joy and relief to go swimming in the rain, their bright cries perpetuating the deathless joke about how they were getting simply drenched, and the children screaming with delight at the new sensation of bathing in the rain, and the joke about getting drenched linking the generations in a strong indestructible chain. And the comedian who waded in carrying an umbrella.

When the others went swimming my son said he was going in too. He pulled his dripping trunks from the line where they had hung all through the shower, and wrung them out. Languidly, and with no thought of going in, I watched him, his hard little body, skinny and bare, saw him wince slightly as he pulled up around his vitals the small, **soggy**, icy garment. As he **buckled** the swollen belt suddenly my groin felt the chill of death.

I Words and Phrases

ringworm ['rɪŋwɜːm]	n.	contagious itching skin disease, caused by fungi 癣，癣菌病
mar [mɑː]	v.	impair the appearance of, disfigure, spoil 损毁，损伤；糟蹋
cove [kəʊv]	n.	small, sheltered bay 小溪
desolate ['des(ə)lət]	v.	make... appear bleak and depressingly empty or bare 使荒凉；使孤寂
groove [gruːv]	n.	long, narrow cut or depression especially for guided motion 凹槽

gunwale ['gʌn(ə)l]	n.	the upper edge or planking of the side of a boat or ship 船缘
crop up		happen or appear unexpectedly 突然出现
chuck [tʃʌk]	v.	pat or squeeze fondly or playfully, especially under the chin 轻拍
dislodge [dɪs'lɒdʒ]	v.	remove from fixed position 使移动
duck [dʌk]	v.	lower the head or the body quickly to avoid a blow 闪避
briskly [brɪsklɪ]	adv.	moving, acting quickly, actively or energetically 轻快地；活泼地
undulate ['ʌndjʊleɪt]	v.	move with a smooth, wave like motion 波动，起伏
cultist [kʌltɪst]	n.	a person who is very enthusiastic about a a particular religion, figure or object 狂热的信徒
flaky ['fleɪkɪ]	adj.	breaking or separating easily into small thin pieces 薄而易剥落的
sag [sæg]	v.	sink or subside gradually under the weight or pressure or through lack of strength 下垂
indelible [ɪn'delɪb(ə)l]	adj.	cannot be removed, washed away or erased 难忘的；擦不掉的
juniper ['dʒuːnɪpə]	n.	even green shrub or small trees 杜松
outhouse ['aʊthaʊs]	n.	a structure such as a shed or barn that is built onto or in the grounds of a house 外屋
sedative ['sedətɪv]	adj.	promoting calm or inducing sleep 镇定剂
purr [pɜː]	v.	make low, continuous, vibrating sound expressing contentment 发出喉音
petulant ['petjʊl(ə)nt]	adj.	(of a child of a person) annoyed and behaving in an unreasonable way 暴躁的
afterglow ['æftəgləʊ]	n.	light or radiance remaining in the sky after the sun has set 夕照；晚霞
whine [waɪn]	v.	give or make a long, unpleasant high-pitched

Chapter 18
Elwyn Brooks White
埃尔文·布鲁克斯·怀特

		complaining cry or sound 发牢骚；哭诉；发出呜呜声
plug [plʌg]	n.	a lure with one or more hooks attached 插头；塞
mooring ['mɔrɪŋ]	n.	a place where ship or boats are moored 下锚；停泊处
premonitory [prɪ'mɒnɪtərɪ]	adj.	giving a feeling or warning that sth especially something bad is going to happen 先兆的，预兆的
rumble ['rʌmb(ə)l]	n.	continuous deep resonant sound 隆隆声；抱怨声
soggy ['sɒgɪ]	adj.	extremely wet and soft 浸透的
buckle ['bʌk(ə)l]	v.	fasten or decorate 扣住；使弯曲

II Reading Comprehension Questions

1. When did the author go to the lake in Maine for the first time? Was the vacation a perfect success?
2. What brought him to revisit the lake?
3. Read the detailed account of his revisit to the lake with his little son. What struck you most among all the details? Why?
4. What is meant by "the creepy sensation of a dual existence"? What continuously sharpened this feeling during his revist to the lake?
5. What happened one afternoon? What did his son do that made his groin feel the "chill of death"?

III Questions on Writing Style and Language

1. Have you noticed any stylistic features of writing? What particular effect is produced by these sentences?
2. Repetition of key words, phrases and sentences may create a dominant impression in our writings. Please analyze the using of repetition in this essay.
3. Discuss the sentence variety in this essay. Why does White use the sentence fragment "Peace and goodness and jollity" at the beginning of a

paragraph? Are there any other sentence fragments in the essay?
4. The author uses many figures of speech in this essay. Can you find examples of simile, personification, parallelism and onomatopoeia?
5. By describing his revisit to the lake, the author subtly explored three pairs of themes in this essay, which may be named respectively as illusion & reality, human & nature, and youth & maturity. Please try to analyze these themes in detail.

Chapter 18

Elwyn Brooks White
埃尔文·布鲁克斯·怀特

Text B

Farewell, My Lovely![1]

E. B. White

I see by the new Sears Roebuck[2] catalogue that it is still possible to buy an **axle** for a 1909 Model T Ford, but I am not deceived. The great days have faded, the end is in sight. Only one page in the current catalogue is devoted to parts and accessories for the Model T; yet everyone remembers springtimes when the Ford gadget section was larger than men's clothing, almost as large as household furnishings. The last Model T was built in 1927, and the car is fading from what scholars call the American scene—which is an understatement, because to a few million people who grew up with it, the old Ford practically *was* the American scene.

It was the miracle God had wrought. And it was patently the sort of thing that could only happen once. Mechanically **uncanny**, it was like nothing that had ever come to the world before. Flourishing industries rose and fell with it. As a vehicle, it was hard-working, commonplace, heroic; and it often seemed to transmit those qualities to the persons who rode in it. My own generation identifies it with Youth, with its **gaudy**, irretrievable excitements; before it fades into the mist, I would like to pay it the tribute of the sigh that is not a sob, and set down random entries in a shape somewhat less cumbersome than a Sears Roebuck catalogue.

The Model T was distinguished from all other makes of cars by the fact

---

1 The essay was originally published on May16, the 1936 issue of *The New Yorker*. 该文最初发表于1936年5月16日的《纽约客》。《纽约客》是美国知识、文艺类的综合杂志，内容覆盖新闻报道、文艺评论、散文、漫画、诗歌、小说，以及纽约文化生活动向等。

2 Sears Roebuck: Sears Roebuck refers to Sears Roebuck & Co., a leading retailer of general merchandise, tools, home appliances, clothing, and automotive parts and services. 西尔斯罗巴克公司，是一家在美国很受欢迎的零售公司，主要出售工具、家用电器、衣服、汽车零件等。

that its transmission was of a type known as **planetary**—which was half metaphysics, half sheer friction. Engineers accepted the word "planetary" in its **epicyclic** sense, but I was always conscious that it also meant "wandering", "erratic." Because of the peculiar nature of this planetary element, there was always, in Model T, a certain dull **rapport** between engine and wheels, and even when the car was in a state known as neutral, it trembled with a deep imperative and tended to inch forward. There was never a moment when the bands were not faintly **egging** the machine **on**. In this respect it was like a horse, rolling the bit on its tongue, and country people brought to it the same technique they used with draft animals.

  Its most remarkable quality was its rate of acceleration. In its **palmy** days the Model T could take off faster than anything on the road. The reason was simple. To get under way, you simply hooked the third finger of the right hand around a lever on the steering column, pulled down hard, and shoved your left foot forcibly against the low-speed pedal. These were simple, positive motions; the car responded by lunging forward with a roar. After a few seconds of this turmoil, you took your toe off the pedal, eased up a **mite** on the **throttle**, and the car, possessed of only two forward speeds, **catapulted** directly into high with a series of ugly jerks and was off on its glorious errand. The abruptness of this departure was never equalled in other cars of the period. The human leg was (and still is) incapable of letting in a **clutch** with anything like the forthright abandon that used to send Model T on its way. Letting in a clutch is a negative, hesitant motion, depending on delicate nervous control; pushing down the Ford pedal was a simple, country motion—an expansive act, which came as natural as kicking an old door to make it **budge**.

  The driver of the old Model T was a man enthroned. The car, with top up, stood seven feet high. The driver sat on top of the gas tank, brooding it with his own body. When he wanted gasoline, he alighted, along with everything else in the front seat; the seat was pulled off, the metal cap unscrewed, and a wooden stick thrust down to sound the liquid in the well. There were always a couple of these sounding sticks kicking around in the **ratty** sub-cushion regions of a **flivver**. Refuelling was more of a social function then, because the driver

Chapter 18
Elwyn Brooks White
埃尔文·布鲁克斯·怀特

had to unbend, whether he wanted to or not. Directly in front of the driver was the windshield—high, uncompromisingly erect. Nobody talked about air resistance, and the four cylinders pushed the car through the atmosphere with a simple disregard of physical law.

There was this about a Model T: the purchaser never regarded his purchase as a complete, finished product. When you bought a Ford, you figured you had a start—a vibrant, spirited framework to which could be screwed an almost limitless assortment of decorative and functional hardware. Driving away from the agency, hugging the new wheel between your knees, you were already full of creative worry. A Ford was born naked as a baby, and a flourishing industry grew up out of correcting its rare deficiencies and combating its fascinating diseases. Those were the great days of lily-painting. I have been looking at some old Sears Roebuck catalogues, and they bring everything back so clear.

First you bought a **Ruby** Safety **Reflector** for the rear, so that your **posterior** would glow in another car's brilliance. Then you invested thirty-nine cents in some radiator Moto Wings, a popular ornament which gave the Pegasus[1] touch to the machine and did something godlike to the owner. For nine cents you bought a fan-belt guide to keep the belt from slipping off the **pulley.**

You bought a radiator compound to stop leaks. This was as much a part of everybody's equipment as aspirin tablets are of a medicine cabinet. You bought special oil to prevent chattering, a clamp-on dash light, a patching outfit, a tool box which you bolted to the running board, a sun **visor**, a steering-column brace to keep the column rigid, and a set of emergency containers for gas, oil, and water—three thin, disc-like cans which reposed in a case on the running board during long, important journeys—red for gas, gray for water, green for oil. It was only a beginning. After the car was about a year old, steps were taken to check the alarming disintegration. (Model T was

---

[1] Pegasus: (Greek mythology) the immortal winged horse that sprang from the blood of the slain Medusa; was tamed by Bellerophon with the help of a bridle given him by Athena; as the flying horse of the Muses it is a symbol of highflying imagination. 珀加索斯，古希腊神话中生有双翼的神马，被其足蹄踩过的地方有泉水涌出，诗人饮之可获灵感，是喷薄的想象力的象征。

full of tumors, but they were benign.) A set of anti-rattlers (98c) was a popular **panacea**. You hooked them on to the gas and spark rods, to the brake pull rod, and to the steering-rod connections. Hood silencers, of black rubber, were applied to the fluttering hood. Shock-absorbers and **snubbers** gave "complete relaxation." Some people bought rubber pedal pads, to fit over the standard metal pedals. (I didn't like these, I remember.) Persons of a suspicious or **pugnacious** turn of mind bought a rear-view mirror; but most Model T owners weren't worried by what was coming from behind because they would soon enough see it out in front. They rode in a state of cheerful **catalepsy**. Quite a large **mutinous clique** among Ford owners went over to a foot accelerator (you could buy one and screw it to the floor board), but there was a certain madness in these people, because the Model T, just as she stood, had a choice of three foot pedals to push, and there were plenty of moments when both feet were occupied in the routine performance of duty and when the only way to speed up the engine was with the hand throttle.

Gadget bred gadget. Owners not only bought ready-made gadgets, they invented gadgets to meet special needs. I myself drove my car directly from the agency to the blacksmith's, and had the smith affix two enormous iron brackets to the port running board to support an army trunk.

People who owned closed models builded along different lines: they bought ball grip handles for opening doors, window anti-rattlers, and deluxe flower vases of the cut-glass anti-splash type. People with delicate sensibilities garnished their car with a device called the Donna Lee Automobile Disseminator—a porous vase guaranteed, according to Sears, to fill the car with a "faint clean odor of lavender." The gap between open cars and closed cars was not as great then as it is now: for $11.95, Sears Roebuck converted your touring car into a sedan and you went forth renewed. One agreeable quality of the old Fords was that they had no bumpers, and their fenders softened and **wilted** with the years and permitted driver to squeeze in and out of tight places.

Tires were $30 \times 3\frac{1}{2}$, cost about twelve dollars, and **punctured** readily. Everybody carried a Jiffy patching set, with a nutmeg grater to roughen the tube before the **goo** was spread on. Everybody was capable of putting on a

Chapter 18

Elwyn Brooks White
埃尔文·布鲁克斯·怀特

patch, expected to have to, and did have to.

During my association with Model T's, self-starters were not a prevalent accessory. They were expensive and under suspicion. Your car came equipped with a serviceable crank, and the first thing you learned was how to Get Results. It was a special trick, and until you learned it (usually from another Ford owner, but sometimes by a period of appalling experimentation) you might as well have been winding up an **awning**. The trick was to leave the ignition switch off, proceed to the animal's head, pull the choke (which was a little wire protruding through the radiator), and give the crank two or three nonchalant upward lifts. Then, whistling as though thinking about something else, you would saunter back to the driver's cabin, turn the ignition on, return to the crank, and this time, catching it on the down stroke, give it a quick spin with plenty of That. If this procedure was followed, the engine almost always responded—first with a few scattered explosions, then with a **tumultuous** gunfire, which you checked by racing around to the driver's seat and retarding the throttle. Often, if the emergency brake hadn't been pulled all the way back, the car advanced on you the instant the first explosion occurred and you would hold it back by leaning your weight against it. I can still feel my old Ford nuzzling me at the curb, as though looking for an apple in my pocket.

In zero weather, ordinary cranking became an impossibility, except for giants. The oil thickened, and it became necessary to jack up the rear wheels, which, for some planetary reason, eased the throw.

The lore and legend that governed the Ford were boundless. Owners had their own theories about everything; they discussed mutual problems in that wise, infinitely resourceful way old women discuss **rheumatism**. Exact knowledge was pretty scarce, and often proved less effective than superstition. Dropping a **camphor** ball into the gas tank was a popular expedient; it seemed to have a tonic effect on both man and machine. There wasn't much to base exact knowledge on. The Ford driver flew blind. He didn't know the temperature of his engine, the speed of his car, the amount of his fuel or the pressure of his oil (the old Ford lubricated itself by what was amiably described as the "splash system"). A speedometer cost money and was an extra, like a windshield-wiper. The dashboard of the early models was bare save for an ignition key; later models, grown effete, boasted an ammeter which pulsated alarmingly with the throbbing of the car. Under the dash was a box of coils, with vibrators which you adjusted, or thought you adjusted. Whatever the driver learned of his motor, he learned not through instruments but through sudden developments. I remember that the timer was one of the vital organs about which there was ample doctrine. When everything else had been checked, you "had a look" at the timer. It was an extravagantly odd little device, simple in construction, mysterious in function. It contained a roller, held by a spring, and there were four contact points on the inside of the case against which, many people believed, the roller rolled. I have had a timer apart on a sick Ford many times, but I never really knew what I was up to—I was just showing off before God. There were almost as many schools of thought as there were timers. Some people, when things went wrong, just clenched their teeth and gave the timer a smart crack with a wrench. Other people opened it up and blew on it. There was a school that held that the timer needed large amounts of oil; they fixed it by frequent baptism. And there was a school that was positive it was meant to run dry as a bone; these people were continually taking it off and wiping it. I remember once spitting into a timer; not in anger, but in a spirit of research. You see, the Model T driver moved in the realm of metaphysics. He believed his car could be **hexed**.

One reason the Ford anatomy was never reduced to an exact science was that, having "fixed" it, the owner couldn't honestly claim that the treatment had brought about the cure. There were too many authenticated cases of Fords fixing themselves—restored naturally to health after a short rest. Farmers soon discovered this, and it fitted nicely with their draft-horse philosophy: "Let 'er cool off and she'll snap into it again."

A Ford owner had Number One Bearing constantly in mind. This bearing, being at the front end of the motor, was the one that always burned out, because the oil didn't reach it when the car was climbing hills. (That's what I was always told, anyway.) The oil used to recede and leave Number One dry as a clam flat; you had to watch that bearing like a hawk. It was like a weak

Chapter 18

Elwyn Brooks White
埃尔文·布鲁克斯·怀特

heart—you could hear it start knocking, and that was when you stopped and let her cool off. Try as you would to keep the oil supply right, in the end Number One always went out. "Number One Bearing burned out on me and I had to have her replaced," you would say, wisely; and your companions always had a lot to tell about how to protect and pamper Number One to keep her alive.

Sprinkled not too liberally among the millions of amateur witch doctors who drove Fords and applied their own abominable cures were the heaven-sent mechanics who could really make the car talk. These professionals turned up in undreamed-of spots. One time, on the banks of the Columbia River in Washington, I heard the rear end go out of my Model T when I was trying to whip it up a steep incline onto the deck of a ferry. Something snapped; the car slid backward into the mud. It seemed to me like the end of the trail. But the captain of the ferry, observing the withered remnant, spoke up.

"What's got her?" he asked.

"I guess it's the rear end," I replied, listlessly. The captain leaned over the rail and stared. Then I saw that there was a hunger in his eyes that set him off from other men.

"Tell you what," he said, carelessly, trying to cover up his eagerness, "let's pull the son of a bitch up onto the boat, and I'll help you fix her while we're going back and forth on the river."

We did just this. All that day I **plied** between the towns of Pasco and Kennewick, while the skipper (who had once worked in a Ford garage) directed the amazing work of resetting the bones of my car.

Springtime in the heyday of the Model T was a **delirious** season. Owning a car was still a major excitement, roads were still wonderful and bad. The Fords were obviously conceived in madness: any car which was capable of going from forward into reverse without any perceptible mechanical **hiatus** was bound to be a mighty challenging thing to the human imagination. Boys used to **veer** them **off** the highway into a level pasture and run wild with them, as though they were cutting up with a girl. Most everybody used the reverse pedal quite as much as the regular foot brake—it distributed the wear over the bands and wore them all down evenly. That was the big trick, to wear all the bands down evenly, so that the final chattering would be total and the whole unit scream for renewal.

  The days were golden, the nights were dim and strange. I still recall with trembling those loud, nocturnal crises when you drew up to a signpost and raced the engine so the lights would be bright enough to read destinations by. I have never been really planetary since. I suppose it's time to say goodbye. Farewell, my lovely!

I. Words and Phrases

axle ['æks(ə)l]	n.	a shaft on which a wheel rotates 车轴
uncanny [ʌn'kænɪ]	adj.	surpassing the ordinary or normal 神秘的，离奇的
gaudy ['gɔːdɪ]	adj.	tastelessly showy 华而不实的
planetary ['plænɪt(ə)rɪ]	adj.	resembling the physical or orbital characteristics of a planet 行星的；（机器）行星齿轮的
epicyclic [epə'saɪklɪk]	adj.	of or relating to an epicycle 本轮的；周转的
rapport [ræ'pɔː]	n.	a relationship of mutual understanding or trust 密切关系
egg on		urge or incite, especially daring or foolish acts 煽动，怂恿
palmy ['pɑːmɪ]	adj.	very lively and profitable 繁荣的
mite [maɪt]	n.	a slight but appreciable addition 极小量
throttle ['θrɒt(ə)l]	n.	a pedal that controls the throttle valve 节流阀，（车辆）风门
catapult ['kætəpʌlt]	v.	shoot forth or launch, as if from a catapult 用弹弓射；用弹射器发射；猛投
clutch [klʌtʃ]	n.	a pedal or lever that engages or disengages a rotating shaft and a driving mechanism 离合器
budge [bʌdʒ]	v.	move very slightly 挪动，微微移动
ratty ['rætɪ]	adj.	showing signs of wear and tear 破烂的

Chapter 18
Elwyn Brooks White
埃尔文·布鲁克斯·怀特

flivver ['flɪvə]	*n.*	an American slang term refering to any small car that gave a rough ride, esp. one that is small, inexpensive, and old 廉价小汽车
ruby ['ruːbɪ]	*adj.*	resembling the color of blood or cherries or rubies 红宝石；红宝石色的
reflector [rɪ'flektə]	*n.*	device that reflects radiation 反射物
posterior [pɒ'stɪərɪə]	*n.*	near or toward the back of something(such as the body) 后部，臀部
pulley ['pʊlɪ]	*n.*	a device consisting of a wheel over which a rope or chain is pulled in order to lift heavy objects 滑轮
visor ['vaɪzə]	*n.*	a piece of plastic or other material attached to the top of the windshield inside a car, that can be turned down to protect the driver's eyes from bright sunshine 遮阳板
panacea [ˌpænə'siːə]	*n.*	something that is believed to solve all those problems 万灵丹
snubber ['snʌbə]	*n.*	a device used to suppress ("snub") some phenomenon 制动装置
pugnacious [pʌg'neɪʃəs]	*adj.*	ready and able to resort to force or violence 好斗的，好战的
catalepsy ['kæt(ə)lepsɪ]	*n.*	a trancelike state with loss of voluntary motion and failure to react to stimuli 僵住症
mutinous ['mjuːtɪnəs]	*adj.*	disposed to or in a state of mutiny 暴动的；反抗的
clique [kliːk]	*n.*	an exclusive circle of people with a common purpose 派系，派
wilt [wɪlt]	*v.*	become weak or tired, losing energy 使凋谢，使枯萎
puncture ['pʌŋktʃə]	*v.*	pierce with a pointed object; make a hole into 刺穿
goo [guː]	*n.*	any thick messy substance 黏性物

awning [ˈɔːnɪŋ]	n.	a canopy made of canvas to shelter people or things from rain or sun 雨篷；遮阳棚
tumultuous [tjʊˈmʌltjʊəs]	adj.	characterized by unrest or disorder or insubordination 喧嚣的；骚乱的
rheumatism [ˈruːmətɪz(ə)m]	n.	any painful disorder of the joints or muscles or connective tissues 风湿病
camphor [ˈkæmfə]	n.	a white substance with a strong smell that is used in medicine and to keep insects away 樟脑
hex [heks]	v.	cast a spell over someone or something 施魔法于
ply [plaɪ]	v.	travel a route regularly 定期地来往
delirious [dɪˈlɪrɪəs]	adj.	marked by uncontrolled excitement or emotion 发狂的；神志昏迷的
hiatus [haɪˈeɪtəs]	n.	a missing piece (as a gap in a manuscript) 裂缝，空隙
veer off		turn sharply; change direction abruptly 突然转向

II Reading Comprehension Questions

1. What did the author feel upon seeing the new Sears Roebuck catalogue that it is still possible to buy an axle for a 1909 Model T Ford? Why?
2. What are some of the facts about the Model T that distinguished it from all other makes of cars?
3. According to the author, "The lore and legend that governed the Ford were boundless". Can you give some examples of the lore and legend?
4. According to the author, why was the Ford anatomy never reduced to an exact science?
5. What is the author's general sentiment expressed by recalling the Model T Ford? Have you ever had similar sentiments towards a particular object?

Chapter 18

Elwyn Brooks White
埃尔文·布鲁克斯·怀特

Quotes of the Author

It is not often that someone comes along who is a true friend and a good writer.

I arise in the morning torn between a desire to improve the world and a desire to enjoy the world. This makes it hard to plan the day.

Luck is not something you can mention in the presence of self-made men.

One of the most time-consuming things is to have an enemy.

Analyzing humor is like dissecting a frog. Few people are interested and the frog dies of it.

Genius is more often found in a cracked pot than in a whole one.